Travels with my ECONOMIST

Encounters with India

Lisa Scott

David Bateman

For Paul
Who took me there.
And more importantly, brought me back.

❖ ❖ ❖

Text © Lisa Scott, 2012
Typographical design © David Bateman Ltd, 2012
Photographs © Lisa Scott, 2012

Published in 2012 by David Bateman Ltd,
30 Tarndale Grove, Albany, Auckland, New Zealand
www.batemanpublishing.co.nz

ISBN 978-1-86953-822-4

Back cover photographs:
Left: Spices piled high in the City Market, Bangalore. Right: Part of the
   ruined Veerabhadra Temple, Matanga Hill, Hampi.
Book design: Alice Bell
Map: Nick Keenleyside, OUTLINE Draughting & Graphics Ltd
Printed in China by Everbest Printing Co. Ltd

Contents

Acknowledgements

I am indebted to the following people:

Professor Rajeev Gowda, Director, Centre for Public Policy, Indian Institute of Management, Bangalore.

G Sabarinathan, Associate Professor, Chairman of the Office of International Affairs, IIM Bangalore and his lovely wife, Lakshmi.

Simon Cunliffe, former deputy editor (News), *Otago Daily Times*

Joanne Wane, deputy editor, *North & South.*

The team at *Next.*

Otago Polytechnic Students' Association

Film maker and journalist Paranjoy Guha Thakurta for his excellent film, 'Blood & Iron'.

Professor Prabhat Jha, MD, DPhil, University of Toronto Chair in Disease Control, Director, Centre for Global Health Research, Saint Micheal's Hospital, Toronto, Canada.

And to the authors and journalists whose books and articles I read during my travels. Thank you for the diversion, education and respite care.

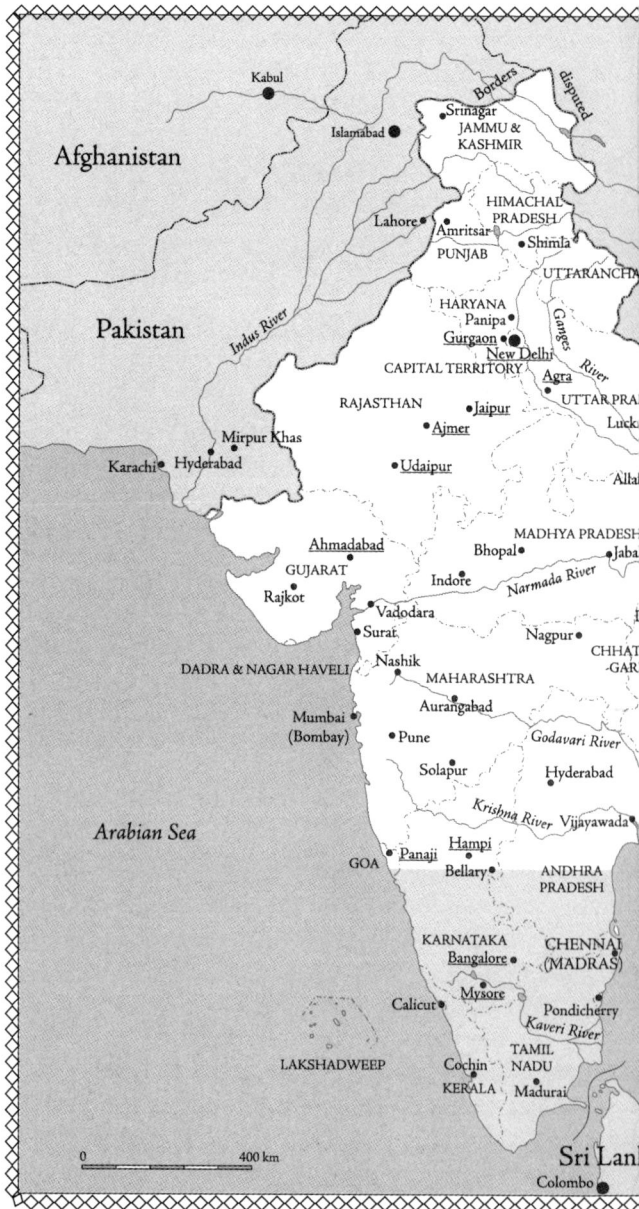

Kabul

Srinagar
JAMMU &
KASHMIR

Islamabad

Afghanistan

HIMACHAL
PRADESH

Lahore
Amritsar
Shimla
PUNJAB

UTTARANCHA

Pakistan

HARYANA
Panipa
Gurgaon
New Delhi
CAPITAL TERRITORY
Agra

Indus River

RAJASTHAN
Jaipur
UTTAR PRA

Ajmer
Luck

Mirpur Khas

Udaipur
Alla

Karachi Hyderabad

MADHYA PRADESH

Ahmadabad
Bhopal
Jaba

GUJARAT
Indore
Narmada River

Rajkot

Vadodara
Surat
Nagpur
CHHAT
-GAR

DADRA & NAGAR HAVELI
Nashik
MAHARASHTRA

Aurangabad

Mumbai
(Bombay)
Pune
Godavari River

Solapur
Hyderabad

Krishna River Vijayawada

Arabian Sea

GOA Panaji
Hampi
Bellary
ANDHRA
PRADESH

KARNATAKA CHENNAI
Bangalore (MADRAS)

Calicut Mysore
Pondicherry
Kaveri River

TAMIL
NADU
LAKSHADWEEP Cochin
KERALA Madurai

Sri Lan
Colombo

0   400 km

Ganges River

India

N **W**—**E** **S**

China

Brahmaputra River

ARUNACHAL PRADESH

pal
Kathmandu
SIKKIM
Bhutan

ASSAM
NAGALAND

Patna
BIHAR
anasi
Dhanbad

MEGHALAYA

Bangladesh
MANIPUR

JHARKHAND
Dhaka
TRIPURA
MIZORAM

WEST
BENGAL
Jamshedpur
Kolkata
(Calcutta)

Mahanadi River

Myanmar
(Burma)

ORISSA

Bhubaneshwar

Yangon
(Rangoon)

ishakhapatnam

Bay of Bengal

Port Blair

ANDAMAN &
NICOBAR ISLANDS

ACES <u>UNDERLINED</u> INDICATE THOSE VISITED
THE AUTHOR AND THE ECONOMIST.

7

Author's Note

In the time since I was in India, the tiger economy has become the elephant economy, proving that even India's boisterous free market must weather the storms of global recession. More than that, Prime Minister Manmohan Singh's government will need to recoup the trade faith eroded by the corruption-bloated Commonwealth Games and the 2G Telecom scandal.

India is a maelstrom of commerce and cruelty. For every NZ$60 tablet developed by innovative companies wishing to bridge the technological gap between rich and poor, a bride is burned because her dowry was judged insufficient. Making change in India is like trying to turn a slow-moving elephant precariously overloaded with ancient codes and fatal superstitions. It will take some doing. Fortunately, in India anything is possible.

About the text:
Travels began as random dispatches, originally published in the *Otago Daily Times*, *Next* and *North & South*. With time to reflect (and aided by a surprisingly emotional travel diary), I've been able to augment these early sketches, give more depth to the initial experiences, all while consciously deciding not to gild the slap of first impressions.
Lisa Scott, Dunedin, April 2012

Tetchy disclaimer:
'I don't know what she's talking about. Plenty of women would give their right ovary to go on a trip like this. I'd just like to say to the people of India that I am very, very sorry. It won't happen again.'
The economist

Marriage, a Fraught Proposal

'Come to India with me,' said the economist.

'I'm not sure,' I said.

'India, how *romantic*,' said Tammy, best friend despite being an ex-model. We were at pole dancing class, another in a long list of fitness flings doomed to failure. Watching long-legged Tammy pole dance is like watching a giraffe try to climb a tree.

'Just think, Scoot — the Taj Mahal!' exclaimed the Tammster, attempting the Carousel. Limbs locked around my own pole, a Beginner's Fireman had gone horribly wrong. 'What a great place for the economist to propose. Why, practically *everyone's* getting married in India these days.' She bent down and either tipped me a wink or grimaced in pain, it was hard to tell.

'I'm stuck,' I said.

❀ ❀ ❀

'You're not getting any younger,' complained Mother, pointing out the bleeding obvious. 'I've got the hat; I just need the wedding.'

Unfortunately, wedding cakes look wonky with just a bride, and the economist so far showed no sign of committing.

Perhaps economists fear matrimony? A Turkish economist I know, informed by his fiancée that she wouldn't marry him until he gave up smoking, now smokes forty a day and has been engaged for fifteen years.

'I am not going to propose to you because you've been proposed to four times before,' said my economist testily. 'But you know I always say yes,' I offered (manners were so dinned into me growing up you could say I'm polite to the point of matrimony).

I tried proposing myself last leap year and just happened to be in the kitchen when I took the plunge. 'You know, we should get married,' I said, slowly and calmly, the way you'd soothe an easily spooked racehorse.

'These cupboards need painting,' said the economist.

For anyone who's at all interested, I've actually already planned the entire wedding, to be held at midnight in the Woodhaugh Gardens with *A Midsummer Night's Dream* theme. The ring-bearer will be Mr Puck the Siamese; all the guests will be dressed as fairies and the groom will wear an ass's head, à la Bottom. People won't forget that in a hurry.

Like cheese, these things take time.

I can wait. I *have* been waiting, for nine years now.

When I first met the economist, I thought he was an unemployed house painter.

I've always loved stupid men. Every one of my boyfriends has been a bad boy and a real thickie, the more tattooed and pierced the better. I wasn't looking for a man with the courage of his convictions, just convictions. You always know where you are with a stupid man, not to mention that feeling of superiority.

My mother would be unfailingly polite to these Neanderthals, over for Sunday dinner and casing the joint, eating with their hands, conversationally grunting.

'Isn't Nail great?' I'd say, doing the washing up, Diane Fossey praising her gorilla.

Nail would be sprawled in the other room, picking his teeth with a chair leg and monosyllabically responding to my dad's, 'How about those All Blacks?'

I believe my thug-hankering stemmed from a misunderstanding of the phrase, 'still waters run deep'. Tall, dark and silent, my brooding hunks were all stare and no substance. (Ridiculous really, if a woman was sullen and uncommunicative she'd be thought boring, not romantic.)

Clapping eyes on the economist, that sheep in wolf's clothing, I immediately noticed his shabby, mismatched outfit as it semaphored in the strobe lights of a dingy bar. Such dreadful dress-sense could only be the result of paint-fume related neurological damage.

'Help me,' blinked his shirt balefully. Rising above this sartorial train wreck was the face of the handsomest man I had ever seen, if the most dishevelled. Out of the goodness of my heart, I went to his aid.

Disappointingly, he wasn't a dole-bludger but a colour-blind economist. His heroes are Adam Smith and Dewey of the Dewey Decimal System (he was once a library monitor). While my bad boys were crashing cars and running afoul of the local constabulary, the worst the economist sustained was a paper cut.

However, I've never pretended to be anything other than a very shallow woman, and the economist is a very attractive man. So I gave up my days of wine and philandering (actually just philandering) to live in Borer Towers with a vomiting cat.

❊ ❊ ❊

Do I get an 'I do?' I don't. Nine proposal-less years later, the time was ripe for some ring-and-kneeling. If navigating the subcontinent would shake that man into matrimony, then I'd do it.

'All right, I *will* come to India,' I said. 'But first we have to find a house-sitter, and that won't be easy.'

'This house is great,' said the economist, gesturing expansively. 'Who wouldn't want to live here?'

The Siamese meowed and hocked up a bit of polystyrene.

'Poor little fella.'

'Meh,' I said.

How relieved I was when shabby became chic. Our whole house is decorated in the 'distressed look'. There isn't a single piece of furniture, cushion, curtain or vase that hasn't been scratched, thrown-up on by the Siamese cat or smashed into pieces and stuck back together with glue.

Stylish dishabille notwithstanding, most people wouldn't live in our neighbourhood were it not for a court order. This is the dodgy part of town, where the inhabitants of rehabilitation halfway houses do the Thorazine shuffle to the BP for ciggies. Dunedin's police call the confluence of the three streets bordering our pallid slum the 'Crime Triangle'. Mongrel Mob members mutter, 'Wanna buy some cannabis?' as you puff up the hill after your morning run.

'Have you got any Botox?' I enquired.

And our house also might not be to everyone's taste — my decorating style probably best described as 'parrot'. Unbearably camp to the average man, the shamelessly ribald upholstery means absolutely nothing to the economist, who is, as I mentioned, severely colour blind.

An ad placed, applicants with various quirks, tics and unlovable personality traits auditioned. The successful appointee, Helena, seemed perfect. When she first came over, the Siamese cat was immediately and violently sick on the rug and she didn't bat an eyelid.

Waiting to leave for Bangalore (where the terrorist bombs went off, near Mangalore, where the plane fell off the runway), I spent the early winter evenings blobbing out in front of the television.

'Does candle wax evaporate?' I asked the economist, as the coffee table blazed with a cathedral's worth of illumination.

'No, it just exudes stinking fumes of industrial solvent,' he replied snarkily, tossing and turning on the couch. 'Why *do* women like bloody candles and pillows so much?'

'Because they are luxurious.'

'It's *not* luxury. It's the depths of irritating frippery,' the economist declared, dislodging cushions and knocking an ornament off the table. Layers of glue prevented it breaking twice.

'Well, what's the male equivalent?' I inquired, looking lovingly into his pewter eyes.

'Knives,' he said sullenly.

And I want to marry this man.

❊ ❊ ❊

As I'd been packed for a month, the week of our departure saw a fluster of panic on the economist's part, complete with shameful examples of the syndrome known as 'man eyes' — release a man from the confines of his living room and he can be trusted to find the South Pole, the Northwest Passage and the outline of a woman's breast through three layers of Kevlar, but never, ever, a set of car keys.

Our bags loaded up with summer-weight clothes, bug spray and sun block were immediately pissed in by the Siamese cat, sensing something was up and expressing his displeasure. Outside, the southerly slapped ears to redness, fog squatted over the Peninsula. Pleased to be escaping the worst of winter's clutches, soon it would be goodbye from him and goodbye from me.

Last-minute functions and bon voyage parties were a blur of glass-in-one-hand-drumstick-in-the-other. I was going to lose tonnes of weight in India, so I figured every chance to eat was vital carbo-loading. The gravy train of gluttony only stopped when I caught sight of my reflection in a sneeze guard, stalled in the act of hoovering up the Otago Foreign Policy School buffet.

Television viewing the night before we left didn't exactly inspire confidence in international travel. 'Survivors of the world's most horrific plane crashes!' screamed the host of '20/20'. Changing channels: 'My Tourist Kidnap Hell!'

If only long-haul flights and the resultant swollen, red-eyed shuffles through immigration mazes were *that* interesting — a visit to Dante's ninth circle of hell, more like: Intercontinental Boredom.

Personally, I would prefer to be chloroformed upon entering the plane, waking up (surely no more groggy) at my destination. This would also take care of any 'crashing, engulfed in flames' heebie-jeebies brought on by aeroplane travel. The economist declared my flight worries were baseless, due to the location of our seats.

'Ever heard of a plane backing into a mountain? We're in the one part they always find.'

At that moment the woman in front reclined, giving the economist the aeroplane equivalent of a lap-dance, with dandruff instead of pasties. The mottled fat of her upper arms bulged between the seat dividers. I revised my aeroplane crash fantasy to 'lost on a tropical island, forced to eat other passengers'. She would keep us going for a while.

The Town of Boiled Beans

It was hard to believe that only a week earlier I had been gobbling chicken drumsticks without any thought for the sanitary conditions of their provenance, and glad-handing Murray McCully who had just flown back to New Zealand for the Otago Foreign Policy School on China.

'I hear you've been in Wales?' I said.

'Whales,' he corrected.

'Minke, cockroaches of the sea,' I countered, meaning to be deeply ironic.

Foreign Minister Murray's eyes indicated the madness of jet-lag, or the suspicion that I had a Tibetan flag hidden up my jumper.

Now here I am in Bangalore, Southern India, about to make a few foreign policies of my own: Lisa Scott, cultural ambassador for New Zealand.

Having considered and rejected Leninism, Marxism, Rastafarianism and Socialism, the economist has come to India with the goal of finding himself. It might be a lengthy search.

'What's Ben Kingsley doing on the money?' he joked.

Gandhi would have forgiven him, but I immediately regretted our viewing certain films before we left. 'Slumdog Millionaire's' railway urchins and the carriage roof-riders in 'A Passage to India' have made an impression I've not been able to shake.

'We could travel for free!' he exclaimed, ungovernably excited.

I can just imagine our return: the economist sporting the dreadlocked hair of a mangy lion, stinky fingered, having renounced both materialism and toilet paper.

They say travel broadens the mind. This is exactly what I'm afraid of. If he opens his chakras, I'm leaving.

We arrived in the 'twilight zone' of morning hours.

'Why are you here?' asked the man at passport control.

'I'm a visiting professor,' explained the economist. After a brief period of crapulous officialising, inspection of our passports revealed different surnames.

'And she is your research assistant?' asked the official with a sly grin. The economist barked with laughter, super-loud in the deserted arrivals hall.

According to some sources, the Hindu god-king Indra was cursed with a thousand vaginas for his seduction and subsequent extramarital affair with Ahalya. The passport officials are delighted by the naughtiness of unmarried sex (as long as they aren't similarly punished), and so we sail into the country on a tide of lascivious winks and nudges.

From air-conditioned chill, the airport's automatic doors open to humidity's slobber. Stepping outside, my ankles immediately swell to ten times their normal size, like those jelly dinosaurs you put in the bath. Faces pressed up against the wire mesh fences enclosing the airport: hundreds of little brown men. The disembarking passengers hesitate; temporarily stop trundling, and the crowd surges against the corral. There is a pause as India waits for us, a warm tidal pool filled with nibbly fish. We jump in.

Driving through the swampy air of the slumbering city we pass skips filled with rubble, bamboo scaffolds and pyramids of sand, but not one digger, dozer or crane. Bangalore has recently experienced massive expansion, yet most of the work is still done by hand, by Dalit families, India's untouchables, who live on site. The suddenness of its own sprouting seems to have caught the city by surprise. Construction sites abound, side by side with crumbling colonial mansions. Such creative destruction, it's hard to know whether buildings are going up or being torn down.

Our taxi lumbers in and out of craters like an elephant negotiating a staircase. The moonlight glimmers over open sewers, the yellow eyes of mongrel dogs and billboards advertising cheap laparoscopic surgery. Behind flapping tarpaulin curtains, on concrete foundations pierced by twists of rusty iron, the workers are asleep.

Bangalore, capital of the state of Karnataka. Almost-but-not-quite also known as Bengaluru (like Calcutta/Kolkata, in the process of reverting to its pre-British name), Bangalore is India's teenage growth-spurt.

Founded in 1537 by Kempe Gowda, a vassal of the Vijayanagara kings, Bangalore began life as a mud fort. Legend has it the city got its name 'Town of the Boiled Beans' when, on a hunting expedition, the eleventh century king Veera Ballala, tired and hungry and lost in the forest without a packed lunch, came across a poor old woman who served him the aforementioned beans. The city has attracted bean-counters ever since: Bangalore was the administrative centre of colonial rule in Southern India during the British Raj.

Once a sleepy town famous for its temperate climate, magnificent gardens, lakes and tree-lined boulevards, Bangalore is now India's third most populous metropolis. Home to 6.8 million souls back in 2006, with today's techno-boom swelling the numbers it's closer to 9 million (they'll know for sure after this year's census, if people could just stop fighting over the questions, particularly the ones regarding caste).

Google, IBM, Yahoo, Oracle and Cisco, Infosys and Wipro — the Godheads of IT are all based here. Thomas Friedman, award-winning *New York Times* columnist and author of the *World is Flat*, wrote: 'When my kids were little I used to say, "think of the starving children in India", to get them to finish their dinner. Now I say, "think of those clever IT professionals in India, they're going to steal your jobs", to get them to finish college.'

Money pours into Bangalore's US$11.62 billion economy from biotech, electronics, telecommunication and defence organisations. The Indian Aerospace Programme was launched here. Bangalore's annual economic growth rate is 10.3 per cent, New Zealand grows at 1 or 2 per cent.

Despite Gandhi's threat, 'industrialise and perish', India is reaping the rewards of its 'planned modernisation', doing in twenty years what New Zealand has been trying to do for the last 200.

'Compared to India, New Zealand is going backwards,' said the economist dolefully. He likens India's rambunctious economy to the industrial revolution of eighteenth century England — all the old certainties changing overnight, the rise of a nouveau riche, higher wages, more consumer goods and a simultaneous desire for them. Millions of Indians have been lifted out of starvation and poverty. Unfortunately, industrial revolutions come with associated horrors: environmental ruin, exploitation of the workforce, a violent clash of values.

The Indian boom began in the 1990s with the liberalisation of the 'License Raj', restrictions on private companies were revoked and new areas were opened to foreign capital. A series of reforms similar to Rogernomics freed things up, allowed for competition and the buds of entrepreneurship and innovation, creating fabulous wealth — for some.

With a significant share of India's fifty-five billionaires and more than 10,000 millionaires, Bangalore is so rich that unlike Kolkata, where 50 per cent of the population live in slums, only 10 per cent of Bangaloreans do. But that's 900,000 people.

India's Silicon Valley, Bangalore is home to the world's call centres. In a strange way this provides a comforting fibre-optic link with home — knowing the very air reverberates with sound particles made by Kiwis complaining about Telecom broadband and Windows Vista.

Computer shops are everywhere. A good thing too, as I've soaked my laptop with bug repellent (ignorant of the effects of airplane travel on pressurised contents) and the fumes are nauseating. Putting it out in the garden of our apartment at the Indian Institute of Management Bangalore (IIMB) to dry, I hope the rarefied air of super-cleverness might do its circuits, and my own, some good.

The IIMB, founded in 1973, is widely considered among the best business schools in the world. Its MBA programme is the toughest to get into: in 2008, 267,000 candidates applied for just 1200 positions. The yearly entrance exam causes nationwide hysteria and suicide.

The students strolling the campus are the smartest people in India, and destined to be the wealthiest. A bidding war is held at the end of each academic year, companies competing to entice graduates. The highest starting salary is published in the newspapers. Last year it was US$350,000 — the equivalent of NZ$10 million, in terms of what you can buy with it.

In the eighteenth century Voltaire wrote: 'I am convinced that everything we know has come down to us from the banks of the Ganges.'

Well, everything *anyone* knows about maths, statistics and economics is known by the students on this campus. There is no doubt I am the stupidest person here, the slowest water buffalo. I'm also the whitest. In fact we are the *only* white faces, not just on campus but in this entire neighbourhood. Bangalore is considerably off the tourist track, so people stare, at first unsmiling and then grinning when we do.

'Can we have your autograph?' kid the auto-rickshaw wallahs.

The IIMB campus is surrounded by a painstakingly cared-for natural forest; gardeners in crimson saris bend over each plant as if they were tending the finest teas. Squirrels skitter and squeak from the treetops — locals say the three black stripes on their backs were caused by a stroke from the trident of the creator/destroyer (and blesser of small things), the god Shiva. Walking the embowered paths, a pair of spotted eagles silently track our progress; crows *wak waa.* The air is thick with dragonflies and jewel-bright butterflies: orange, cobalt and emerald, some as large as my hand. Only thirty years ago the entire city was like this; progress's recent advances have beaten nature back to a tonsured fringe.

The land seethes with life. Somewhere in this vast country are tigers and elephants. *Jungle Book* vines coil around the faculty buildings and termite temples rise up out of the red earth. Shy Mowglis, the gardeners' children, spy on us from behind palm leaves. The forest insinuates itself against our 'married' quarters — an airy apartment on two levels with polished marble floors which are death to fumbled drinking glasses. The beds are bed-boxes: sleep on top, store your saris below.

We are the only couple living in these sought-after accommodations who *aren't* married, and had better keep that quiet. Blushing on my behalf, hibiscus flowers riot in pink and red. Ladies in gold-trimmed saris with a pinch of vermilion powder skilfully dotted on their foreheads sweep the paths. Hundreds of workers from the 'backwards castes' clean, cook, garden and stand sentry outside the campus buildings. Unskilled labourers, they are legally entitled to earn Karnataka's minimum wage: Rs100 per day (NZ$3) but the reality is probably closer to Rs20 (70 cents).

The air is hot, heavy and wet. It rains three or four times a day in sudden showers, sometimes a kiss of warm precipitation, sometimes a hair-flattening torrent, flooding the paths. The maroon earth dries almost immediately into red mud sculptures. A broom runs a wet comb through, leaving tracks like those in a rockabilly pompadour.

It's the rainy season, the first monsoon. The second monsoon season will come when this one finishes circling around the country and returns in October. Monsoon, but no sign of a wedding yet. I'm hoping Tammy is right and the Taj Mahal might prove inspirational. Should there be a proposal, I'd best be ready.

'I hope you don't fall foul of the food,' said the Tammster before I left.

Little does she know this is *exactly* what I plan to do. In the absence of her ectomorph metabolism, I'm off to find the dirtiest, most disreputable-looking food stall in Bangalore, in the hopes of catching a slimming bout of dysentery.

As New Zealand's unauthorised ambassador to India, I can't promise to be as debonair as Mr McCully, and I certainly won't be as diplomatic. But I'll be the more memorable.

Just like Mrs Moore in Forster's *Passage*, the susurration of my name echoing against the hills long after my visit has passed. 'Eeessa ott, eeessa ott . . .'

Filth & the Fourth Estate

The house-sitter emails. Mr Puck is constantly throwing up (sometimes the thought that Siamese cats live for up to twenty-five years can reduce me to tears), the neighbours are dodgy, the house is an icebox. Have we ever been burgled? Yes actually, and by the neighbours — though she needn't worry: one is still doing five to seven for stabbing her flatmate. Think better of mentioning this.

While the house-sitter loses the plot in the criminal gloom of Maitland Street, I'm adjusting to the atmosphere of India. 'Teeming' is a good word for it. The cockroach squatting on the bathroom floor was enormous, until I flattened it with the economist's size 11 jandal. Ants carried the carcass away, leaving only a smear. Hearing my step on the stairs, the lizard living in the kitchen fled into a crack. The wet, mushroomy mould on the bedroom walls tries not to call attention to itself: the mosquitoes aren't so coy.

Packs of skinny dogs howl down the night, wild boys out on the streets; scavenging, snarling. India honks and shrieks outside the window while under the mosquito net I dream of pirates scrambling up the university's perimeter walls, knives held in their teeth. At 4 a.m. the muezzin broadcasts a call to prayer from the mosque's loudspeakers.

Early morning, stepping outside the compound, we leave the safe haven of our pre-lapsarian Eden and smack up against India. My first impression of the country I'll be living in for the next six months is care of a man in a tattered shirt who mounts the meridian, drops his trousers and squats with an expression of religious contemplation, oblivious to the rush-hour traffic. I can't look away, and realise I've never seen another person poo before.

The air is dry, dieselly and dusty. It gets in your eyes, mouth, fouls your hair. Out on the street, pretty girls tip-toe past piles of stinking debris. Young men toot appreciatively. The main thoroughfares are a pageant where the audience turns a blind eye to the rotting food and starving dogs, and don't smell the stink. There is rubbish everywhere: plastic in all its forms, empty books of matches, medical waste, car tyres. It's as if a landfill has exploded.

Auto drivers (the parking-meter wardens of India, universally hated) stop and piss without qualm into the roadside ditches. The smell of shit from these runoff ditches/open sewers is overwhelming, even when breathing through your mouth. A housewife hitches up her sari to expose flat cracked grey feet and throws a plastic bag of household rubbish into the sewer. The bag temporarily blocks the flow of dirty water, and something unspeakable eddies around the obstacle.

I get into a routine where most mornings I go out to buy *The Times of India* and a *Bangalore Mirror*. Handing over my Rs5, I exchange 'Good Mornings' with the tea wallah and everyone else standing about reading their choice from a plethora of newspapers in a multitude of languages (India had 3805 dailies in 1993 and the number has since risen), and drinking hot chai.

Indian journalism follows the pyramid model; one need only read the first two paragraphs of any story to get the gist. Salacious headlines scream death and scandal. Indian newspapers revel in gory pictures of violent crime, accidents and self-immolation. Charred corpses, blood and guts shine wetly in full colour above the fold. While photographs of decapitated train-crash victims would never make the newspapers in New Zealand, it seems there are few restrictions on the Indian media. Some days the stories are sad and bizarre:

Dogs Eat Corpse
Surat: In the early hours of Thursday, dogs ate large parts of a human body on the New Civil Hospital campus. It is not known whether the man was already dead when he was attacked. Reports said that around 1.15 a.m. attendants of patients noticed six–seven dogs eating the body of a man near the trauma centre. Authorities believe that the victim was

amongst the large number of homeless people who spend their nights on the hospital campus. Bangalore Mirror

In the arts and culture section: lists of Bollywood hits and flops, and scathing reviews. One face features every day: Amitabh Bachchan. Flamboyantly spectacled and expertly streaked, the deeply baritoned 'Big B' has spent decades as the country's Number One film star, and done everything from play Lear to hosting India's version of 'Who Wants to be a Millionaire?' He can do no wrong, unlike his poor son Abhishek, whose 'Raavan' is this year's filmi failure (being married to former Miss World Aishwarya Rai probably takes the sting out of it).

On the fashion pages: flowing ankle-length garments, without a hint of bare leg but plenty of naked torsos. Lukewarm society gossip speculates about various film stars hooking up, claims they are 'spending every moment together,' although there is NO WAY they are having sex outside marriage; the fans (not to mention their families) wouldn't have it. Every now and then a movie star couple will flit to London, where presumably they get to at least kiss without the Indian media panting outside, faces pressed up against the windows.

Some days, what passes for titillating says more about India's social mores than any serious commentary could.

Risheeka is determined to glam things up in Sandalwood, which is why she wore a bikini in her upcoming debut, Kanteerava, *in which she sings a song titled 'Bithri' (Sexy Bitch). 'It wasn't easy wearing a two-piece,' she says, herself the first among the GenNext heroines to don a swimsuit in a film. A hue and cry is made when a heroine shows so much flesh in the south.* Bangalore Mirror

Today's top story in *The Times of India* concerns a leading Karnataka list MP who, together with several of his relatives, abducted and raped a university student. I think of New Zealand's name suppression laws, especially when public figures are charged with a crime. Not so here. Politician, businessman or movie star — the Indian media have a field day. The difference being that high-profile rapist/murderer/embezzlers just don't seem to ever get caught, charged or serve any time. Many abscond to the United Kingdom, from where it appears almost impossible to get them back again.

❖ ❖ ❖

The *Bangalore Mirror*'s 'Ask the Sexpert' is my favourite newspaper column. Possessing, as I do, a fourteen-year-old boy's sense of humour, I sometimes cry with laughter while reading it. People write in with their sexual queries, which are then answered by Dr Mahindra Watsa, who must have the patience of a saint.

Every day I am staggered anew at the ignorance of the contributors. How can anyone be so utterly innocent in the twenty-first century? There are 1.2 billion people in India; somebody has to know how babies are made, but you wouldn't think so if you read 'Ask the Sexpert'.

According to a nationwide survey, half of India's women are married before the age of eighteen to husbands just as inexperienced as they are. In the absence of sex education in schools, most Indians rely on their friends (59 per cent) for sexual knowledge, followed by magazines (58 per cent) and the internet (46 per cent). One thing's for sure, nobody in India is getting 'the talk'; only 18 per cent said they had received any sort of guidance from their parents.

The country, it seems, is filled with young men of marrying age who are totally repressed and childishly innocent, an extremely dangerous mix. A UNICEF survey found that only 17 per cent of Indian males and 21 per cent of Indian females were aware of HIV. The number of AIDs cases in India has overtaken that of Africa, and UNAIDS/WHO estimates that the majority of people suffering from AIDs in the country have no idea they have it.

The letters to Dr Watsa are written, in the main, by prospective grooms who worry endlessly about the length, girth and colour of their penises:

Q: My penis is black. I want it to be fairer. What should I do?
Q: I am 28 years old and my parents are forcing me to get married but I

am not interested as my penis is only three inches long and one inch
thick. Will I ever be able to satisfy a woman?

Q: My girlfriend swallowed my semen while we were engaging in oral
sex. Is it true this causes cancer?

Q: I am a 36-year-old single man. Six months ago I had sex with a
housewife. Then, I made as many as 220 strokes in the 40 minutes
of our intercourse. Today, I could only reach 180 in the same time.
Please reply. I am worried.

A: Do take part in the Commonwealth Games, since you seem like
an athlete. My advice is to enjoy the act and stop counting. Give a
thought to whether you are satisfying your partner or not.

I often picture these men, standing in bathrooms across India, holding
the guilty appendage in their hand, sorrowfully contemplating its lack
while simultaneously stumped by its purpose. For them, the penis is a
mystery item, as unfathomable as a diaphragm — is it a little hat? —
danged if they know what to do with it.

India has a puritanical and hypocritical attitude towards sex, tangled
by centuries of religious and cultural mores. Sex is demonised as evil
and dirty. Safe sex messages are believed to promote promiscuity. This
prudish, peevish ignorance makes for rampant sexual frustration.

Despite damning statistics telling of a high rate of teenage
pregnancies and child sex abuse, India shows little sign of shedding
its conservatism about matters sexual, a baffling stance best summed
up by this quote from a parliamentary committee: 'Social and cultural
ethos are such that sex education has absolutely no place in it.'

Compared to those writing to Dr Watsa, the average New Zealand
man is a paragon of pleasure. How can this even be possible? For
goodness sake, Indians invented the *Karma Sutra*!

Many of the correspondents show a clear ignorance as to the location
of the female reproductive organs. Most don't care. Dr Watsa often
cautions against sex before marriage. If you ask me, lack of sex before
marriage appears to be the root cause of the problem.

The economist admonishes my slutty ethics. Hardly *my* fault: Kiwi
women are the most promiscuous in the world, according to the

Durex Sexual Wellbeing Global Survey, so I'm obviously the victim of an ethical osmosis. The economist boldly speculates that population rates soar in poor countries lacking sex education, until I point out that we didn't have sex education at my school, either. We had frogs in biology; I thought all those pregnant seniors waddling the halls were going to spawn.

'I knew not to even *talk* to girls,' he says, 'and I never got anyone pregnant.'

If we take 'Ask the Sexpert' as an example of the sexual proclivities of Indian men, then there must be an awful lot of wanking going on:

> Q: *I have been masturbating for five years. Now I am 28 and my penis seems smaller than what it was. I want to restore it to its original size in a month as I am getting married.*
> A: *Your penis is not shrinking* (writes Dr Watsa . . . you can almost hear him sighing).

I know it's the sentimentality of the morally bankrupt, but, regardless of the obvious pitfalls of reproductive ignorance, there is still something very sweet about a society where sexual innocence remains.

The porn sensibility of the Western media — tits and arse selling everything from ice-cream to car insurance — has made us so jaded. A part of me (the fantasist) is charmed by the idea of not knowing it all, not having seen it all. The alternative: a six-year-old in hot pants and a tiara lisping 'Happy Birthday, Mr President'.

In a world suffering the effects of the global village, cultural folkways watered down to a blasé gruel, these differences are a comfort.

Pain in the Asana

Bangaloreans are well-dressed people and, for the most part, demonstrably affluent. Anyone who doesn't drive a car has a motorbike. There are few bicycles, the choking blue pall of exhaust hovering over the roads testimony to the city's vehicular wealth.

Everyone stares as we stroll past open, poo-filled sewers on our way to the campus shop to buy some groceries. Even the lowliest Indian wouldn't do that; they walk on the road instead. We just haven't got there yet — unable to surrender our footpath bias, too scared of the lunacy of traffic. Once inside the shop, we're unable to figure out what anything is and resort to bhaji mix. It's so hot. Not the bhaji mix (surprisingly bland), the temperature.

Really, compared to the rest of India, it's not hot; we're just nelly. Bangalore's elevation on the Mysore plateau is the reason for the city's salubrious climate, milder and less extreme than the rest of India, with a balmy high of 36°C in summer, a low of 17 in winter. Still, walking for twenty minutes leaves us drenched in sweat, and when that evaporates, as sun-baked as the empty lemon drink bottles littering the roadsides. Plastic pontoons, they bob and sway, clogging the waterways. Drying out over decades, in some places they form a crackling polyethylene leaf-mulch, crunching underfoot. Warming the world, one Limca at a time.

Due to the heat, the economist wears 'formal' board shorts and jandals. Men come up to him on the street, shake his hand and ask where he's from. How long have we been married? How many children do we have?

After first trying to explain that, while we're not married, 'we have both been married before, to other people' (and meeting nothing but blank stares), the economist gives up and makes me his conversational wife. Groups of teenage boys ring-fence him at elbow height, yelling excitedly. Is he from the Netherlands? He does look Dutch, with his long blonde hair. The Dutch have just beaten Brazil in the World Cup.

Following his lead, I resolutely wear Western dress (albeit of a dowdiness that would satisfy even the most conservative religious sect). Men of all ages stop and gawp; drivers turn their heads a dangerous 180 degrees. Perhaps I'm simply their idea of a freak, with my red face and dribbly hair. God forgive me but for a brief, delusional moment I actually think, 'I'll miss all this attention when I get back to Dunedin'.

'The fair skin of the foreigner is associated with everything clean, regal and desirable,' write Sudhir Kakar and Katharina Kakar in *The Indians*. 'This, together with memories of being ruled by fair-skinned invaders and the presumption of wealth makes most Indians fawn over the goras (whites).'

Walking down the street wearing a calf-length skirt and T-shirt (all right *and* lipstick and mascara, hair washed and brushed — after all I want India to like me), I am approached by an elderly dhoti-wearing man, legs akimbo. I smile. Old man smiles to reveal no teeth. I get ready for some fawning.

As he passes, the old man punches (not a pinch but a bouncing punch) me on the arse. Boink.

'What the hell!?' I yell, turning to glower. I've just experienced 'Eve-teasing'.

In the afternoon I am pinched in the same place (physically, not geographically), but this time I'm not alone. 'Pinch me, and my boyfriend will pinch *you*,' I say to the culprit who, like most Indian men, is about the size of a twelve-year-old New Zealand girl. Flimsy shoulders, twigular wrists. He holds his hands up, 'folded' in the attitude of begging forgiveness.

'You are a very naughty man,' scolds the economist.

'Wear local dress,' advised a friend, when I complained on Facebook. After a quick visit to the nearest Reliance Mart (India's Warehouse), I discover that even in kurta and churidar (long loose top and baggy pant/tights) I am an irresistible object of pincher movements. My poor bum is soon yellow, green and purple with bruises at various stages of blooming.

Indian men's predilection for bottom-touching might be known by the harmless sounding tag of 'Eve-teasing', but Indian girls obviously don't think it's harmless, and ride motorbikes and scooters to work and university rather than brave public transport.

After a week, I've had enough. Time to ugly up. Hair unwashed and scrapped back, no makeup, legs unshaven — success, of a sort. The whispering continues, and cars still slow to drive-by-shooting pace, but I'm now too plain to inspire hands-on lust. Huzzah!

Why *are* Indian men such bum-punching/pinching perverts? Indian's blame Western morality and young Indian men's obsession with Western media. The globalisation of social mores (the 'American Pie' effect) resulting in an increasingly dangerous environment for Indian women.

Not only are movies to blame but also, apparently, cigarettes: 'It is a biological fact that smoking stimulates the oral erotic zone and the mind starts wandering,' opined a government minister, but there don't seem to be that many smokers in Bangalore, so nicotine dementia can't be the explanation for this city's happy fingers.

India was and continues to be a patriarchal society, with all the general subordination of women and the disempowerment that patriarchy entails (although caste will always trump gender in the sense that a Brahmin woman will have higher status than a low-caste man). As per Hindu tradition, a wife is part of her husband. In the ancient and long-abolished custom of sati, widowed women were forcefully placed on the burning pyre of their dead husbands. Some widows even did it voluntarily, perhaps attempting to escape the modern alternative: a penniless widowhood viewed with the superstitious horror we save for black cats. Daughters were rarely seen, and never heard.

While the barrier between the sexes is no longer the formidable purdah curtain it once was; and despite the post-Independence Indian Women's Movement of the '70s and '80s, antiquated, feudal views of women as the home-held chattels of men persist. Pubescent girls are not allowed to play with boys and are confined to the company of their own sex. There are many prohibitions with regard to the kind of clothes they may wear and recreational activities such as visiting friends, going to the market or the movies, anything which may bring her in contact with the opposite sex, are rigidly curtailed.

The girl has to be protected — from herself as much as from men — in the highly vulnerable period between puberty and marriage, a period to be kept as short as possible. Meanwhile, men are brought up to believe that girls who go out are loose. An unaccompanied woman is dirty. Dirtiness occludes respect. A loudly laughing, boldly gazing woman endangers the honour (izzat) of her family. From a tap on the bum things can rapidly get out of control, depending on the reaction of the victim and the complicity of onlookers, making Eve-teasing the ostensibly harmless tip of a very nasty iceberg.

Unfortunately, not many complaints of harassment are registered because of a fear of humiliation and public exposure, the deep dishonour of perceived 'wantonness'. Parents will ask their daughters to forget the incident to avoid shame and embarrassment. Faced with constant social barbs, many of the preyed upon simply commit suicide.

❖ ❖ ❖

Even though 'Eve-teasing' is now illegal, violence against women is the fastest-growing crime in India. The fine for Eve-teasing, Rs2000 (about NZ$60), is rarely enforced and for those who try to prevent it, defiance can be dangerous. A Dalit youth was shot dead in Muzaffarnagar last month for opposing a group of men passing lewd comments about his sister.

The Indian government has attempted rather pointless solutions to these close encounters of the worst kind, sporadically rounding up teenage boys for talking to girls in the street. In Lucknow, one harried police inspector admitted to more direct action: speaking to *The Times of India* he said, 'I just take them to the lockup and thrash them'.

Inevitably, someone will counter with a charge of 'Adam-teasing'. One Romeo, complaining about girls' gauzy saris, low-cut cholis and flimsy salwar, wailed: 'There is always too much visible!' She was asking for it, your Honour.

'We forget that all countries go through these periods of intolerance, periods of immaturity,' says the economist — I think of the stubborn religious bigotry of New Zealand in the 1940s, the homo-bashing years before homosexual law reform, the congenital racism of the United States before the Civil Rights movement.

'With economic growth and democracy, over time they kind of grow up,' he reassures me.

'But India's had 4000 years to grow up!' I protest.

Yesterday, an American aid worker was raped at knife point in her apartment.

'No property was taken,' said the investigating officer.

New Zealand women are supposed to be staunch, but the stories of gang rape in the Indian papers have me cowed. After only a week I have adopted a head-down, fast and angry way of walking — the complete opposite of my usual aimless wandering.

'God, if a woman molested me I'd be *so* happy,' said the economist. I remonstrated with him physically.

'I'm just saying, Darling . . . ow! I think you're being a little judgemental.' He backed away, clutching his nipples, for the first time in his life the victim of a double standard.

Can't Touch This

'Do be careful of the culture shock,' warned mother-in-law before we left, several times, as if it were a cobra under the bed. I may just be in massive denial, but I was used to squalor and poverty — I live in Maitland Street after all. Well, maybe not squalor and poverty on such a grand scale, not forgetting I am in one of India's wealthiest cities, the silicon-coated heart of India.

The difference being that, unlike the residents of our very own Crime Triangle, debilitated by nothing more serious than learnt helplessness and a propensity for drink, Bangalore's most wretched cope with the seemingly unendurable: legs bent like paperclips, arms missing, cruel scars. Brown skin speaks of being sliced by machete, showing crimson in the slashes. Empty-eyed women mutely proffer filthy babies with lolling, too-big heads.

India has the biggest number of prostitutes of any country in the world. Many of them are children. Eighty per cent of the children trafficked into the sex industry in India come from Bangalore. There is an enormous seedy underside to this city that we either don't see, or are too blind to notice for what it is. Thousands of children go missing in Bangalore every year and are never found. The offspring of migrant labourers who have travelled to the city for construction work, they are kidnapped, drugged with cough syrup and forced into child labour, begging or brothels. The going rate for full sex is US$2.

In 2005, the World Bank set the global poverty line at US$1.25 (NZ$1.66) a day, meaning 80 per cent of India's population lived below it. The Indian government, in the dwindling light of 'India Shining' (a US$20 million advertising campaign launched in 2003, intended to promote India internationally and widely criticised for glossing over social problems) and a growth rate of more than 8 per cent, has set the poverty line at 87 cents a day, claiming that a family of five could get by on Rs4824 per month (NZ$120). This seems almost impossible to believe, but according to the 2007 National Commission for Enterprise in the Unorganised Sector, 836 million Indians survive on Rs20 a day, which equates to roughly 87 cents.

Somehow they abide. They have to, life for them is to endure or die.

❖ ❖ ❖

Historically, Dalits (people who work with their hands, and other 'backward castes'), rarely changed social groups — occupations and career prospects were clearly segregated. The word 'Dalit' comes from Sanskrit and means 'ground', 'oppressed', 'crushed' or 'broken to pieces'. Efforts to help the Dalits began in the nineteenth century during British colonial rule and later under India's independent government, with the implementation of a reservation policy; a form of affirmative action, where a certain percentage of the available places at educational institutes and jobs in government departments are set aside for people from scheduled tribes and castes. Now every year tens of thousands of the best government jobs and university places are reserved for Dalits. From the Dalit perspective, the state and public sector are emancipators, but with liberalisation grows resentment.

While the reservation policy was designed to end centuries of social discrimination, the stain of untouchability made reform difficult and Dalits in many parts of India remain targets of discrimination and abuse. The system has stirred growing resentment and criticisms from middle-class educated Indians who feel they have been excluded from jobs despite being better qualified.

Despite, or perhaps because of, these reservations for the poorer castes at elite institutions, caste prejudice persists and remains a highly controversial issue. Most Indians will still not eat with, talk to or touch lips to a glass, bottle or cup touched by a member of an inferior caste. While the few exceptions such as India's sole 'backwards' billionaire,

ABOVE: The Vidhana Soudha, seat of the Karnataka state legislature. Home to some of India's most corrupt ministers, the building bears the shamelessly sacrilegious inscription: Government's Work is God's Work.

LEFT: Flower sellers at the entrance to Bangalore's City Market.

BELOW: Roadside dentist, Bangalore. Crowns, dentures or extractions — no appointment necessary. No anaesthetic either.

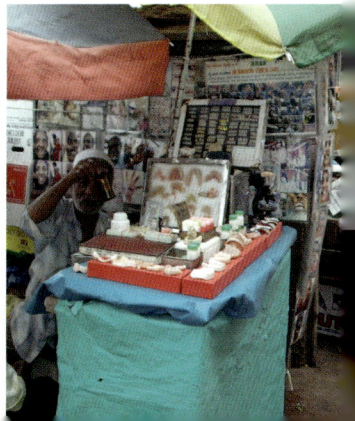

LEFT: Nandi the bull lies nestled in foliage, 1000 steps down the winding path that leads from the top of Chamundi Hill, Mysore. Female travellers are advised to take another person due to the quiet surroundings, blind curves, leopards and male walkers.

BELOW: The economist grows daily more spiritual!

ABOVE: The Baroque Church of Our Lady of the Immaculate Conception, Panaji — overlooking the villas, cobbles and cashew trees of Goa's capital since 1541.

RIGHT: The ruined belfry of St Augustine's, Old Goa. Abandoned in 1835, the church once boasted a vast nave covered by a barrel vault whose enormous weight hastened its own demise.

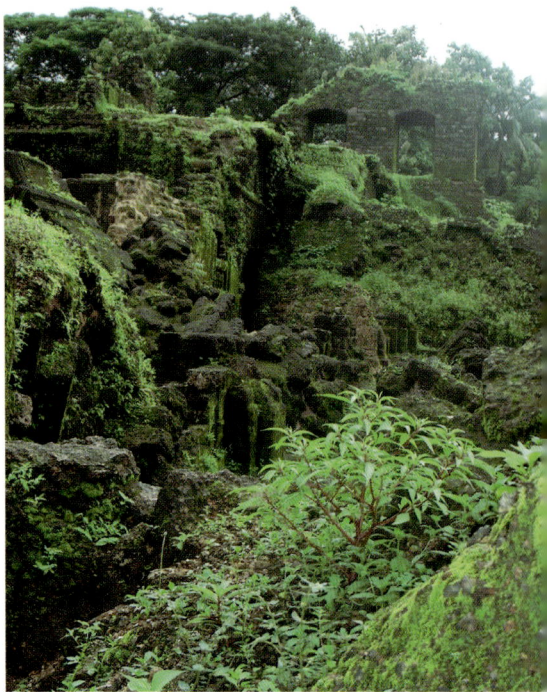

RIGHT: The Goan jungle keeps its secrets. Somewhere here, at the ruined convent of Our Lady of Grace, Old Goa, lie the bones of the martyred Georgian queen, Ketevan.

BELOW: The monsoon lashes Vagator Beach, home of Goa's trance scene.

Rajesh Saraiya (who, despite demonstrating considerable business acumen, setting up a multinational company in Ukraine, is regarded with the astonishment one would save for a talking dog), and the odd scholarship student from the slums are held up as examples of progress, most Indians are still circumscribed by language-based specifics and determinates of professional success such as skin colour (belonging to the 'creamy layer'), being part of a particular marriage group (kin-based units with rigid rules about which lineages are allowed to marry) and speaking convent English.

Meanwhile, the poor wait — staring into space, chewing betel nut. Tuk tuk drivers wait on the side of the road, labourers wait for someone to ask them to do some tiny job, shopkeepers wait for a customer to come along.

A man at the railway station fixes zips. What does he think about while he's waiting for one to break? Outside the Centre for Executive Education, a professor's driver waits for him all day in the car. So much time alone with your thoughts, waiting, waiting . . . it would do your head in.

I asked one of the IIMB professors whether the Indian poor have good lives. He looked slightly disturbed by the question. 'Of course they are happy,' he said. 'They are too stupid not to be.'

As obvious as the loitering poor, there is also no getting away from the Indian need for hierarchies. You must be somebody to survive with dignity in the anonymous throng of India, eminence the only substitute for money. In their book *The Indians*, Sudhir Kakar and Katharina Kakar say what makes this a particularly Indian phenomenon is that a person's self-worth is almost exclusively determined by the rank he occupies in Indian society. 'Is this person superior or inferior to me?' remains very near the top of subconscious questions evoked in any interpersonal encounter. 'Indians are perhaps the world's most undemocratic people,' maintain Sudhir and Katharina, 'living in the world's largest democracy.'

The most pervasive dimension of Indian identity is that measurement of social- and self-worth, that ultimate hierarchical scorn: caste. The term 'caste' derives from the Portuguese casta meaning race or descent, which has come to signify the strata of Indian society. The vertical order of castes isn't static; it changes from village to village and region to region, although a Brahmin will always be at the top of the pecking order. The ranking of a caste in the social order is according to the notion of purity versus pollution. A Brahmin is the purest, and an untouchable, the Dalit, the most polluted.

Today's cynical Indian youth (who nevertheless still believe it) included, many Hindus think the Brahmin caste, the teachers, have a direct hotline to God. Add to that an emphasis on the value of the knowledge economy, the evolution of the IT tsars, and it's no surprise many Brahmins are billionaires.

He may not be a billionaire, but our host at IIMB, Professor Rajeev Gowda, is a Brahmin.

'Caste. A despicable history of inequality,' he says.

Of the firm opinion that, if you're living at a university you may as well learn something, I took up an invitation to sit in on Rajeev's class: The Politics of Identity. 'What is an Indian?' he asks. The class is made up for the most part by extremely well-off Hindus who live in an India where your servant's children become your children's servants. 'An Indian is someone aware of the rules,' Rajeev answers. 'Rules at village level. Rules at government level.'

'Confront the reality of India,' Rajeev encourages his privileged, well-fed, well-born students — tomorrow's billionaires. 'Get out of your air-conditioned car, see the real India on the pot-holed roads. Only you can do something about it.'

According to Rajeev, 'India' is a construct held together by both rules and elaborate social structures around food, marriage and prejudice. A certain social dynamic allows for moving up, but not by all. If it is a given that mixing outside these unspoken social parameters is a kind of pollution, then this creates a society that governs itself.

There isn't a strict segregation of church and state in India but a general acceptance of many, multiple religions and sects. It all comes down to 'Dharma' — your place in the world, your raison d'être. Historically, not everyone has adhered to a belief in this cult of multiplicity.

'India is a mere geographical expression. It is no more a country than the equator,' said Winston Churchill. But what would he know?

The preoccupation of the caste system with high and low has been associated with suffering and humiliation for millions through the centuries. As the Marathi poet Govindaraj put it, Hindu society is made up of men 'who bow their heads to the kicks from above and who simultaneously give a kick below, never thinking to resist the one or refrain from the other'.

The Constitution of India provides 'certain special safeguards for the welfare of Scheduled Castes, economically backward people and other weaker sections of the population, so that they can take their rightful place in the community. As citizens of the Republic of India, they are fully entitled to certain rights and privileges denied to them in the past on grounds of the Caste system and the practice of Untouchability.'

In Bangalore, the reality of these noble intentions sees beggars, alcoholics, tuberculosis patients, the physically disabled and elderly dementia sufferers rounded up and forced into the police van which comes around once a week, to be put away, indefinitely, at the Beggars' Rehabilitation Centre in Hegganahalli, better known as the Beggars' Colony. Provided with a meal and uniform, eventually allowed back out on the streets (if they have the Rs500–1100 needed to bribe officials), their 'rights and privileges' seem to be no more than permission to slump in a doorway with one hand held out, the other hiding their eyes.

Recently, thirty beggars died within twenty-four hours at the Beggars' Colony, their bodies immediately cremated without autopsy. 'Food poisoning,' said officials, a tainted kesari bath (a type of dessert made with semolina). The death certificates, however, were wildly contradictory, stating cause of death as anything from prolonged illness to anorexia and epilepsy.

The colony occupies prime real estate. A place where life and death have lost all meaning, it has been shrinking lately as a result of determined land grabs, and most suspect deliberate poisoning. Not that anyone is driven to action.

'There was no need to conduct a post-mortem,' said Bangalore's Police Commissioner. In the silence, an unspoken 'Who cares?'

Snakes & Lathers

There is a mongoose living in our garden. At night he capers about, moon-dancing; brindled fur shimmying, pointy nose held high. His little claws clack on the paving stones. How I would like to gaze into his big round eyes and tell him I adore him, my Rikki-Tikki-Tavi.

In the United States, the Big Four are television networks: ABC, NBC, CBS and Fox. A New Zealand Big Four would, undoubtedly, be All Blacks. In India, however, the Big Four are not cricketers but venomous snakes: the cobra, the krait, Russell's viper and the saw-scaled viper.

Monsoon season is also snake season, as babies from the breeding time (and their annoyed parents) are washed from their homes by rivers of rain water. With the economist not being a doctor of anything useful and yours truly voted most likely to panic in an emergency, our only hope is the one animal able to defeat them all — the mongoose, with his lightning reactions, thick fur and built-up immunity to snake bites.

The short story 'Rikki-Tikki-Tavi', written in 1894, appears in Rudyard Kipling's *The Jungle Book*. A fantastic allegory for the Raj's fear of both India and Indians, a heroic young mongoose saves an English family from the murderous intentions of Nag the cobra and his even more dangerous mate Nagaina, who want to kill them so cobras can once again rule in the garden.

Many of the English colonialists trembled at all things Indian; animal or spiritual — djins driving them to gins — so the myth of a deep abiding love on the part of the natives for the imperialists must have been extremely comforting. Hence, Rikki also takes on and kills a krait, a dust brown snakeling even more lethal than the cobra, out of love for the boy, Teddy.

Hoping to encourage the same devotion, this morning I left an offering of chocolate chippie biscuits outside our mongoose's burrow.

The economist, having read far too much about the Big Four on Wikipedia, is suffering from ophidiophobia, the abnormal fear of snakes, shying like a pony on the motorway, harking at every rustle, and nervously checking under the bed.

I don't blame him. Quite frankly, there is nothing abnormal about fearing a creature that will bite and bite and bite, delivering a gratuitous dose of neurotoxin when a mere prick will do. One can only surmise that snakes bite because they enjoy it, and the snakes of India are particularly happy. According to the BBC, as many as 50,000 people die from snake bite every year in India, that's 137 per day.

As an aside, it might interest you to know that in America, home of the brave, a surprising number of snake-bite deaths (40 per cent) are alcohol-related. Forget drinking and driving, if you drink and handle snakes, you really are a bloody idiot. Or an American.

❈ ❈ ❈

The Herpetologist's Guide to Avoiding Death by Serpent:

'When encountering a snake, it is recommended to leave the vicinity.' (No argument there.)

'Remain silent and motionless.' (Difficult to achieve when screaming and waving your arms around, but okay.)

'If the snake fails to move on, step away slowly and cautiously.' (Ignoring the rivulets of pee running down the inside of your trews, your backward steps making a wet, *shooka shooka* noise.)

Even a seemingly dead snake isn't to be trusted. 'They will actually roll over and stick out their tongue to fool a potential threat,' claims one snake expert.

Wait, there's worse: if by some miracle you succeed in killing it, you're still not in the clear, as a snake's detached head contains vast amounts of toxin and can bite reflexively.

Whump it, stomp it, cut off its head and it still wants to hurt you. Snakes are a bit like ex-husbands really.

If unfortunate enough to become envenomated, *do not* attempt any of these outmoded treatments:

Tourniquets are completely ineffective and can even cause gangrene.

Cutting open the bitten area doesn't work either.

Sucking out the venom, ditto and *ew*.

'Use of electroshock therapy has been shown to be useless and potentially dangerous.' (Surely being bitten by a snake is bad enough?)

❀ ❀ ❀

Joseph Rudyard Kipling was born in Bombay (Mumbai), British India in 1865. Taken to England by his parents when he was five years old, the die was cast — while he spoke English when around his parents, he thought and dreamed in the world sung and told to him by his ayah. He returned to India as an adult, sailing from England in 1882, arriving back in the city of his birth where, he said, 'his English years just fell away'.

Kipling worked in India as a columnist for various newspapers, first at Simla (Shimla) hill station, the summer capital of the Raj, and later in Allahabad in Uttar Pradesh. It was recollections of this time that he would later draw on during cold winters in Vermont, leading in 1894 to the publication of *The Jungle Book*.

I read *The Jungle Book* over and over as a small child, but Disney's 1967 cartoon adaptation is the real reason for the prevailing appeal of characters such as Mowgli the man-child raised by wolves, Shere Khan, a royal Bengal tiger, Baloo the bear, Bagheera the black panther, Kaa the python, the monkey tribe Bandar-log, and evil cobras Nag and Nagina.

Rudyard Kipling has flipped and flopped in and out of fashion as a writer, for some decades derided as a dirty old Imperialist, then revisited and re-appreciated — ending up beloved as a sentimentalist and lover of all things Indian. The sad truth is Kipling's books are one of the few remaining places to see the animals his stories anthropomorphise, as they have been hunted and persecuted to near extinction in India.

Robert Baden Powell petitioned Kipling to allow the scouting movement to adopt *The Jungle Book* as a motivational text, then and forever naming all senior scout leaders 'Akela' (an Indian wolf) — and making one of Kipling's strangest legacies the generations of odds, bods and occasional deviants who have at one time answered to it.

In 1907 Kipling won the Noble Prize in Literature. He kept writing right up until the end of his life, dying of a perforated duodenal ulcer on 18 January 1936. His death had in fact been previously announced in a magazine, to which he wrote, 'I've just read that I am dead. Don't forget to delete me from your list of subscribers.'

Rudyard Kipling, a member of the white hegemony, was forgiven by the Indians for belonging to such a bunch of heatstroke-prone, gin-swilling snobs because he loved India so.

The economist and I aren't part of any ruling class, barely have any class at all (which is why we recoil when people call us Sir and Madam), but we love India too. I can only hope the mongoose stoops to save us.

❈ ❈ ❈

'And another interesting thing *is . . .*' said the economist, in a sonorous, professorial voice.

The King Cobra, *Ophiophagus hannah*, is not a member of the Big Four. This famous species can inject large quantities of potent venom, is deadlier than smaller species but actually shy, and lives mostly in dense jungle where it rarely comes into contact with humans. It feeds only on other snakes, rather than mice and rodents, hence its scientific name, which means 'snake-eater king'.

The Big Four, on the other hand, are all quite common, mean as hell and bite readily (the bite of a Russell's viper makes you bleed from every orifice, which seems a bit unnecessary). They are often found in proximity to human habitation, as they are attracted to the associated rodent populations on which they feed. These species are all primarily nocturnal; most victims are bitten at night after accidentally stepping on them coming back from the loo.

A polyvalent serum that effectively neutralises the venom of all of the Big Four snakes is widely available in India. There are two types of antivenin made specifically to treat King Cobra envenomations. The Red Cross in Thailand manufactures one, and the Central Research

Institute in India manufactures the other. All Indian hospitals carry these antivenins.

I asked the guard outside our quarters whether we could make it across the road to Apollo Hospital (about 200 metres) in time for a shot of antivenin, should one of us get bitten. He smiled and shook his head. No chance.

But Lunch is Only 70 Cents!

It isn't easy keeping up appearances when strange heat-related blisters are popping out all over your freckled skin and you're being molested from backside to breakfast. *You* try being fabulous while skirting open sewers and coping without the necessities of life: chardonnay, Whitestone cheese, tampons. Forget Kashmir, a country without tampons is a country in crisis.

But less of the hysterical white woman shtick. I'm loving the ubiquitous Indian head wobble. Described by travel journalist Stephan Wilkinson as 'a vague cock of the head', it can be a little disconcerting until you realise it simply means the listener is in agreement with what is being said. Very graceful and, unsurprisingly, not at all like the media stereotypes of Indians past and present: the Burma Babus and blackface punka wallahs of the 1970s British sitcom 'It Ain't Half Hot Mum', the obsequious 'Thank you, come again' of the Simpsons' Abu. Instantly contagious, you're wobbling your own head before you even realise it.

No race can escape being stereotyped, but is there any truth in the cultural tropes associated with Indians?

Ridiculously smart? Check.

Profoundly hierarchical? Yes, Madam.

Skinny and puny? Yes. And no.

The first rule of every Indian's life, according to Indra Sinha, author of *The Death of Mr Love*, is: Agodar potoba, nantar vittoba! First Mr Gut, then Mr God.

There are few people as concerned with food as Indians are. Food taboos abound. Diet is viewed as the mainstay of physical and mental health, balance only achieved by consuming the right foods at the right time in the right season. The most common Indian preoccupation with food relates to its digestion and defecation. Stools are carefully observed. Constipation is taken very seriously.

With the burgeoning middle class flush (no pun intended) with spending cash and gluttonous for everything Western, India is currently in the grip of a KFC, Dominos and McDonalds-spawned obesity epidemic. Numbers of the overweight have increased by 20 per cent over the last seven years, meaning almost one in five men and over one in six women are now seriously fat in a country where, in the state of Maharashtra alone, 45,000 children die of malnutrition every twelve months.

Newspaper ads flogging diet products to the rich and flabby are unintentionally hilarious. A full page illustration shows delighted parents posing with the garlanded newlyweds. Mother has contributed the endorsement beneath the picture: 'I cannot count how many good marriage proposals we lost because of her obesity.' Fortunately, thanks to Dr Satheeesh Kodakatti's Ayurvedic tablets, their daughter 'lost seven kilograms in three months and became beautiful and attractive. Her marriage was fixed in the fourth month.'

If only.

In India, you are what you eat, literally. The strict vegetarianism of Jains and Vaishnava Hindus is dictated by an appreciation of the extreme terror of the animal being slaughtered, the pain becoming part of its flesh. The vegetarian kitchen is the most important part of the house, an altar to purity: all meat-eaters and people of inferior consciousness — Dalits and Europeans — must be kept far away, so that they do not contaminate it.

Southern Indian food is predominantly vegetarian, soupier and hotter than the cuisine of the north, and is rice-based. Rice is combined with lentils to make dosas, idlis, vadas and uttapams (earth and water). Southern chutneys are a flavoursome mix of tamarind, coconut, peanuts, dhal, fenugreek seeds and cilantro, more commonly known as fresh coriander (earth and fire). A thali, or platter, is the commonest item on the menu, varying slightly from restaurant to restaurant but nearly always consisting of a set meal of rice, chapathi, dhal, curried vegetables and yogurt bath served on a cool green plantain (type of banana used for cooking) leaf or, in lowlier establishments, in a compartmentalised circular tin tray reminiscent of prison ware.

After a few hiccups involving ordering nothing but sickly sweets, we settle into a routine of businessman's lunches eaten standing shoulder to shoulder with the locals. The economist (ironically the inventor of decision software) finds decision-making extremely difficult and so loves the simplicity of the system: point at the picture, pay, get your food. No complicated choices involved. Price is also a consideration.

'Lunch is only seventy cents!' he exclaims, looking like he might cry. He'd heard there was no such thing as free lunch, but this got pretty close.

'That man just touched my bottom.'

'Darling, I don't think you're listening. Seventy cents! God, I love India. If there was just a beach, I could live in Bangalore forever.'

In comparison to the history and variety of Indian food, 'Masterchef New Zealand' is a backyard boil-up with nothing on the menu but pork bones. I cringe, thinking of the way we Kiwis bray on and on about our 'cuisine'. Poor Indian New Zealanders, to suffer such patronising gits, always asking smugly, 'So, what do you think of the country?' Indian immigrants must be thinking, 'It's a cultural backwater, your children are morons, and I can't get a decent masala dosa'.

❖ ❖ ❖

Even though almost everyone in Bangalore speaks English, sometimes I just can't take in what they are saying, as if my ears are blocked with a dense plug of cultural cotton wool. This might explain why foreigners always seem to shout at people whose language they don't understand — it's an attempt to clear the blockage, or maybe they are just trying to be heard over the rain.

And boy does it rain. Nature here is wet and seething. The flowering vine *Thunbergia mysorensis* (or Indian Clock Vine) swaths the concrete colonnade leading to the library with red trumpets that capture the water in their little bucket-like flowers, which then overflows onto the towering termite hills. Termite hills are snake ganglands, local vipers congregating beneath the shadow of the tower blocks; smoking, sharpening their fangs and hitching up their pants. No one seems to object to these red-mud estates. For all the multitude of staff tending the gardens, pulling out plants and installing new ones, not one, it seems, is assigned to termite eradication.

Of India, Mark Twain said: '. . . land of dreams and romance, of fabulous wealth and fabulous poverty, of splendor and rags, of palaces and hovels, of famine and pestilence, of genii and giants and Aladdin lamps, of tigers and elephants, the cobra and the jungle, the country of a thousand nations and a hundred tongues, of a thousand religions and two million gods, cradle of the human race, birthplace of human speech, mother of history . . .'

It's this terrible wonderfulness, this ancient and forever, that makes for the colossal mind-fuck of it all. At the moment I'm reading *Midnight's Children* by Salman Rushdie. This dense and intricate tome, weaving a sky carpet of politics and magic realism, makes slightly more sense in India. Accosted by a group of beggars, one of the female characters says that 'it's like being surrounded by some terrible monster, a creature with heads and heads and heads'.

It's all too easy to imagine India as a many-headed monster, crushing you by accident, squashing you with need and amiable curiosity. A veritable sense-tsunami and in the vacuum at the centre of it all, the many-armed Shiva, whose nature is emptiness. This hydra of contradictions causes periodic bouts of a condition I've started to call TMI, or Too Many Indians. A masala-flavoured panic attack, TMI is brought on by the sheer number of people, the staring, the noise, the awful press of bodies. A slightly milder version of a full-scale freak-out, the too-muchness of India creeps up and throws a black bag over my head. The only reprieve: two aspirin and a wee lie down.

Maybe this is just what happens when a spoiled, sheltered, middle-class girl collides with an alien enormity, and is devastated by her own banality.

Waxing Hysterical

Exploring Bannerghatta Road and the IIMB's immediate environs, you could be forgiven for thinking there are no public toilets in Bangalore. No street signs, either. Of course there *must* be; they're just not obvious.

Bangalorean footpaths are cracked, shattered or absent; walking them requires a dedicated up-and-down, hop-on-hop-off gait, and high levels of concentration. Heavy concrete slabs are tilted up like henge stones, shoved aside like vandalised graves, exposing the sewers underneath. They rock when you walk over them, threatening to spill you into the filth below.

In a re-occurring nightmare, I drop my wallet into the ooze beneath the concrete carapace. I wonder if the economist would fish it out for me.

'I wouldn't,' he says.

Where *do* Indian women go to the toilet? Indian men happily piss and spit all over any and every available wall. Heeding the call of nature, the economist gleefully unzips, saying, 'When in Rome . . .'

The 2007 World Toilet Summit, held in Delhi, concluded that over 700 million people don't have access to a toilet in India. The absence of bathroom facilities guarantees you wander hot, lost and busting — fantasising about catheters — for hours on end through a maze of shanty shacks and suburban brickwork before you give up looking for both a loo (and the lake that is apparently somewhere around here) and walk back home, clenching. I've become extremely good at holding on, even though my mother always said this was bad for you.

'Whatever you do, don't make me laugh,' I tell the economist.

Bangalore used to be a city of lakes and we are trying to find one of the last remaining, naively thinking we would be able to walk down to it. Where is Hiranandani Lake? The lake is lost somewhere behind houses, shops and vacant lots. 'This land is owned by . . .' blare skull and cross-boned signs, stabbed into the overgrown grass to discourage squatters who might throw up a condominium overnight.

Dusty streets are home to skinny, scabrous mongrels who follow us briefly through the labyrinth only to flop down exhausted. There's a chemist on every corner, selling pills in ones and twos. The air is so thick you can taste it, clagging and rasping at the back of your throat. Burning pats of cow dung send up wisps of smoke. A herd of buffalo nod and snort, driven languidly down the narrow red-dirt road, balding chickens peck at rubbish mounds. The houses are squished up against each other, wiring atrocious, drainage medieval. Bucktoothed balconies are home to washing, naked children, a goat.

Residences are painted in vibrant '50s teal or hot pink, the effect only a little spoilt by paan spatters from passing spitters. Burnt-out rubbish skips sit next to big holes filled with crap. A rat the size of Mr Puck forages under a fruit stall. Paint peels from walls in sunburnt sheets, or blisters and snows the ground below in a scabby dandruff. It's communal living, no privacy, but behind the passive-aggressive blank stares they save for foreigners, people seem genuinely happy. The street life stretches across three generations; parents, children, grandparents, everyone living in each other's pockets. You would never hear of a body being discovered here months after the person had died.

This neighbourhood isn't a slum by any means, these candy-coloured bungalows are the cramped accommodations of the working class made good, the supervisors and managers of India's cheap labour force — the foremen of exploitation.

I get lost every day. Ask for directions and someone will always eagerly give them to you, but they don't know where anything is any more than you do.

In the first of the three novellas that make up *The Elephanta Suite*, travel writer Paul Theroux describes this ever-ready Indian advisor rather unflatteringly: 'Whenever you hesitated anywhere, looked thoughtful, an Indian would step forward to explain, usually an old man, a bobble-headed pedant, a man urgent with irrelevancies.'

A chronic case of TMI if ever I saw one.

Travelling as I am with my own pedant, a man urgent with printed-out pages from Wikipedia, I hardly need the helpful meddling of the locals. But Indians are kind to a fault. Stranded, cast on an intersection in a sea of traffic, little old Indian grannies come up and take my hand in their soft monkey paws and help me across the road.

Theroux's uneasy American tourists are constantly on the alert for 'the India they'd been warned about, the India that made you sick and fearful'. For them, India is not a place to enjoy, but to endure, like going down a dark hole to find jewels.

I hope I never feel that way.

❖ ❖ ❖

All this wandering about is a prelude to eventually finding the local beauty salon. Long, too long, have I gone without a little personal maintenance. As a trip to Goa is on our agenda, I tentatively put my bikini on in front of the full-length mirror upstairs, only to find a monkey in the bottoms. Small children innocently building sandcastles on the beaches of Goa will be frightened or psychologically scarred. Time for a wax.

Trawling the streets of our neighbourhood for days on end, I finally notice a discreet sign: 'Beauty Parlour Downstairs'. Descending wet steps into the gloom of a daily power cut, at my knock the door opens a crack and worried little Asian faces peer out. The total darkness and their alarmed appearance briefly made me think of a shipping container jimmied open by customs officials to reveal a traumatised group of illegal immigrants, blinking at the sun.

'Closed,' said the Korean boss-lady, slamming the door in my face.

Increasingly desperate (and reassuring myself that some notion of a service industry must exist), I return a week later and use sign language to convey my need — wiggling my fingers into spider legs to denote hairiness. Escorted by two women into a small cubical completely taken up with a Nazi-gynaecological-experiments style gurney covered in dirty blue vinyl, I peel off my jeans, revealing bikini bottoms worn as a guideline.

'Just around the outside,' I explain, getting up on the bed/trolley.

'You don't need those here,' said the smaller one.

Her large associate, a mute, held my legs down and apart, proving herself the strong silent type.

The following moment, as the two disapprovingly contemplated the job before them, was probably the most embarrassing of my life and certainly the first time I had been knickerless in front of strangers without a medical reason, or closing-night party.

'You are married?' asked the short one.

'Yes,' I fibbed.

I should probably mention at this point that it is traditional for Indian wives to be completely hairless, both for reasons of comfort and hygiene in a hot climate, and because Indian men notoriously prefer it.

I did not know this at the time.

Applying boiling hot wax to my tender bits, the two women began to rip off every hair. Eyes filled with tears, I made gasping sounds and the occasional yelp. Every time I squealed, an Asian voice over the wall echoed it back, followed by a giggle. At one particularly painful juncture, unable to help myself, I yelled, 'Jesus Christ!'

An uneasy silence followed. I was faced with a cultural dilemma. These two were clearly not doing what I had asked them to. Lifting my head, I could see they were in fact deforesting the entire knoll. My crotch looked like one of those stressed cockatoos that pluck at themselves.

The problem was, I was raised to be polite and to avoid drawing attention to other's failings. Fearing I might cause real offence, I gritted my teeth and said nothing, until the agony finally drove me to leap off the table, tears dribbling down my face.

The waxers regarded me with astonishment. Talking non-stop nonsense to fill the void, I babbled, 'Goodness me, haven't you ladies done a splendid job, terribly late . . .' Hunched over, I grovelled on the floor for my jeans.

'Not finished,' the short one said. The tall one waved her spatula about.

True, I wasn't finished. Chewbacca had stopped shaving at Tom Selleck. I didn't care. Hauling up my bikini bottoms (where they would immediately set in the residual wax) I thrust a bundle of rupees into the big one's hand, pulled on my jeans and fled.

That evening, the whole area throbbed, swelled up monstrously and turned purple. I lay on the couch clad only in a baggy T-shirt, moaning, the living room windows opened onto the garden providing a meek, post-rain breeze.

'Darling, you're rather breaking the fourth wall,' complained the economist, retreating upstairs.

I really needed a bag of frozen peas to bring down the swelling, but the only thing in the freezer was a bottle of vodka. Chronic pain forcing my hand, I clutched the icy glass to my privates and groaned in relief.

It was at this moment the campus security guard walked past our back gate on his nightly rounds. Our eyes met.

I looked away first.

Mutton Dressed as Lamington

Villagers Save Boy from Sacrifice

Bangalore. Offering human sacrifice to propitiate the Gods may not be a novelty in Karnataka, but the incident which took place in Yadgir district on Thursday night can jolt the most cynical heart. A spine-chilling attempt was made to sacrifice a 13-year-old boy by his father; to unearth a treasure purportedly hidden in his fields. And here's the shocker: the child's mother knew about the ghastly ritual and his stepmother was party to it. However some alert villagers came to know about the nefarious designs of the parents and their 'tantrik', thwarting their attempt in time. The Times of India

From the ridiculous (and terrifying) to the sublime. Tonight we are invited to dinner with Rajeev Gowda, his wife Shamilla and their two children. Rajeev is a professor at the IIMB, Director of the Centre for Public Policy and aspiring politician. He was having a few people around, would we like to come? Yes please.

'Try being on half-Lisa,' suggests the economist, as we are dressing. 'Just until we know the lay of the land.'

Rajeev's Bauhaus apartment overlooks the tree-filled, genteel part of Bangalore. Tiled floors, antique furniture. This neighbourhood is one of the rare slices of the old city. Those present are the Indian upper class at its most elite: journalists, professors, entrepreneurs, a fashion designer, a famous photographer.

The assembled are all opinionated, globally aware and uber-educated. And me. Rajeev's spacious, marble-floored apartment would cost a million dollars in any major city in the world; surrounded by one-hundred-year-old oaks, the wide palatial balcony so above it all, the traffic below is but a murmur. Rajeev's unmarried cousin, the fashion designer, is dressed in one of her own creations, a white-jewelled salwar with tight white silk leggings. Slender, with long black hair, huge brown eyes and turmeric-golden skin, she is quite possibly the most beautiful woman I have ever seen. So poised, so cultured. So quiet.

My face a boiled bean hue, wearing my cheap, too-tight cotton kurta from Reliance Mart, I feel like a squat dung beetle in comparison. Rajeev's family and friends are New India — cosmopolitan, urbane. We are sweaty oiks from the colonies, but everyone is terribly kind, feigning interest in our points of view, asking what we think of India so far.

'Love it!' we gush.

New Zealanders know the rules of *that* game.

Rajeev is a tall, handsome man with a boyish lisp that makes him even more attractive. Possessing the insouciant languor of the aristocrat, he has political aspirations in the Nehru–Gandhi Indian National Congress — the largest and oldest democratic party in the world, founded in 1885 by the occultist Theosophical Society. Currently low on the party's totem pole, despite his own high social rank, Rajeev breaks off his party duties to humbly 'Yes, Sir' phone calls from the leader.

'One day, hopefully, someone will "Yes, Sir" me,' he says. 'But for now . . .'

Strangely, for such a chauvinistic environment, women do very well in Indian politics (usually as a result of being the daughters, nieces, or wives of feudal political dynasties), the formidable Sonia Gandhi being a good example. She is an Italian who married an Indian (not just any old Indian: the son of the then prime minister, who became prime minister himself), and is now one of the most powerful people in the country. 'We just call her Madam,' says the politician-in-waiting.

Rajeev's family are Brahmins and long-standing movers and shakers in local politics (and let's not forget, a Gowda founded Bangalore). Their two live-in maids, tiny women in pink and red saris, peek out from the kitchen where they are preparing the food in concert to the artful conducting of Shamilla. Short and dark with doll eyes, the servants have the frail physiognomy of adult survivors of childhood malnutrition.

It's not really a dinner party as we Kiwis would know it — there's a distinct lack of drinking too much, talking at the top of your voice and hitting on other people's wives. Ironically, Bangalore has a reputation throughout India as party central, and is thus nicknamed 'Beergalore', but all the bars and restaurants close at the ridiculous hour of 10.50. There *is* no night life. The New Zealand equivalent of a raunchy night out in Bangalore would be a post-christening sherry with a slightly tipsy vicar.

Indians can't drink anyway, well certainly not by our binge-drinking standards. In Bollywood movies there is always the obligatory 'drunk scene', where the leading man and his loser buddy get plastered, sing, slur and eventually fall over before passing out. Women *never* drink or smoke in Bollywood movies and forget kissing — they might decadently share a piece of fruit, bite for bite, with the leading man, but that's as naughty as it gets.

In a recurring theme, the Indian media lament the influence of shonky Western morals: 'What's wrong with young women today?' writes Disgusted of Hyderabad. 'Being seen in public drinking! Wearing jeans! Smoking! Well, I never.'

Needless to say, the high-born ladies at Rajeev's soiree don't drink, merely hold their glasses, always full, as props denoting Western cool.

I drink and, despite my cheap apparel and too-red face, am immediately found very interesting by the men. I bum a smoke off a debonair young chap who makes an almost imperceptible moue of distaste. Resigned, he demonstrates an old-fashioned chivalry. Flourishing a Zippo he tells me his family have harvested Arabica coffee from a hill station in the Baba Budan Giri ranges since the seventeenth century. Smoking *and* drinking, I prove myself the very epitome of wanton Western womanhood. White mischief, or damp pink mischief at the very least. Nobody told them it was going to be that kind of party. There is a polite swarm.

How long have the economist and I been married?

'Oh, we're not married,' I glibly tell the assembled.

Husbands covertly send the economist 'dodged-that-bullet' admiring glances. The gentlemen have a real thing about foreign spirits, particularly American whiskey. Kentucky bourbon is the night's tipple of prestige. In the old days, British booze was the esteemed snort and servants would be sent to the local grog shop to buy a bottle of the best Scottish whisky (real, as opposed to Indian-made) as loudly and obviously as they could, so that their master's exquisite and expensive taste would be made public knowledge.

Outside, on the balcony, the adults share snake stories in answer to our fascination. Inside, the children are behaving impeccably. One fourteen-year-old girl, the daughter of Rajeev's friends, modestly tells us of her plans to get into India's top law school. Waiting for her parents, she sits patiently on the couch, ankles crossed, reading a biography of the Indian mathematical genius, Srinivasa Ramanujan. I think of myself at fourteen: sullen, inarticulate, a sebaceous cyst of misplaced revolt.

Delivered home to the IIMB, the economist and I are giddy with the glamour of the evening, as excited as country mice returning from a rare jaunt to the city. Before turning in under the mosquito net, I read a little from *The Adventure of the Dying Detective*, particularly taken with Sir Arthur Conan Doyle's description of Sherlock Holmes. Despite Doyle's tales being set in Victorian England, Holmes is very like the handsome, affected, Indian coffee-bean heir I met at Rajeev's. 'He had a remarkable gentleness and courtesy in his dealings with women. He disliked and distrusted the sex, but he was always a chivalrous opponent.'

I imagine the bean heir, himself retiring for the evening, tossing his starched shirt on the floor for the servants to pick up, thinking: 'That New Zealand woman, what a dreadful parvenue.'

I laugh out loud.

'Did you tuck the net in properly on your side?' asks the economist.

City Market

I've decided on my method of dispensing alms. Based on my average weekly income (which, after Visa repayments and direct debits, is about NZ$30), I'll give one beggar loads of money (Rs200 = NZ$6) once a week, rather than peeling it off in dribs and drabs of Rs10 at a time.

I *am* Lotto.

'Women of a certain hip-to-waist ratio were best in the colonies,' declares the economist, as we quaver at the intersection.

He's right, I think (I've had plenty of time to think, we've been standing here for twenty minutes now). No faint-hearted ninnies or shrinking violets could possibly have coped, pre air conditioning, with a country where temperatures soar as high as 54°C. It's a very good thing indeed that, during our courtship, the economist put me through a stringent battery of girlfriend suitability tests involving dirt, depravity and camping without pillows. Conducted with the aim of not making the same mistake twice and including a pea under the mattress (Darling, I couldn't sleep a wink), thanks to this instilled buffering, I am able to cope with our visit to Bangalore's City Market.

City Market is gained by passing through a dangerous convergence of eight roads. No traffic lights, no road rules, just go when it looks okay. It never looks okay. It looks like vehicular manslaughter.

Cows loll in the middle of it all, entirely unconcerned. Somehow, despite the absolute bedlam, nobody gets hurt, there aren't that many accidents and most of the time all the individual crossing currents of buses, auto rickshaws, lorries and pedestrians weave and dart and pass in and out and through each other like a perfectly choreographed ballet.

Motorbikes carry whole families: dad, mum and three kids lined up on the seat like peas on a knife. In defiance of the clouds of red dust, the schoolchildren perched in front of their fathers' chests have immaculate uniforms; white knee socks, the girl's hair in ribboned bunches. Lopsided and overloaded, colourfully painted trucks with 'Horn Please' painted on the bumper muscle between cars, bicycles and cows.

Driving four abreast, everyone constantly sounds their horn in warning. There is no such thing as indicating — the give way rule in India consists of giving way to the oncoming vehicle travelling the fastest. This lack of rule-following is made up for by the aplomb with which the drivers swerve and career, madly tooting, missing annihilation by a buffalo hair's breadth.

The Indian techno-boom has made the Bangalorean standard of living rise enormously, meaning that instead of antique Hero bicycles, today's smart young chaps ride Tata scooters and Hero Honda motorbikes. Family men drive Nanos or Suzuki Zens — all this new metal makes navigating the congested roads even more horrendous. The wide, potholed asphalt supports eight 'lanes' of cars, bikes and trucks, waves and waves of them. The mayor of Bangalore was stuck in traffic last week and he was livid. He now insists on driving in a cortege with a car in front and a car behind, though just how this will prevent that from happening again is anyone's guess.

As a pedestrian, by moving forward, you are signalling your intention to others. If you change direction or halt out of fear or nerves, woe betide you. He who hesitates is mowed down. We jerk and flop about, and the economist stood in cow poo, until eventually we got the hang of just going for it. You could wait politely by the side of the road for a break in the traffic for the rest of your life.

As you enter the market proper, the fresh, lemony smell of coriander in huge bundles greets you, mingled with the stench of rotten vegetables from yesterday's transport strike. Laid out on the ground there are pyramids of persimmons, corn cobs, tomatoes, cucumbers, coconuts and aubergines. It's a visual splendour: sight fighting smell for sensory overload.

The stench of shit and urine from terrified animals is sweetened by intermittent wafts of incense, shaped into dozens of vermilion cones and piled up on the counters like a psychedelic mountain range. Tied to the fence, nervous calves root in the rubbish. A stalled truck carries a massive statue of Shiva, blue as a new Smurf, a cobra wrapped around his neck like a dandy's scarf. Rusty axel bare, the driver changes the tyre, and the tilting, towering Shiva casts a benevolent shadow over the straw scattered on the ground.

While the City Market is on the 'what to do in Bangalore' map, it's definitely a real market, not a tourist bazaar. Despite this, it is brochure-beautiful, if coloured using a lunatic's paint box, everything in clashing colours: crimson, gold, turquoise, vermilion shouting for attention. So many people, and all the while the traffic roars and bashes you about the ears.

Time for some peace and quiet.

Escaping the madness, we make our way to Mahatma Gandhi Road to have lunch upstairs at the very swanky Ulla's Refreshments. Two mains, drinks and coffee for the incredibly expensive price of NZ$9. 'Let's push the boat out,' says the economist. Maybe he thinks it's my birthday.

Scandalising the staff with our unorthodox combinations of food ('Is Madam *sure* she wants dharwad pedha with her aloo chaat?'). We find it all delicious and finally feel like we are making it. Thanks to New Zealand's stellar performance in the 2010 FIFA World Cup, there's plenty to talk about.

'Who will go to the final?' asks Ulla's rotund manager. Germany and Holland, we decide. Germany have performed outstandingly, but as the manager points out, 'the World Cup is anyone's cup,' after Brazil and Italy got the shuffti.

The economist sips his third mango lassi. From Ulla's balcony one has a good view of the unfinished Mahatma Gandhi Road section of Bangalore Metro's elevated mass transit system, jutting out into nothing like a broken freeway in a disaster movie. The Bangalore Metro Rail Corporation has so far nominated and missed four deadlines for inaugeration of the line since work began in 2007.

In this posh, touristy part of the city most people don't bother you. They are just doing their thing, you, yours. Apart, of course, from the bloody auto-rickshaw wallahs. Loitering on the street corners in their vile khaki pantsuits, just waiting to begin some hard-core haggling. Bored, betel-stained traders on a red-dirt exchange floor.

Currently striking (on Tuesdays and Thursdays only), they are protesting at the rise in the cost of LPG and the fact that they have had no corresponding rise in their per-kilometre fare. The government refuses to move on the issue, so, with other transport workers going out in solidarity, airports are closed down, buses not working, disruptions to trains and on it goes. A few of the rickshaw wallahs have covered themselves in petrol and threatened to strike a match. Nobody intervened . . . Indians hate the auto-rickshaw wallahs.

'I'd shoot them the way you shoot rabbits over here,' an Indian friend emails from Dunedin, 'they're bastards.'

Whatever the personality shortcomings of the drivers, tuk-tukking is still a great way to navigate the traffic (although you do breathe in a considerable amount of carbon monoxide as you go) and it's also a cheap way to get around the city, costing less than NZ$4 to travel as much as 20 kilometres.

Taking advantage of our ignorance, the driver usually dumps us out at an uncle's knick-knack shop and quickly disappears. The shopkeepers must be sorely disappointed — the poorest and tightest tourists they could possibly have the misfortune to find outside their door, yet we're the best currently on offer, as, due to terrorism heebie jeebies amongst Europeans (the bomb explosion at Pune's German Bakery still fresh in everyone's minds), there just *aren't* any tourists around right now. So far we have been confused variously for Netherlanders, Germans, English.

Until we open our mouths, of course. Nobody could mistake that nasal twang. 'Australia!'

Hailing another tuk tuk, we ask to be dropped off outside the Vidhana Soudha, the many-pillared Karnataka Houses of Parliament. On this torpid, breezeless afternoon, the Indian flag droops against the pole. Saffron, white and green hang downward, obscuring the ashoka chakra, the twenty-four-spoke wheel at the flag's centre. The ice-cream vendors plying their trade outside the Houses of Parliament are too hot to pester anyone, slumped on the footpath beside their mobile freezers, listlessly flapping a hand to indicate their range. Iceblocks are only 70 cents. Three go down pretty easy.

Walking the length of the railings, we notice strange things scattered on the footpath near the members' entrance: a broken pumpkin, feathers, bangles, a handful of vermilion and turmeric, a lemon pierced with four nails. The other pedestrians are giving this queer assembly of objects a wide berth.

These are the remnants of kaala jaadu, a Black Magic ritual. One of the politicians within these hallowed walls has earned the ire of his constituents, it seems. The minister had better shape up or the chicken gets it.

Blessed are the Bovines

'If you ever want to know who owns a cow in India,' says Rajeev, 'put a rope around its neck and try to lead it off. The owner will instantly appear.' Cows in India only seem to be ownerless. A city girl, I've always been a bit of a stranger to cows and their ways, we non-farmers only ever seeing them through car windows, black and white against the green. However, cows make steak and for that I will remain forever grateful.

In India, cows are sacred. They own the roads. And you don't eat them.

The sheer number of cows in India comes as a bit of a shock. They are everywhere — on the footpaths, in front of the newspaper kiosk, standing outside the ATM's bullet-proof glass, eyeballing the armed guard. Moseying, chewing, plonked at the intersections. Contemplating their holiness. Cow poo (gobar) doesn't sit around for long. Eagerly scooped up, the dung is used as a disinfectant, and once dried, as fuel in lieu of firewood. Cow urine is commonly used in India for medicinal purposes, distilled and consumed by patients seeking treatment for a wide variety of illnesses. At present, there is no conclusive evidence this has any effect.

India has the world's largest population of cattle (283 million, according to *TIME* magazine) and twenty-six distinctive breeds including Jerseys imported by the Raj, Indian-born Red Danish out of sires from Denmark, beautiful beige Brahmans and long-horned Zebus. All of them in your face, up close and personal.

Every morning, buying a newspaper, I have to push a certain Friesian heifer out of my way as she placidly yet stubbornly holds her favourite spot outside the tiny newsagent kiosk. The locals are feeding her a breakfast of bananas. 'You again?' she telegraphs with unconcerned brown eyes, turning to see who is shoving at her bum.

'Mooove,' I groan.

The newspaper readers smile, revealing teeth stained red by paan.

Indian cows wander the highways with utter disregard for the traffic. They graze unmindfully on the roadside verges, munching vegetables thrown out by street vendors. Drivers swerve to avoid them and no wonder; the penalty for killing a cow was once death, these days jail or a fine equivalent to three years' salary. The cows of India know they're holy. They roam unchallenged and uncaring, road-hogging.

'What is the greatest traffic hazard in Delhi today? Cows,' affirms Bibek Debroy, a columnist for India's *Financial Express*. To solve the problem Bibek suggests kitting the cows out with safety appendages and means of identification: 'Let them have reflectors . . . license plates.'

Although in recent years New Zealand dairy farmers have become vilified and dairying blamed for polluting our waterways, since the days of Indus valley (Bronze Age) civilisation dairy farming has been the most important occupation in India. While the early Hindus ate the meat of oxen and bulls sacrificed to the gods, the slaughter of milk-producing cows, as symbols of wealth for a largely pastoral people, was prohibited. Over time the cow became seen as a maternal figure, the sacred female, its flesh taboo. By the early centuries AD it was said that killing a cow was equal to killing a Brahman.

As the lamb is to Christianity, the cow is to Hinduism. The country's 900 million Hindus revere the cow and the bull god, Nandi, Shiva's mount (most Indian gods have attendant animal vehicles. Elephantine Ganesha rides on a poor wee mouse). Stray and homeless cows are supported by their neighbourhood temple. There is no gift more pious than the gift of a cow, symbol of the earth, 'Mother' of civilisation, its milk nuturing the nation. The tiger may well be the national animal of India, but the cow is more noticeable.

Ghee (clarified liquid butter) and milk form the core of all Hindu rituals, meaning the cow holds a central place in religion. Although Hindus follow no single set of rules, reverence for cows can be found throughout the religion's major texts. Some trace the cow's sacred status back to Lord Krishna, one of the faith's most important figures.

He is said to have appeared 5000 years ago as a cowherd and is often described as bala-gopala, 'the child who protects the cows'.

In India the cow is viewed as an animal to be esteemed, not eaten. In a bid to bolster support, some of India's Hindu politicians are proposing cow-protection ordinances and, in Karnataka, going so far as to propose a ban on beef butchery. While this hasn't happened yet, even the McDonalds of India daren't serve anything redder than a processed chicken patty.

Gandhi once wrote: 'If someone were to ask me what the most important outward manifestation of Hinduism was, I would say that it was cow protection.' Delhi's 13 million residents, sharing the streets with 40,000 cows, might disagree. Complaints of ripped-open rubbish bags and snarled traffic have led city officials to employ cow catchers — one hundred urban cowboys tasked with gently rounding up and relocating the bovine battalions.

But the cows aren't going easy. They have sharp horns and a bad attitude. Life on the streets has made them smart and ornery, and they perform a backstreet dance of defiance.

Squished and occasionally gored, perhaps the Delhi cow wallahs dream of a country like New Zealand, where cows live outside the cities and feed on grass, not plastic bags; a country where, if you put a hoof out of line, you might just get served up with minty peas.

New World, Dark Ages

There has been another honour killing. The fifth couple murdered by their own families in a fortnight.

Romeo and Juliet were hacked to pieces, their bodies hidden in a rubbish pile next to school grounds, left to be discovered by children. In other news this week, India has launched a billion-dollar, state-of-the-art satellite. The new world and the Dark Ages, cheek by jowl.

Waking to a worm of worry, we have only two days left to register with the Commissioner of Police or become illegal aliens, without a residential permit. Off we set.

The Bangalore traffic is an ocean and you a drop within. The auto-rickshaws all bear the same number plate; KA 05 (KA for the state of Karnataka) but I always read it as KAOS. And it is. The blaring horns, cratered tarmac, a river now a cesspit; sidewalk drivers, dead or dying dogs, wandering cows, puddles of red spit from paan-chewers, beggars missing a hand, eye or pants.

The smell: excrement, marigolds, incense and coriander.

Negotiating this madness, we arrived at the Commissioner of Police to find a queue stretching round the building. Forms had to be filled out. The criteria were stringent and multitudinous. An air of threat and sullen time-wasting exuded from lounging officials. One guard, armed with a lathi (a cane used to beat people), seemed to have nothing to do but make the hundreds stand up, move left, move right. His voluminous stomach had been belted into the groin of his khaki pants, where it bulged menacingly, like two angry coconuts.

'This is the fault of those bloody terrorists,' declared the economist. He was getting that face he gets — part peevish, part berserker.

'But we're New Zealanders,' I reassured him. 'We have such cute accents.' New Zealanders, the world's Labradors.

Did we have four additional passport-sized photos? Nope. Leaving the commissioner's compound, we passed the statue of Sir M Visvesvaraya, an engineer and one of India's most influential thinkers. A strict vegetarian and teetotaller, Sir MV even has his own day, 15 September, Engineer's Day.

'See, other countries have engineering, space programmes . . . what do we have? Baristas. Our sole contribution to civilisation? Good coffee. Oh, my computer's not working, I'd better take it to a barista . . .' the economist went on and on in a nasty falsetto. He always gets a bit pissy when things don't go his way.

After walking for an hour and not a photo booth in sight, we finally asked someone. Kind to a fault, Indians will always give you directions. Perhaps the word 'photo' explained our being directed to an MRI clinic. We eventually had our pictures taken, between power cuts, at a camera shop in a nearby mall: both ears visible, hair scraped back. The results best described as 'modern revolting'. I complained at length.

'Ugly pictures are the least of our worries,' said the economist, in the tones of Eeyore contemplating his burst balloon.

Returning to the queue, a man being led off in iron shackles answered the question of what would happen if we decided not to bother.

'I lost my passport!' he protested.

The thin-lipped official wasn't buying it.

Tomato-soup air, the total lack of public toilets, mosquitoes the size of ham sandwiches . . . being deported sounded lovely.

The economist oozed his way into the commissioner's office on a slick of charm.

'And this is my wife,' he said.

Funny how, whenever we're being messed around by petty bureaucrats, he upgrades me to legitimacy. As wifey, my role was to say nothing. I regarded the paan-stained floor, hiding my supercilious smile. In that moment I suddenly understood the burka.

Aware of the caste society in which we dwelt, the economist attempted an academic finagle.

'I'm a professor,' he said, immodestly.

The official gave him a look which said, 'We kicked people like you out in '47,' chucking our passports back across the desk, face down like dirty pictures. 'Come back tomorrow.'

Tomorrow and we queue for five hours with our fellow sufferers from Senegal, Nigeria and Sri Lanka. The whole thing seems an exercise in bullying and stupidity. For the first time in our lives, we sovereign Kiwis are desperate and stateless, our fortunes hostage to the caprice of a government employee. How the other half lives.

Weary and close to tears, I read the sign in front of me twenty-five times: 'In case of undue delay or harassment caused by officials in attending to official work, the same may be brought to the notice of the registrar.'

Presumably as a foil to bribery, our papers are checked by three different officials in three different queues. We are photographed again, our faces are grim.

'Who is she to you?' the clerk asks the economist.

'My partner,' he replies.

This makes absolutely no sense.

'Your wife?' she tries.

'One day, if she plays her cards right, she might be,' he jokes. Neither the clerk nor I think this is funny.

'Come back at 4.30.'

Finally we have our papers. From the sacred cow of documents, an excerpt: Bureau of Immigration Bangalore. Registration Certificate/Residential Permit (RC/RP). Form 'A' (RULE 6). Lisa Anne Marie Scott, colour of eyes: OTHERS.

Occupation: WRITETR

LEFT: Kiwi tourists are all class!

BELOW: The Annual Independence Day Flower Show held inside the Lal Bagh glasshouse. Featuring over 250 varieties of flowers and plants; the star attraction was a replica of Delhi's India Gate made from 250,000 roses (partially seen at top right).

ABOVE: A Zebu or Brahman, a breed of cattle adapted to high temperatures and resistant to pests and diseases. Plastic bags will still make them froth at the mouth, however.

LEFT: Reflecting pool in the courtyard of the Jama Masjid, the principal mosque of Old Delhi, which is able to accommodate up to 25,000 worshippers.

RIGHT: Hotel Capital (Deluxe) and Guest House. Government approved.

BELOW: Delhi's Red Fort or Lal Qila, a sandstone monument to pomp and splendour at the peak of Mughal power. The enormous, now empty octagonal fort was once a mini-city protected by a moat, turrets, bastions and ramparts.

ABOVE: The tomb of
the Mughal Emperor
Humayun, Delhi.

LEFT: Arcaded cloisters,
Red Fort, Delhi.

Transported by Divine Intervention

In India, women are supposed to ride on the front half of buses, men at the back. Not chivalry, rather an attempt to avoid undue and unwanted stimulation on the part of the menfolk. It turns out Indian men are highly suggestible. Having your hair down or uncovered is erotic, as is exposing your lower leg. A sleeveless blouse is considered extremely risqué in India, naked shoulders as shocking as a bare breast.

There is no snogging on Indian television or in Indian movies. Couples get to first base by pressing their foreheads together and staring deeply into each other's eyes — they never kiss, it's too rude. A Bangalorean teleported to an Antipodean beach in summertime would probably explode at the sight of such untrammelled exhibitionism.

All this repression means sex is all some Indian men ever think about. Presented with a female backside in tantalising proximity, they are helpless against the urge to grind against it. Just so you know, bus frottage isn't a prelude to romance.

Actually, riding the buses is mostly okay, once you let go of petty Western constructs such as 'personal space'. Contrary to Indian public transport's reputation for sly perversion, the first time I travelled by bus I experienced not one pinch, poke or fondle (mind you, the economist *was* standing right beside me). Disappointed and not a little insulted, I went and sat up front. 'Ladies and the Physically Challenged' read the sign above my head.

Today, after a lurch, I'm suddenly sandwiched in the middle, cut off from the women by the last heave of extra people getting on, and now surrounded by men. After twenty minutes I'm forced to say, 'Get any closer and we'll have to get married', to the man behind me who has been rubbing against my arse. There is a big wet stain on the front of his trousers.

Meanwhile, the economist is having a jolly time, leaping on and off the bus at every stop, hanging outside by one arm, nose to the breeze. His face glows with happiness. The other men slap him on the back and shout encouragement.

'This is the worst experience of my life!' I wailed into someone's armpit. My whingeing went unheard.

As far as I'm concerned, riding a bus in India is only great in retrospect, like German Expressionist movies and bungy jumping. 'The Indian transport system is proof that God exists,' said an old Bangalorean. 'How else could it work, but for divine intervention?'

Speaking of transcendence, it seems the economist is a bit of a celebrity here. Everywhere we go, groups of young men stop to take his photo. Do they mistake him for Brendon McCullum, I wonder? Sir Richard Hadlee? (We later discover many people believe he is Bret Michaels, the lead singer of '80s hair metal band, Poison).

The economist has been watching a lot of the God Channel lately and becoming increasingly obsessed with it. After my first husband's born-again phase, this makes me very uneasy. The God Channel's fervent congregations scream out 'Jesus! Jesus!', tear their clothes, cry and faint, while Bible-thumping pastors bellow that gays in the army are destroying America. The ranting preacher is African American. Watching a black man persecuting a minority using quotations from the same book the Klan once used to prove *his* race was inferior is horribly funny.

To stop the economist watching nothing but the God Channel and growing daily more spiritual, I have to steal the remote. He's not particular about which religion he subscribes to, he likes them all. Sheltering under a tree during monsoon rain, he became convinced that the snaggle-toothed man with the enormous nose standing next to me was Ganesha.

'He wants you to finish your book,' he whispered, wiggling his eyebrows.

Giving vast sums of money to the beggars, the economist is finding himself, and (I have to say) himself is a pretty nice guy. I prefer to run my lottery system, giving one unsuspecting unfortunate an enormous sum once a week. They often flee, fearing a change of mind. Round and round she goes, where she stops nobody knows.

❧ ❧ ❧

On the luxury train to Mysore, once people realised we weren't American they stared with less hostility. We sampled the delights of a small round pear seasoned with a liberal pinch of chilli powder (the pear is so hard it reminded me of crab-apples stolen as a kid from the garden next door to ours — the subsequent tummy ache is comfortingly familiar) and watched the antics of the hijra, the cross-dressers or 'Children of God'.

Announcing themselves with a loud clap, the hijra sweep into the carriage, anklets a-jingling, ruby nails flashing. Faces white with rice flour, pouting lips smeared with Maybelline Red Comet, their kohl-rimmed eyes are mischievous.

Viewed with superstitious dread, and familial disgust, hijra are often disowned and discarded, left to earn a living by entertaining at weddings or begging in twos and threes. Made understandably bitchy by this exclusion, money is the only way to appease them. In return they sing a song, tell a joke and forgo cursing your family.

Cackling in derision, rupees clutched in their large hands, the hijra eventually tinkle away, making for the next carriage, a powdered flock of stand-over crows.

Mysore is the second largest city in the state of Karnataka, located approximately 146 kilometres south-west of Bangalore. A centre for the production of sandalwood, incense and silk, Mysore is also known for yoga retreats and Ayurvedic medicine.

'Mysore' is an anglicised version of Mahishuru, which means the abode of Mahisasura, a demon from Hindu mythology, half man half water buffalo. Mysore is most famous for the Dasara festival, possessing a wobbly date somewhere around September/October. A resplendent carnival of pomp, Dasara consists of ten days of richly costumed elephants, idols, liveried retainers and marching brass bands, all celebrating the victory of truth over evil and culminating in remembrance of the day, 5000 years ago, when the bloodthirsty Goddess Chamundeshwari, wearing her garland of severed heads, slew the demon Mahisasura (who had been terrorising heaven and earth) by chopping off his. The festival observes the nine day battle, during which Mahisasura's army was decimated, with his death under the waxing moon of the tenth.

A brain spasm (which would make my history of art lecturer very happy) brings to mind Artemisia Gentileschi's seventeenth century 'homage' to decapitation, 'Judith Slaying Holofernes'. Proving a woman wielding something sharp is a timeless terror, I read of a woman from a village called Makkapurva who used the sickle she was cutting grass with to cut off the head of a man who tried to sexually assault her, and then paraded the head through the village. Never, ever, sneak up on a woman using a large blade in an isolated field.

When it's not Dasara, Mysore is a quiet, clean city slumbering at the foot of the Chamundi hills. 'Helloschoolpen?' ask the Mysore children at dawn, relieving us of every one of our Biros, so that I have to write my travel diary in maroon lip-liner, which I have packed for some reason — anticipating a 'Rocky Horror Picture Show' party perhaps, or a Naomi Campbell impersonation contest.

Everything in Mysore is tainted by the all-pervading, acrid smell of wees. As the sun rises, the *hoick, hoick* of cleared throats heralds the start of another day. Everyone in India does this early morning loud spitting thing, clearing the pipes — it sounds like hangover retching, or someone hawking up a budgie.

We give our breakfast to the monkeys — the sacred cows can take care of themselves — and feed biscuits to the skinny stray dogs. Their soulful eyes say, 'Take me home'. The economist seems to push me forward whenever a pack crosses our path. Could this be because he knows something I don't (85 per cent of all yearly human deaths from rabies occur in India)?

The former seat of the Wodeyar maharajas, Mysore Palace makes Dunedin's Larnach Castle look like a handsomely decorated urinal. The royal family returns there once a year, just for the Dasara festival. The Wodeyar dynasty ruled in the Kingdom of Mysore until Independence, but are now much reduced in numbers, possibly as the result of a curse of barrenness placed on the family by the widow Alamelamma, after the Raja Wodeyar tried to divest her of a fine pearl nose-stud.

The old palace was gutted by fire in 1897; the one standing today was completed in 1912 by English architect Henry Irwin. An Indo-Saracenic (an architectural style popularised in late nineteenth century British India, drawing on elements of Islamic, Indian, Gothic and Neo-Classical architecture) marvel, it is a kaleidoscope of stained glass, silver mirrors and gaudy colours. Its carved wooden doors and mosaic floors, Golden Howdah, Doll's Pavilion, and great bronze tigers all add to the over-the-top-ness of it all. Elton John would love it.

Outside the palace a flash mob of forty men elbow the economist out of the way to have their photo taken — with me for a change. I'm so pleased; I don't even slap the hand that squeezes my bottom.

The fact that the next golden age (heaven on earth) was 2500 years away didn't stop the economist's search for enlightenment. Chamundi Hill, one of the eight holy hills of southern India, is home to a temple to the emasculating, eight-armed, bull-riding, demon-slaying goddess Chamundi. After prevaricating for some time about whether we are allowed to, we enter the temple and have our third eyes blessed with sandalwood paste, to the sound of little bells. Afterwards, we both experience a warm rush of feeling — it could be religious illumination, it could just be relief that nobody yelled at us.

Listening intently to the guru at the Godly Museum on Mysore's Chamundi Hill, the economist looks both sage and demented. I fear an intervention is called for, before he's off on the next astral plane. Ever since my aforementioned ex became a fire-and-brimstone Old Testament ranter, complete with spittle-flecked proselytising and speaking in tongues, I've had a steady dislike for religion. Now here's the economist showing signs of liturgical fever. It makes me very nervous.

Later, at lunch, all eyes are on us. Not by reason of our pale skin, but the messiness of our munching as, in the total absence of cutlery, we attempt to eat with our hands. The economist makes a particularly entertaining display at the vegetarian tearoom of the Mysore railway station. His long, inflexible spatulate fingers flick rice everywhere — on the walls, the floor, in his hair. The two Benedictine nuns at the table behind us laugh into their wimples, effortlessly spooning up their dhal with dainty fingers. Blushing, we wash our hands under the communal tap.

On our return journey the economist swings out the train door, sniffing burning plastic from trackside fires and waving to the locals. Smiling like a naughty Krishna, he never seems to need the toilet. Outside the window houses with huge holes in their sides, as if they've been shelled in a recent battle, sag against each other, exhausted. Cavalierly hopping off at every small station and then jumping back on at the last minute, the economist provides the passengers with marvellous entertainment. At one point the entire carriage leans out the windows, yelling, 'Get back on! Get back on!' as the train begins to pull away from the station while he buys onion bhajis from a platform stall. There is worried silence when he fails to reappear, until he pokes his head around the wall of our compartment, wiping a hand across his forehead, miming 'phew!' Everyone bursts into relieved applause.

Show off.

Resolutely staying in my seat because I have jandal burn, I can't help but notice that the sari is not the most flattering of garments, although SBF (Sari Back Fat) is surely an indication of the rising standard of living in India.

Disembarking, and now a lot less tolerant (all he has to do is hang off the train door and everybody loves him), woe betide anyone who touches my bum.

'All men are perverts,' says the economist. 'Some just hide it better than others.' If this pragmatism is meant to be comforting, it isn't working.

An unseen hand snakes out. Pinch.

Sick of all the sneaky pinching, punching and poking, I seriously lose the plot. Standing on the platform of the crowded bus station, I yell, 'Fucking stop touching my bum you fucking arseholes!!' at the top of my voice, flailing my arms around like an agitator washing machine.

The economist is mortified.

'You're being extremely culturally insensitive,' he tsks — groping my arse being just a quaint old Indian custom.

We head back to our apartment via auto rickshaw, grit in our eyes, carbon monoxide in our lungs. The rickshaw drivers have just won a 26 per cent fare increase after their nationwide bundah (strike). Does it stop them trying to rip you off? Of course not. None of the manual meters have been recalibrated or replaced by digital ones, and their broken seals indicate widespread meter-tampering. You have to figure out the fare with the aid of a chart prepared by the Department of Legal Metrology.

As we pull up outside the IIMB, our driver, moustachioed like a 1970s Bollywood star, asks for Rs270 ($9). 'Ha!' says the economist, paying the correct fare ($2) and including a tip, 'nice try'. Beaming at each other, they share a look of mutual recognition, the driver doing a 'but-of-course' head-wobble. I go to find a sticky plaster.

After a rest from our Mysore adventures, and the application of some topical cream, we might contemplate a trip to Goa . . .

Fair & Unlovely

I like to watch the soaps on Star Plus and the Colours network and make up the dialogue. The men are always crying. It's quite sexy.

But the ads are the best.

'Main average nhi hoon,' (I'm not average) announces movie-star god Shahid Kapoor, lounging around a swanky apartment in a black bathrobe. Well of course he's not average; he's Shahid Kapoor, baby-faced actor and dancer perpetually cast as the dim-but-hot romantic lead. To the delight of millions of swooning Indian girls, his pants are always tight and his shirtsleeves rolled up to reveal muscular forearms.

Today the tightness of Shahid's leather pants proves no obstacle to his riding a motorbike. His passenger is an incandescently pale sylph who leans over his shoulder to caress his cheek as they zoom about the cityscape. Looking directly into the camera, Shahid holds up the reason for his uniqueness, a tub of fairness cream for men. With the help of this product, he says, anyone can be prepared. Thanks to Shahid, Indian men don't want to be tall, dark and handsome anymore; they want to be Fair & Handsome.

A few minutes later, another ad, this one starring Anushka Sharma. Gravely, she warns that some parts of our bodies are actually darker than our faces. This is definitely not true in my case (unless you count bruises) but as she speaks, legions of Indian women are hastily adding fairness cream to tomorrow's shopping list.

One might well ask, 'Why would anyone want to apply a fairness cream?' In the southern hemisphere, despite the ozone roasting us to jerky, a tan is still considered sexy. Dark skin is exotic, lusty and a totem of the holidaying classes. Those of us who aren't lucky enough to be of

Maori or Polynesian decent are often ashamed to be so white.

'Fish belly arms,' I lamented to the Tammster (herself a pleasant shade of biscuit) when, previous to pole dancing, mid-winter disrobing revealed acres of pasty.

'Freckles like flies on a dead trout.'

'Oh Scoot,' she said, 'You're pale and interesting.'

At the time I took her word for it — after all the Tammster knows her chic from clay — now I'm not so sure. While I slather on the self-tanner, achieving a shade of orange not intended by God, all across Asia the demand for skin-whiteners is soaring.

I am firmly of the opinion that, tanned or fair, pink or olive-skinned, all women are beautiful — it's just that changing room strip lighting is so unflattering, sometimes we forget our own fabulousness. Well not in India. My delusional mantra of self-belief won't hold here, where, if you listen to the marketing jungle drums, dark equals ugly and dull. For the growing Indian middle class, fair skin, beauty and success are directly correlated.

Making me a goddess of gorgeous, right? Nope. Pale-skinned and green-eyed I may be, but this fairness = beauty rule doesn't apply to foreigners. Even though it seems my bottom is damn near irresistible to a certain segment of the population, pale skin will never be enough to make me attractive in India. I'll forever be a freaky-looking white girl in a brown nation. However these tonal rules of attraction matter a great deal to people of Indian heritage, some of whom are literally dying to be white.

The Fair & Lovely ads ask, 'Do you want success, do you want confidence, do you want your lover to propose? Use fairness cream.' Even though I'm an Irish Colleen of carpet-matches-the-curtains variety, the 'white is right' message is so shrilly pervasive, the not-good-enoughness so bludgeoning, I go out and buy a pottle of Ponds White Beauty.

I *know*.

Applying a smear in the morning, by lunchtime my cheeks were en flambé — a combination of third degree sunburn and bike-crash rash. A sulphuric acid peel might have been gentler. For two weeks my face sported angry red blisters. A couple of freckles were permanently erased.

When it comes to third-wave feminism and *The Beauty Myth*'s concept of 'beauty' as a normative value entirely socially constructed, Naomi Wolf should have considered stupid is as stupid does.

Many consumer commentators posit that the Indian obsession with fair skin is a hangover from colonial masters, but the truth is Indians have long had a prejudice against dark skin and a poor tolerance towards swarthier races. When Gandhi addressed a public meeting in Bombay on 26 September 1896, he had the following to say about the Indian struggle in South Africa:

'Ours is one continued struggle against degradation sought to be inflicted upon us by the European, who desire to degrade us to the level of the raw Kaffir, whose occupation is hunting and whose sole ambition is to collect a certain number of cattle to buy a wife with, and then pass his life in indolence and nakedness.'

Indian and Pakistani cab drivers in New York caused controversy in 1999 when they refused to take actor Danny Glover, on the grounds that they were scared of him.

With these black-skin bugbears, India presents a phenomenal market for fairness cream, and its value to companies like Hindustan Lever — flogging bleaching products to 1.2 billion people with a coffee-coloured chip on their shoulders — is estimated at Rs800 crore each year (a crore is 10 million rupees).

United States beauty-care multinationals first became aware of this rich vein of social stigma ten years ago, when marketing executives from a large American skin-care conglomerate stumbled across an enormous, untapped niche for a whitening product which had previously tanked in the United States.

An imaginative, satirical reconstruction of this epiphany was published in the writing compendium *Sulekha Select* in the form of an inter-office memo from the said conglomerates' marketing department: 'If we could get Michael Jackson to endorse the product in India, that would work wonders. Showing him in his Thriller days and comparing that Michael Jackson to the new one would prove that even the darkest of dark people can become fair with the right attitude and skin-care products.'

Fair, fairer, fairest. A cursory study of the classified matrimonial columns in the local papers shows ads that endorse this obsession and that follow a set pattern: 'A fair, good-looking Gujarati/Sindhi/Punjabi/Tamil lady wanted for an educated, well-settled man . . .' Southern Indians are often tarred by their northern brethren with the prejudicial descriptor 'small and dark', while taller north Indians advertise themselves as the fairest in the land. A 'wheatish' complexion is a euphemism for a girl who is on her way to fair, 'chalky white' being the epitome, a colour so unrealistic and unachievable amongst a people high in melanin, it's almost as ridiculous as the concept of 'skinny jeans' is for me.

Billboards, magazines, newspaper ads, the message is everywhere — white is right. Fair and lovely commercials preach acceptance and promise assimilation into the bourgeois modern world. 'You're nothing but a peasant' is the subtext, 'if your skin is dark.' The same way the Western media portrays fat people as stupid and unworthy of love.

In Bollywood movies the comic roles are often played by dark-skinned actors; failed leading men. Dark skin is synonymous with the lower classes and associated with the toil and sweat of hard labour in the fields, while fair skin is identified with genteel, upmarket living. In India, nobody wants to be immediately done down at first glance by being too brown. No wonder millions reach for a pottle of bleach every morning.

The problem is, fairness cosmetics are incredibly dangerous, causing discolouration, photosensitivity, red rashes, burns and blisters. Most whiteners act to suppress the production of melanin, moisturise and eradicate spots and marks, which sounds very nice. However, the main ingredient of bleaching creams, hydroquinone, causes cancer. Mercury toxicity is another nasty side effect. What price white?

Goan, Goan, Gone

'You were a bit of a goer before you met me,' says the economist. He does love his jokes.

We travel to Goa on the sleeper bus. Needless to say, it's not very expensive. The bunks are surrounded by red velour curtains and are Indian-people-sized, so the economist and I have to spoon; slick and sweaty, steaming up the windows. It's very romantic. 'Now we have travelled by bus, train and tuk tuk!' he says excitedly, like a small boy who collects modes of transportation.

Tiny Goa, sandwiched between the Western Ghats, Karnataka, and the Arabian Sea, is India's smallest and richest state, with a gross domestic product (GDP) per capita two and a half times that of the country as a whole. Goa was once a legendary stop on the 1960s and 1970s hippy trail. When the flower children washed their patchouli off and became investment bankers, a core group remained — dedicating themselves to concentrating on developments in music, yoga and recreational drugs.

In the late '80s and early '90s, Goa became home to Goan Trance, a kind of dance party where the music is so boringly repetitive, large amounts of narcotics are required to enjoy it. Fashions change and the fickle trancers have largely moved on (although New Year's Eve is still a biggie with the Brits), with new global hot spots for Goan Trance popping up, including Brazil, Japan and . . . New Zealand. Go figure.

Goa, once a glorious hibiscus bloom, is these days a little tattered from being plucked and worn behind the ears of so many. And with the soaring murder rate, it's not a very safe place for tourists.

As we staggered off the rickety local bus, three men were being detained for the rape and murder of fifteen-year-old British tourist

Scarlett Keeling. Scarlett's death was initially listed as drowning by the Goan police, despite the autopsy revealing she had more than fifty wounds, and had been sexually assaulted before her death. Her mother insisting on a second autopsy, the Goan tourism minister was forced to admit that Indian police had attempted a cover-up, fearing that registering a case of murder would affect the Goan tourism industry.

Questions were asked in the Indian media about the parental fitness of Scarlett's mother, revealing an unfortunate Indian/Goan morality. What sort of mother (asked the editorials) lets a fifteen-year-old stay in Goa without her (she and the rest of the family were travelling nearby in another state while Scarlett stayed with her tour-guide boyfriend)? Police allege loose morality and drug-taking on Scarlett's part led to her demise.

In addition to the three men arrested, four others were wanted in connection with Scarlett's death. One of those arrested was her boyfriend.

Also in the news was the trial of charming serial killer Hatchand Bhaonani Gurumukh Charles Sobhraj. A psychopath of Indian and Vietnamese descent, Sobhraj preyed on Western tourists throughout South-east Asia during the 1970s. Nicknamed 'the Serpent' and the 'Bikini Killer,' he posed as a dapper, cultured, man-about-world or mysterious drug dealer, befriending and defrauding backpacking couples on the 'hippie trail' and then poisoning, drowning, strangling and burning them.

Skilled at deception and evasion, Sobhraj is a real-life Ripley who committed at least twelve murders that the authorities know of as a means of sustaining his lifestyle of adventure — using his victims' passports and money to move from country to country. Sobhraj had many followers (including several policemen). Assembling a 'clan', he wanted to start a criminal family in the style of Charles Manson and the Manson family.

Interrogated by Thai police in Bangkok, Sobhraj was let off the hook because, like the Goans, authorities there feared the negative publicity accompanying a murder trial would harm the county's tourism trade. Not so easily silenced, however, was Dutch embassy diplomat Herman Knippenberg, who was investigating the murder of two Dutch backpackers, and suspected Sobhraj — even though he did not know his real name. Searching Sobhraj's apartment, Knippenberg found a great deal of evidence, such as documents belonging to the victims and poison-laced medicines. He spent decades accumulating evidence against Sobhraj, despite a lack of cooperation at the time by law enforcement authorities. Meanwhile, Sobhraj continued to get away with murder.

Sobhraj was eventually tried and convicted and was jailed, in India, from 1976 to 1997, leading a life of leisure in prison. After his release, he retired as a celebrity in Paris but unexpectedly returned to Nepal in 2003, where he was again arrested, tried and sentenced to life imprisonment on 30 July 2010 for murders he had committed there.

His girlfriend, the beautiful eighteen-year-old daughter of his lawyer, tearfully protested his innocence. Sobhraj loves all this attention, charging large amounts for interviews and film rights. The subject of four books and three documentaries, his narcissistic overconfidence and overweening belief in his own intelligence is probably what led him to return to a country where authorities were still eager to arrest him. He just couldn't help himself, like the pyromaniac, stinking of petrol, who returns to the blazing warehouse, standing in the crowd of onlookers.

So . . . into the heart of darkness we go. The city of Old Goa (Velha Goa) was abandoned to cholera and malaria in 1835, the inhabitants fleeing by palanquin or on foot, never to return. Today all that remains standing are magnificent, empty churches built in laterite (rust-red, iron-rich earth bricks) and lime plaster.

Everything sweats in the heat. Scaling the lower portions of the baroque Basilica of Bom Jesus (Good Jesus), suspended from the roof by vine harnesses, workers scrub off the day's lichen and clip the border plants. Fanning out from the Basilica's monolithic girth, teams of gardeners attempt to beat back the jungle's voracious appetite. Crows in dark vestments hunch in the niches.

Girded by Ionic, Tuscan and Corinthian pillars and pilasters, Bom Jesus boasts a marble floor inlaid with precious stones, complementing the elaborate gilded altars. Buttresses of light fall from the high windows. Ironically, this opulent, sumptuous construction was built to protect the mortal remains of a man who lived in self-imposed penury: Saint Francis Xavier, who died of fever on Shangchuan Island, off the south coast of China, in 1552.

The saint is said to have miraculous powers of healing. When Saint Francis' body was exhumed, seventy-six days after his death, it was found fresh — incorrupt; no embalming had been done. Before it was placed in a silver reliquary, two years after his death, the doctors of Goa examined the body again and it was still fresh.

Born into the castle of Xavier and an exceptional student and athlete, Francis Xavier dropped out of university in Paris to travel the world, devoting himself to the poor and needy. Thrice shipwrecked, starved and attacked by pirates, he wrote of his time in Goa, '. . . never have I been happier, nor more continuously'.

But then saints are all about mortification of the flesh — and Xavier's oft-exhumed corpse has been subjected to some tribulations. One of his big toes was bitten off in 1554 by a Portuguese lady who took it away as a relic. In 1890, the other toe fell off and a good portion of an arm was severed and sent to Rome. What's left rests under a crocheted blanket of silver stars.

My own flesh is quite mortified, thank you. A committee of physicians would never describe me as 'fresh'. The Goan air is a bathtub of lukewarm water which you slosh through. It drags at your steps like dreams of running away. Fetid, dank and mildewed, Goa smells like a bach closed up for winter. Surrounded by purgatorial jungle; coconut trees, bamboo, teak and cashew alive with kingfishers, mynas and parrots, and you can almost hear the trees panting with the effort of absorbing the hot breath of skulking foxes and bug-rooting boar. Goa has a high snake population but, on the upside, there aren't that many rats.

❈ ❈ ❈

In the sixteenth century, compelled to found a base from where they could control the seas, and thanks to Vasco de Gama's discovery of a sea route, the Portuguese came to Goa to convert the heathen, wearing puffy-sleeved embroidered capes made of beaver fur, and tights. From a land of brimstone they brought the Inquisition and, despite their ridiculous dress, the Portuguese 'subdued' the Goans, carrying out a wave of conquest, colonisation and enforced conversions.

Water torture and the rack proved extremely successful (nobody laughed at their Van Dyke beards after that), and Goa remained Portuguese territory for the next 450 years, until reclaimed by India with the help of the British in 1961. In the state museum, amidst the wooden pietà and portraits of Portuguese governors, the Inquisition's black wooden table squats like a malevolent beetle. Seen from the front, the table is supported by two upright lions and a rather squat, pot-bellied eagle. A reminder that the committee's purpose was to strike fear and compliance into the hearts of those about to be interrogated (and a sneaky inside joke), the rear of the table is festooned with carvings of faces racked with pain.

In the portrait gallery, painted life-size on lacquered wood, viceroys and governors pose, pompously futile, in elaborate horse-hair wigs, coloured hose and velvet frock coats. Beringed hands hold steel helmets and heavy swords. Once a year a new batch of Portuguese settlers arrived by ship, fervent with political ambition, to replace their fellows fallen to disease or snake bite. Outside, it's 35°C with 98 per cent humidity. Curious, I buy some paan from a roadside vendor. It tastes like minty dirt wrapped in a dock leaf.

Wandering the empty cathedrals under the pious gaze of mould-patina'd saints and cardinals, witnessing Christ's agony on the elaborately carved, gilt-framed Stations of the Cross, you wonder at the relentless religious zeal of the Jesuits, Franciscans, Dominicans, Augustinians, Carmelites and Theatines.

All this frenzied decoration, all this gold, silver, ornate chandeliers, jewelled lanterns, stained-glass windows. All the icons, saints and marble angels, the very Portuguese-looking Jesuses, the smoke-stained oil paintings of the Devil being thwarted — all this stuff speaks of the staggering hubris required to bend an entire population to your will — only for these considerable monuments to your success: chapels, churches, convents, monasteries and cathedrals, to stand empty four centuries later.

Once, you thought yourself so important. Time passes and you are reduced to nothing more than a rich man's bones, lying forgotten and unprayed-for beneath the remains of the ruined altar of the church of Saint Augustine. The elaborate carved headstone bearing your coat of arms is now just a weather-beaten flagstone in a roofless ruin, scuffed by the feet of atheist tourists.

Somewhere beneath all this moss and tendrils of vine lie the mortal remains of the martyred Queen, Ketevan of Georgia; long searched for, never found.

The main road bisecting the Old City, Rua Direta, was once lined with stately buildings where bankers, jewellers, slaves, musicians, embroiderers and tobacconists provided the Portuguese with everything their hearts desired. Carriages rattled and Arabian horses high-stepped. The pleasure fest was short-lived and towards the close of the sixteenth century, Goa was already in its last flourish. The Dutch were taking over the world and the Portuguese couldn't afford to keep up the luxury and splendour of Goa. Ships stopped coming, an epidemic of cholera broke out, wiping out both the population and any hope of continued commercial activity. The city was reduced to a ruin. The monuments remaining today are 'protected and nurtured by the Archaeological Survey of India', but even this esteemed society cannot prevail against the ravages of those cruel twins, Nature and Time.

❖ ❖ ❖

It's not tourist season. The skeleton staff at our accommodation consists of two wide boys, two shy ladies and a baby. Monsoons batter the beach, whipping the sea into a raging, frothing, pounding monster chomping at the sand dunes. Swimming in this maelstrom would be madness. However, we island dwellers have been land bound for almost two months now and miss the smell of the ocean and the sound of the waves so much that in defiance of the conditions, we put on our togs and clamber down the cliff path to go for a dip.

The first thing we see on the beach is a highly venomous yellow-lipped sea krait — either dead or playing dead. We're so fascinated by the snake it's a while before we notice a shadow the size of a skyscraper looming over us. Lurching in the gale, weeping rust, is the *River Princess*, run aground ten years ago, the tonnes of sand in her hold pining her to the bottom.

'Let's swim out!' exclaims the economist. I pretend not to hear his lunatic suggestion, which is whipped away by the tempest.

A metre up the beach, as the sea continues to devour the foreshore, waves crash down on the body of a dead cow with one horn dug into the coarse yellow sand and one eye balefully regarding the heavens.

'It's like removing a twelve-storey building,' say the salvage experts of the *Princess*. Battered by the unkind sea, she shivers and creaks. Apparently her massive metal carcass is causing a deadly current, lethal to local fishermen, so she *must* be removed. A tender stoush is raging. 'We'll do it for free,' says the shipping line that used to own her. By 'free' they mean they won't pay the Goan government for the privilege of collecting their own ship. In true corruption style, it looks like the highest bid (US$30 million from a rival company) will win.

Snakes, malaria, mossies and tourist murderers all cast a pall, but the biggest killer on the beaches of Goa is the Arabian Sea, or drowning. The lifeguards, terrified of another European death on their watch — the English papers make such a fuss — follow us up and down the coast nervously clutching their red Baywatch floaters as we frolic in the waves. The economist (who started surfing when he was fourteen) is personally affronted. 'This is nothing,' he harrumphs as the storm-sea growls and thumps. 'They should see Saint Kilda in a sou'wester.'

Hardcore Goan Trance still exists, in fact he never left. There he is, propping up the bar of the Mango Tree — the remnants of his hair scraped into a ponytail. The sound system plays irony rock: remixed hits from the '80s, and he's still dancing. His sagging tattoos, too, are from another era: rainbows, unicorns, acid head's smiley face. Sunken cheeks from a paucity of teeth. You only get bones that carious by doing a lot of drugs. Acid, ecstasy, cocaine, charas (hash) and all other forms of recreational drugs are illegal in India but widely available in Goa. No coincidence then that Goa's Fort Aguada jail is filled with foreigners serving lengthy sentences.

Outside the Mango Tree, the road dust is kicked up into clouds by helmetless white tourists roaring past on rental motorbikes far too powerful for them. Inside the Mango Tree, Hardcore teams his own heavy leather biker jacket with Crocs. Trance-chic. 'Hee hee,' he wheezes. His laugh is frightening. The Goan bar staff think he is a pathetic loser and don't bother trying to hide it.

Thoroughly enjoying some grope-free people-watching, eyeing up the mostly European clientele, I order another Kingfisher and a bowl of chilli prawn noodles. The economist looks pale and queasy, regarding my dinner with one rolling fish eye. I offer some. 'Not hungry,' he says, recoiling. Doesn't feel well. Cue: a two-day hiatus involving moaning and periods of unconsciousness punctuated by sprinting to the toilet. Turns out that while I had been standing under the shower rose with all orifices clamped, he had been gargling.

Waiting for him to recover, I read *The White Tiger* by Aravind Adiga. Set in Bangalore, it's about a rental car driver in the high-tech industry who kills his boss and steals his money to fund a start-up company of his own. He goes unpunished and becomes wildly successful, proving that the 'New India' has no morality.

The economist seems to rally: it's false dawn.

Delirium producing no proposals, while the economist groans and sweats I read the best-selling novel *Five Point Someone: What not to do at IIT!* by Chetan Baghat. My version is pirated, scanned and faithfully copied right down to the 'reproduction is forbidden' warning.

The plot concerns three mechanical engineering students who end up with a five-point something GPA (Grade Point Average, the means by which the elite and the mediocre are measured) out of ten, ranking near the bottom of their classes. In India, a pass is not a pass is not a pass.

Five Point Someone laments the fact that, in India, creativity is stifled by a 'grades-above-all-else' mentality — the rather hokey ending nevertheless illustrates the sad reality of the near-suicidal pressure felt by Indian Institute of Technology students.

'Why don't New Zealand students experience the same stress?' I ask the economist, during one of his more lucid moments. 'Some do, at a personal level, because they are very competitive,' he says. 'But there just isn't the same incentive — pass or plunge your entire family into debt — here, the alternatives to success are pretty dire. Plus, it's just not part of our culture. Our heroes are all sportspeople, not academics.'

❖ ❖ ❖

In the end, Goan independence was hard won. The Portuguese didn't leave voluntarily. British and Indian forces stepped in when it suited them after years of guerrilla warfare and resistances squashed and reborn.

Although now absent of villainous mustachios, horse-hair wigs and velvet frock coats, Goa is still Portuguese in many ways. Illuminated by a shaft of sunlight, the curtained canopy of the jungle momentarily draws aside to allow a glimpse of low, symmetrical houses with high plinths, tiles used as corbels and large ornamental windows with stucco mouldings. Balcoes (covered porches or balconies) and verandas allow the owners to be seen and to see the passers-by.

The startling colours washed over the plaster walls are a legacy of an unwritten rule during Portuguese occupation that no house could be painted white, as it was associated with churches and the Virgin Mary. Fresh popsicle tones of pink, lavender and yellow show that the Goan Hindus continue to respect this idea, competing for the most colourful house. Inside, icons of Mary and baby Jesus beatify the sala.

A lassez-faire attitude to the doings of others persists in Goa — sossegado, laid-backness — a malleable morality markedly absent in the rest of India. Goans are prepared to adopt, not annihilate: Templar crosses top altars to Ganesha; Mother Mary might as well be Lakshmi, sitting as she does in an alcove on the side of the road, daubed with the red incense of the Hindu temples. Portuguese and Indian, Colonial and Hindi, Islam and Catholicism — let it be. There is nothing new or remarkable under the sun in Goa.

Goans are also immune to the conduct of tourists, and the shameless tourists are why Goa is so popular with busloads of Indian men on package holidays. Playing soccer on the beach and never going into the water, they covertly take cell phone photos of the foreign females in their bikinis. Posing in front of a target and pretending to be snapping a group shot with their arms around each other's shoulders, they give themselves away completely by their obvious glee at having found another image for the gallery.

Surreptitiously stealing a picture being the whole point of this escapade, confusion reigned when the economist started giving it away.

'Want a photo?' he asked, after I pointed out that the boys standing in front of us weren't merely blocking our sun.

'Of course!' he boomed to requests. 'Come on, Sweetie, over here.' Within seconds we were mobbed by a coachload of engineering students from Hyderabad. 'Gather round boys, gather round,' invited the economist avuncularly. 'Take as many photos as you want!'

'Excuse *me*! That's my nipple!' I protested.

'So sorry, Madam,' said a young man who clearly wasn't. What happens to all these pictures, I wonder? I decided I didn't want to know.

❁ ❁ ❁

Invasions, Inquisitions, Independence. New Year's parties, pink and peeling Anglo-Saxons. The Goan jungle is oblivious to the puny endeavours of both conquests and Contiki tours. As far as the primeval morass is concerned, all human life is meaningless.

'The horror! The horror!' shouted the economist, before I could even think of it, as we walked up the beach in the orange dusk.

I hate it when he does that.

We spent our last night in Goa drinking Kingfisher beer at the Mango Tree. Walking back to our hotel, a little tipsy, we wandered off the path, lost, and had to bushwhack through the pitch-black jungle. Standing stock-still, widening our eyes in an attempt to let more light in, we sense snakes lurking all around, just waiting to be stepped on.

We got lucky, finding the path after an hour of stumbling about and thus avoiding the mortifying headline: 'World's Stupidest Tourists Die on Way Home from Pub.'

Till Khap Do Us Part

More honour killings. Not, however, in a remote village, but this time, in Delhi. The well-to-do family of a nineteen-year-old woman who fell in love with a taxi driver from a different caste responded to the couple's declaration of love by torturing them to death. Neighbours trying to intervene after hearing screams were turned away by the girl's uncle who told them 'family business' was being taken care of. The never-weds were eventually found bound, beaten and electrocuted.

'We had agreed to the marriage but her family did not,' said the murdered man's aunt.

The parents, after murdering their daughter and her nineteen-year-old fiancé, said that 'they had been left no alternative and they didn't regret killing the couple'. Friends were shocked. 'God knows what came over them . . . they were such good people.'

In medieval times, women from Rajasthan's royal families set themselves on fire as their men rode out to meet adversaries on the battlefield. During the 1947 partition, fathers put their daughters, brothers their sisters and husbands their wives to death to avoid 'dishonour' at the hands of the enemy.

'"Honour" has often been enforced through violence on women,' wrote Monobina Gupta in the *Sunday Times of India* shortly after this incident, 'but to fully understand the recent spate of honour killings . . . we need to ask additional questions about individuals within communities. Just recently, a teenage couple was hanged to death in Haryana for marrying within the same gotra [an unbroken male line from a common male ancestor] while three men in their early twenties killed one of their sisters and her husband for marrying outside their caste.

'These killings do not occur in pre-modern feudal villages. These killings happen in some of India's biggest, most modern cities. In the 70s and 80s the streets of Delhi witnessed a dynamic, if controversial movement, with women's groups taking on the perpetrators of gender-based violence, particularly dowry and rape. The streets have fallen silent since but crimes against women have multiplied, just gone underground.

'Is the silence one of complicity?'

To be fair, honour killing isn't just an Indian phenomenon. According to a 2002 United Nations brief, honour killings have been reported in Egypt, Jordan, Lebanon, Morocco, Pakistan, Turkey, the Gulf countries and even among Asian, Arab and Muslim communities in the United Kingdom, France, Germany and New Zealand. Honour killing for marrying outside caste is, however, specific to Indians, home and abroad.

Inside India the majority of honour killings occur in the states of Punjab, Rajasthan, Haryana, Bihar and Uttar Pradesh. Honour killings are rare to non-existent in southern India and the western states of Maharashtra and Gujarat. In West Bengal honour killings all but ceased 100 years ago, thanks to the pervasive influence and activism of early reformists like Vivekananda, Ramakrishna, Vidyasagar and Raja Ram Mohan Roy who demanded the abolition of sati and the enfocement of property inheritance rights for women, in 1828 setting up the Brahmo sabha, a Bengali reformist movement formed to fight social evils, the liberal sway of which is still keenly felt today.

The issue of honour killings says much about the extremes of life in India — not just from rich to poor, but from city to village — and what happens when an ancient moral code perseveres, despite changing economic environments and outside influences. While India's cities are progressing at a rapid rate, and love marriages are becoming more and more prevalent, in many villages the caste system remains as strong as ever, and the reputation of the caste is of utmost importance.

The perpetrators of honour killings believe that the victim has brought dishonour upon the family or community by marrying (without their families' acceptance) outside their caste or religion, or into a social group deemed inappropriate.

Among Rajputs (a landowning north Indian clan, the Rajputs of Rajasthan) marriages with other castes can provoke the killing of the married couple and all immediate family members, because of ingrained notions about purity of lineage. Like caste, racial purity is entrenched in the particular notion of honour, nationhood, social or familial status quo.

According to Marsha Freeman, Director of International Woman's Rights Action Watch at the University of Minnesota, at the root of honour killings is 'the outmoded concept of a woman as a vessel of the family reputation'. A large part of this problem is due to the strong presence of a khap panchayat, a caste council, or informal village court, which consists of members of the same caste deciding on all matters relating to their community. A khap panchayat in Muzaffarnagar in Uttar Pradesh recently banned girls from wearing jeans, village elders blaming the attire for provoking Eve-teasing and encouraging young people to elope.

Although there was no village court in the affluent Delhi neighbourhood where the honour killing mentioned earlier occurred, a perception persists that violence against family members is a family issue, not a judicial one. In the absence of a village court, females in the family — mothers, mothers-in-law, sisters and cousins — frequently support the attacks. 'It's a community mentality,' said Amnesty International's Zaynab Nawaz of this collective punishment. The sentence always far outweighing the crime, this rough justice is no justice at all.

Hours after its release, Ajai Sinha's provocative film about honour killing, 'Khap', was banned in theatres across Punjab and Haryana. Protestors surrounded cinemas, demanding the film be destroyed, and director Sinha received a barrage of hate calls.

'If the country's censors have no objection to "Khap", why should we take the objections of self-appointed localised moral police groups seriously?' said Sinha. 'Let them do what they can.

'The khap rules were conceived 200 years ago. How and why are they still applicable? Personally, if my child announces that she wants to marry a cousin, I'd object. But I wouldn't kill her.'

Bouquets & Bullets

'The unity of India was no longer merely an intellectual conception . . . it was an emotional experience which overpowered me,' wrote India's first prime minister, Jawaharlal Nehru, in his book *The Discovery of India*, written during his imprisonment in Ahmednagar Fort (1942–46) for his part in the Quit India movement.

The Indian Independence Day, commemorating the end of British rule, is celebrated on 15 August and while we were in Bangalore, it happened to be the sixty-fourth Independence Day. Ironically, it fell on a Saturday which also saw the start of the annual and terribly English flower show at the Lal Bagh Botanical Gardens (kick the British out of India by all means, but if you don't mind we Anglophiles will keep the flower shows, gentleman's clubs and an obfuscating civil service).

Lal Bagh, 'the red garden', was commissioned in 1760 by the ruler of Mysore, Hyder Ali, and finished by his son, the great military administrator, torturer and Anglophobe, Tipu Sultan. Originally based on the Mughal gardens that once stood at Sira, 100 years later the 240-acre gardens became very English indeed with the construction of their most famous landmark, the Lal Bagh Glasshouse. The foundation stone for the glasshouse, modelled on London's Crystal Palace, was laid in 1898 by Prince Albert Victor. An implacable enemy of the British, Tipu Sultan must have been spinning in his tomb.

Mounting Lal Bagh rock, 3000 million years old and looking every day of it, one trundles the walking paths beside lovingly tended beds containing thousands of different kinds of flora, shaded by trees imported from Persia, Afghanistan and France — an assembly demonstrating the very best in eighteenth century collecting ethic.

On the garden paths, honeymooners pass, brides tinkling and golden-bangled, flanked by a supporting cast of ladies in their best saris. A sweaty young man bowls up, bursting with the news that he's on his nuptials. We stop our perambulations at requests for pictures. Most wedding groups do not own a camera, so we stand there, smiling politely, while one of the party runs off, looking for the park's roaming photographer.

'Your bride is very beautiful,' I tell the husband. He beams with proprietary pride, covering his mouth to hide bad teeth. His young wife laughs with joy, eyes flashing, taking us in in snatches. Mother-in-law clutches the bride's tiny, mehndi-decorated hand possessively, as if she is an expensive handbag and likely to be stolen.

Mother-in-law speaks excellent English. Discovering I am over thirty and thus way beyond marriageable age (most girls get married off at eighteen) she tuts and pokes me in the belly announcing, 'Those eggs aren't there forever'.

Indian couples do not live together before marriage. After the wedding, the bride's entire new family will pray, eat, cry, gossip and fight together for the rest of her life and she will never be alone again. Strangely, nobody smiles for the pictures. The economist and I do, of course, grinning like baboons — everyone else poses like a Victorian studio portrait of the recently deceased.

We are *so* popular as honeymoon souvenirs that we cannot sit down for five minutes without being mobbed again and have to keep doggedly walking, round and round, prisoners on exercise duty. Trapped though we may be, it is a delightful kind of attention, sweet and generous. All over India there are wedding albums with the two of us in them.

'Who's that?' asks aunty, flicking through the Polaroids.

'Just some goris we met in Lal Bagh gardens. Aren't they hilarious?'

❊ ❊ ❊

The Lal Bagh Glasshouse is filled with gladioli, chrysanthemums and roses, all decked out for the flower show. A massive model of Delhi's

India Gate pricked out in 'mums and marigolds stretches to the vaulted, green-glazed ceiling. The sunlight is defused and liquid. It's like being in an enormous aquarium filled with flowers instead of fish.

Due to the Indian climate the plants and their blooms are all monstrous, triffid-like. Crowds dressed in their best (and two Casual Friday Kiwis) parade through an oversized English country garden, past vast arrangements of peonies and roses so gloriously abundant and haphazardly placed they appear the floral tributes of a careless, brobdingnagian hostess. In the rear of the garden is the world's largest *Ceiba pentandra* or kapok tree. Limbs flowing up from the earth like volcanic lava, its canopy dwarfs the tiny people standing beneath it. The squirrels who have made this gigantic tree home have an inflated sense of entitlement, snootily skipping up and down its arms like courtiers carrying truffles.

On television that night there were back-to-back screenings of Richard Attenborough's 'Gandhi', starring Ben Kingsley. We watched in awe and even cried a bit. Afterwards, we seethed with hatred for the British — before remembering that they made us too. 'Gandhi' the movie isn't just the story of Gandhi, but of India, made with support from the Mountbatten Trust. Louis Mountbatten, First Earl of Burma, was the last English Viceroy, charged with overseeing the transition of British India to independence no later than 1948.

Mountbatten was a great fan of Congress leader Jawaharlal Nehru and his liberal vision of an independent India but had to admit: 'If it could be said that any single man held the future of India in the palm of his hand in 1947, that man was [Muslim leader] Mohammad Ali Jinnah.'

Mohammad Ali Jinnah is always painted as the obstinate villain of the piece, but whatever the reason, Muslim and Hindu could not and would not agree. There were riots and chaos, and in the end the British just wanted to get the hell out. Mountbatten conceded to partition and, in a thrown-together approach, concluded that the situation was too unsettled to wait any longer than 1947. This was to have disastrous consequences for the people of both India and Pakistan. The slapdash handover of power would unleash an orgy of violence and retribution never before seen in the Indian subcontinent, and millions would die on the blood-soaked trudge to Pakistan.

Among the Indian leaders, Gandhi emphatically insisted on maintaining a united India and although he ultimately failed, for a while he successfully rallied the people to this goal by guilt-tripping them with periods of self-starvation.

The subject of Gandhiji is still extremely contentious in India. There are many who thank God he was killed — and thank God doubly it was by a Hindu extremist, and not a Muslim, although the sectarian bloodbath this avoided was merely delayed — as his ideas for Muslim rights were hated by many Hindus and his calls for passive resistance, satyagraha, were a nightmare for freedom fighters, not to mention anyone persecuted by the Third Reich (Gandhi suggested that the Jews walk into Hitler's guns to shame the Germans into stopping).

Hitler wouldn't have been stirred by Gandhi's tactics, but the British were. Non-cooperation, the Salt March and civil disobedience drove them up the wall — though the British *really* left because of mounting public condemnation, after stories of the massacre at Amritsar (and images, most famously Eduard Thony's *Amritsar Massacre*) began to circulate.

It is 13 April 1919, the public holiday of Baisakhi, and crowds are gathering at Jallinwalla Bagh despite the British-imposed martial law restricting a number of civil liberties, including freedom of assembly. Groups of more than four people are banned.

On hearing of this unlawful gathering, General Reginald Dyer, the 'Butcher of Amritsar', leads his troops through the narrow alleys bordering the park and, once reaching open ground, begins shooting without first issuing a warning or order to disperse, instructing his troops to target the densest part of the crowd: to get the most bangs for their bullets.

Some 1650 rounds were used on the crowd of Sikhs, Hindus and Muslims, including women and children. The soldiers kept firing until their ammunition was exhausted, leaving 1500 people wounded and approximately 1000 killed. Trying to escape, hundreds were crushed in the resulting stampede. The wounded could not be removed as a curfew had been declared, and many died that night. In the days following, 120 broken, bloated bodies were pulled from a well in the garden, now known as The Martyrs' Well, where many had jumped to avoid the slaughter.

General Dyer appeared before the Hunter Commission Enquiry, where he stated that he had gone to the Bagh with the deliberate intention of opening fire if he found a crowd assembled there.

'I think it quite possible that I could have dispersed the crowd without firing but they would have come back again and laughed, and I would have made, what I consider, a fool of myself.'

The General told the commission that 'he would have used machine guns if he could have got them into the enclosure, but they were mounted on armoured cars, and the garden was unfortunately bounded on all sides by houses, with few entrances'.

He made no effort to tend to the wounded after the shooting: 'Certainly not. It was not my job. Hospitals were open and they could have gone there.'

Dyer's actions were condoned by his various superiors and no disciplinary action was called for. The General was finally found guilty of 'a mistaken notion of duty', and relieved of his command.

Just like modern-day Middle Eastern dictatorships attempting to ban blogs and cell phone video depicting government troops assassinating protestors, the British tried to block any and all media portraying the Indian people's struggle for Independence, and failed, epically.

Life magazine's 1947 photo essay on Gandhi's self-sufficiency movement (including Margaret Bourke-White's iconic photograph of Gandhi at his charkha or spinning wheel) had an enormous effect in America — the first real example of manipulation of social media, sort of the 1940s equivalent of a Facebook campaign.

In the end the British left worn out and a bit embarrassed; the withdrawal from India being the first sign of a weakening empire, the beginning of what Oxford University historian Dr John Darwin called 'an imperial endgame from which every exit was blocked except the trapdoor to oblivion'.

Etiquette Hell

We caught the bus home from the movies. It was one of those truly outrageous Indian buses. Chrome-ceilinged, windows hung with velvet curtains, a television over the door blasting an old '80s Bollywood movie — complete with that high-pitched filmic music that sounds like a dyspeptic cat.

Marigolds hung across the driver's view. Glittering in the corners, electric candles hiccupped imitation flames above altars to Ganesha. It was packed, a sauna. Dribbles of perspiration ran down the backs of my legs. Everyone seemed to be smiling. One man in green tracksuit pants was especially friendly, asking which stop we needed, telling us how many stops there were left to go, and moving a little closer to talk over my head to the economist about places to visit in Bangalore.

Intrigued by the film, I only glanced over at him once — he was a bit smelly, had terrible brown-stained teeth and his green tracksuit pants were spotted with stains — and went back to enjoying the show: here comes the baddie in his mullet and enormous mustachios, here was the heroine, now it's time for the dance-off. Just like 'West Side Story', without the kissing.

❖ ❖ ❖

Indian film stars are gods. In the films made by the mainstream Bollywood studios operating out of Mumbai, the male leads are all tall fair men called Khan. Flying in the face of northern fashions, movie stars in southern India are invariably short fat men with handlebar moustaches and toupees. *If* they still have their own hair, it's dyed black and backcombed like John Rowles'.

Film stars in southern India may occupy a different end of the 'handsome' spectrum, but they are ten times more beloved than the average Bollywood star, because they represent the triumph of the common man. Five people died in Bangalore, one a policeman, when police opened fire on rioting mourners following the death (by natural causes) of southern Indian film legend Rajkumar in 2006. The policeman was beaten to death by the mob.

As a blessing, fans pour milk over billboards advertising the latest releases of southern Indian film stars and go to their movies twenty-five times. The Indian film industry as a whole is booming, with Bollywood in Mumbai and Tollywood (the Telugu film industry) in Andhra Pradesh, Kollywood (Tamil cinema) based in Chennai, as well as Sandalwood — films made in the Kannada language, currently undergoing a renaissance, proudly spoken and violently rioted over in the south.

❖ ❖ ❖

Anyway, as I said, the bus movie was a sort of 'West Side Story' in MC Hammer pants. I had no idea what language it was in, but I was enjoying every ridiculous moment of it. I had an epiphanic flash of appreciation. Here we were in the real India and wasn't it marvellous.

Something was bumping against my thigh.

Because the bus was so crowded and continuously lurching in and out of potholes, I assumed the jouncing was some part of the bus, the back of a seat perhaps, whacking against my leg with the pulse of our progress. Anyway, a slow realisation came over me that the rhythmic bump, bump, bumping against my thigh wasn't the natural movement of the bus, but something else entirely.

I turned to look at Mr Friendly only to discover he had both hands in his tented pants, and that he was, in fact, pleasuring himself against my leg. For a moment I couldn't quite believe it.

'That man!' I squeaked at the economist.

'Wha?' he said sleepily, startled out of his reverie. Probably thinking about algorithms and how important they are.

'That man is wanking on me!' A high titter escaped my lips.

The economist didn't seem to understand, looking at me blankly.

I made it as plain as I could. 'That. Man. Is. Wanking. On. Me.'

'Hmmm,' said the economist. Craning his neck to peer around my shoulder, he surveyed the problem area. It was then that he made a distinction which will stay with me always.

'Yes, but he doesn't *actually* have his cock out,' he said pedantically.

The bumping increased its tempo.

I felt this was no time to quibble about inside/outside pants. I was staggered by the economist's parameters of social outrage — tweak at yourself by all means chappie, but don't wave it about. I tried to collect myself.

Just what *is* the correct code of behaviour when someone performs the five knuckle shuffle against a part of your body? I was stumped. What would Emily Post do? If only I had her 1922 guide to social intercourse, *Etiquette in Society*, with me. Maybe this would come under Essential Manners for Men, Beyond the Handshake?

I so wanted to emerge from this feely faux pas with my poise intact, in the sure and certain knowledge that I had done the right thing — however, the gentleman in question wasn't chewing with his mouth open, using the wrong fork or wearing a hat indoors. He was wanking on my leg.

To my shame I did nothing — other than back into the protective girth of a large economist and peek at the man's exertions beneath the arm holding the bus strap, fascinated, like a chicken caught in the sway of a very short cobra.

The economist too stared in horror, unable to look away. Things had gotten very quiet. Any passenger close enough to possess a decent view was also watching Mr Green Pants. Having an audience didn't seem to put him off his stroke.

'We must be close,' said the economist, as we neared our destination.

'So must he,' I replied. 'Let's get off before he does.'

As we walked back to the campus, I lambasted the economist for not coming to my defence, for failing to protect me from the slings and arrows of outrageous tracksuits.

'Darling,' he remonstrated, 'what a man does in the privacy of his pants is entirely his own business.'

❖ ❖ ❖

Days later, after posting an abbreviated version of the bus experience on my blog page, Nasty Jill leaves a comment: 'The third world is the only place men find you remotely attractive, and this bothers you.'

If by 'remotely attractive' you mean a dehumanised wank receptacle, then yes, it does bother me, Jill.

Dilli/Delhi

Day one

Everything looks better on the internet. We travelled to the Hotel
Capital on the narrow red vinyl seat of a bicycle rickshaw pulled by
an emphysemic pensioner. Bouncing and jouncing along the late
afternoon's incapacious streets, a passing schoolboy grabs my left boob
and yells, 'Welcome to Delhi!'

Our rickshaw peddler looks as if he might be having a stroke,
shaking and stuttering upon the pedals like an old racehorse trembling
towards the knackers. Sweat rolls down his skinny flanks. 'Would he
manage the Tour de France?' wonders the economist sardonically. I
plead for us to get off, spare this doddery old man the burden and pay
him to rest awhile.

'That's no way to do business,' complains the economist.

The rickshaw peddler hasn't a clue where the Hotel Capital is but
indicates wearily that it's 'somewhere around here'. 'Here' is a maze of
warehouses and wooden carts parked with their arms in the air. Criss-
crossing muddy intersections, we eventually find the Hotel Capital, a pink
rotunda hidden between the lorry yards and stagnant pools of water.

This vile part of town boasts a lovely surprise — beautiful cows.
Curved horns, pendulous ears: aristocratic Brahman rest from the
day's exertions, shaking their white humps at the biting flies. Through
centuries of exposure to inadequate food supplies, insect pests,
parasites, diseases and the weather extremes of tropical India, these
native cattle have developed some remarkable adaptations for survival.
The 'sacred cattle of India', Hindus will not eat them, will not permit
them to be slaughtered, and will not sell them. Will not feed them

much either, by the look of their toast-rack ribs and jutting pelvises, beef bones cradled under a thin layer of hide.

I try not to cry at the mosquito-filled swamp that is our room.

Our first night in Delhi, we have been invited to dinner in Gurgaon, thirty kilometres south, by a company interested in using the economist's decision-making software. After twenty days of monsoon rain, the traffic is gridlocked. According to the uncooperative Sikh concierge — grudgingly delivering bite-size pieces of disconnected information — getting to the restaurant would take at least four hours, *if* we made it. We have to cancel. I'm starving and covered in mean red bites, which I've managed to scratch into weeping sores.

Where can we buy something to eat? Nowhere. It seems we are in the industrial zone.

Explains all the cows.

'Is this *really* India's capital?' I ask crankily, for the umpteenth time, as we mope along the back streets looking for food. The lack of infrastructure, the wrecked roads, crooks, touts: words actually fail me, for all I whinge on. It seems impossible to believe. They're about to host a global sporting event, for Pete's sake.

'Imagine what Kolkata is like,' says the economist.

'Well, we're not fucking going there!' I snap.

Malaria and dengue fever are currently epidemic in Delhi. Using towels and spare clothing, we block any and all mosquito access to our room and burn a coil. Unfortunately this quickly fills the tiny space with eye-searing smog and blocks off all our air, so the economist has to periodically waft the door open and shut with his foot to prevent asphyxiation. It's a long night.

So, what is Delhi like?

It's horrible.

Absolutely a disaster.

A shambles. Not in the Old-English meaning of the word, 'a place for the slaughter of cows', (obviously) but a wrecked ship, a zombie apocalypse. Terrorists shouldn't bother coming to Delhi with a view to messing up the Commonwealth Games, things will most likely collapse unaided.

My 'passage to India' is fast becoming a narrowing tunnel, black at the periphery, a progressively inward looking iris. I experience Forster's claustrophobic echo in the medieval mayhem, the horrid press of humanity: 'The more she thought over it, the more disagreeable and frightening it became . . . the echo began in some indescribable way to undermine her hold on life . . . to murmur "Pathos, piety, courage — they exist, but are identical, and so is filth. Everything exists, nothing has value." '

I was on deadline for a *North & South* article about Delhi's preparations for the Commonwealth Games. Initially, like many, I believed all the stories about the Games were unnecessary tamasha (drama) on the part of the media. I had every intention of writing a positive piece about Indian attempts to pull it all together despite the chaos, assuming the fuss was a beat-up. To be then faced with this weird calm, this slough of inaction: abandoned bulldozers, rusting cranes, piles of building material lying about uselessly, seemed surreal. If this were Auckland, and the Games scheduled to take place there, Aucklanders would be moving to Invercargill to avoid the shame.

In the pauses between expostulations, I'm reading *Q & A*, by Indian diplomat Vikas Swarup. The story of an uneducated urchin from the slums, Jamal Malik, who wins the Indian version of 'Who Wants to Be a Millionaire?', the novel was adapted to become the phenomenally successful movie 'Slumdog Millionaire', directed by Danny Boyle.

'Slumdog' was heavily criticised by Booker-prize-winner Indian writer Salman Rushdie (famed for *Midnight's Children*, ostracised by many for *The Satanic Verses*), who said, 'It just couldn't happen'. This, from a man whose hero (in *Midnight's Children*) is telepathic.

The film went on to make tons of money and caused some Bollywood sneering. Bollywood royalty Anil Kapoor, who played 'Slumdog Millionaire's' corrupt quiz master, is sick to death of being eternally asked about this one particular movie by foreign journalists (too ignorant to realise he is the head of one of India's most successful film dynasties), even though it was his breakout role, enabling him to win a part on the hit show '24' — as an Iranian terrorist. I bet Cliff Curtis was annoyed.

After twenty-four hours in Delhi, 'Slumdog Millionaire' is starting to look like an upbeat tourist brochure.

✦ ✦ ✦

Day two
What a difference a day makes. Actually, what a difference moving to a better hotel makes. The economist, unable to take the sight of my pitiful scabs and silent weeping any longer, insists we decamp to the Bombay Orient. The Bombay Orient is located down an alley bang smack opposite Delhi's most important Islamic site, the Jama Masjid, rising up like a red stone castle above the tenements of the congested old quarter.

(In the meantime, and as an aside, emails of condemnation about the 'bus incident' were coming in thick and fast from friends and family. 'What were you thinking? Stand up for your woman' being the common tone. The economist, shamed into a kind of chivalry and with a nagging fear of another dent to his already perilous boyfriend reputation (forever besmirched after breaking my leg by buying me roller-skates for Christmas), is forced into asking worriedly, 'You won't tell your mum about the Hotel Capital, will you?')

Ah, the Muslim quarter, vibrant, colourful — filled with meat-eaters. I don't expect anything as miraculous as a steak, but I'm all set for a chicken tandoor, until we pass a cage of silent balding chickens — the chickens of vegetarianism. Here in the markets everything is displayed au naturel, so you know exactly what you're getting, right down to the hooves, claws and flensed cow skulls with cloudy eyes. In the alleyways behind the stalls, rats scuttle atop the rotting vegetables. Flies swirl everywhere in the hot still air. Blood grouts the cobblestones. This is reality, more real than ever before — if you let it, it makes you sick to your stomach.

The quarter's inhabitants are friendly, for the most part. Five days later, a pair of motorbike-riding terrorists open fire on a busload of Taiwanese tourists outside the Jama Masjid, killing two.

Even as the city was put on high alert, New Delhi's chief minister,

Sheila Dikshit, attempted to calm people down. 'I appeal to everybody, please do not panic,' she urged. 'An incident like this is something worrying but nothing to panic about.' I'd hate to see something to panic about. Godzilla maybe.

With the start of the Commonwealth Games just two weeks away, the shooting understandably reignites concern over whether India — still haunted by the vulnerability displayed in the devastating Mumbai terror attack of two years ago — is ready to provide adequate security for visiting athletes and spectators.

❁ ❁ ❁

The customer service at the Bombay Orient is so forceful, I flash the towel-bearing factotum as he barges in not bothering to knock. Hastily wrapping the bed sheet about my person, I have to manoeuvre him out of the room with my foot. His shoes squeak in resistance as he skids backwards on the tiles.

I love room service almost as much as I love lying under a fan that blows the mosquitoes away, but I can't make the canteen understand me when I call for a pot of that divinely sweet Indian coffee made with condensed milk. Someone answers and instead of saying 'Hello' or anything at all, just breathes heavily before hanging up. 'Coffee!' I shout, 'Room 21! Coffee!!' It isn't until the day we leave that I figure out that I have been ringing the laundry.

Mughal, Muslim, Hindu, we don't care — most New Zealanders have no allegiance to anything beyond rugby anyway; just give us some culture. Water bottles, sun block and Wikipedia print-outs in our backpacks. Saddled up, jandals on, off we go — walking, walking, walking. We don't take taxis or tuk tuks. We don't ride buses. 'Air-conditioning is cheating,' says the economist.

On our agenda today, Humayun's Tomb, the Red Fort and the Jama Masjid, Raj Ghat and the Gandhi museum. The economist is also in charge of itineraries.

The mausoleum of Humayun is the earliest example of mature Mughal architecture in India. Dominated by two features derived from the Persians — the three great arches on each side and the high, emphatic dome, the entire structure is supported by Hindu pavilions. Indian architecture had no domes until the Muslims overran north India in the thirteenth century. Keen to replicate their domed buildings here, it took a while for local workmen to master the technique.

The second Mughal emperor of India, Humayun was uncommonly superstitious (he never entered a room left foot first). Sadly his ambulatory precautions couldn't prevent him dying by falling down the stairs of his library in Sher Mandal. While he was alive though, he achieved marvels — expanding the empire, championing language, literature, and architecture.

Red sandstone, white marble inlay, perforated stone jail screens, and rose walls and minarets opening into bloomed lotuses — Humayun's Tomb is a fusion of styles, an outstanding amalgamation. We stand admiring, intensely jealous of a people legacy to a civilisation so outstanding. 'Paradise' is a Persian word meaning walled garden. This paradise is laid out like parquet flooring in tones of green, with long, contemplative walkways demonstrating the Persian ideal: plenty of water cleverly engineered to run hither and thither along raised canals, gurgling into pools.

Other important personages are entombed here too, and the grounds are filled with ruined sepulchres. Death made exquisite.

Away from the throngs, neglected by the other tourists, is the pretty and self-contained tomb of Isa Khan, the ruler of medieval Bengal. It's a bit shabby. Somebody has been camping here, leaving the scorch mark of their fire on the floor stones. A peaceful secret garden where the toenails of stray dogs tick against the paving stones, pigeons coo, having made their home in the dome of the roof, their guano streaking the fire-blackened walls white. The calm is narcoleptic. We stay a while.

❁ ❁ ❁

The Red Fort (Lal Qila) is a UNESCO World Heritage Site. The Yamuna River once fed the moats of this barricaded behemoth, a synthesis of Persian, European and Indian art, constituting the unique Shahjahani style (Shah Jahan was the Mughal Emperor who also built the Taj Mahal and the Jama Masjid).

Big and political, the Red Fort is one of the most popular tourist destinations in Old Delhi and the site from which the prime minister addresses the nation every year on Independence Day. Outside, hawkers shrilly tout their wares, forcing you to side-step their dogged pitches before you can enter the gates.

'Maybe you come back later?' they ask. 'Sure.' I say, meaning See Ya Later as in Never.

'You shouldn't have done that,' says the economist, as if I have just injected monkeys with a brain-cell-growing serum.

At one time, more than 3000 people lived within the Delhi Fort complex. Following the Sepoy Mutiny of 1857, the fort was captured by Britain and the residential palaces destroyed. After India gained independence in 1947, the Indian Army took control, handing the Red Fort over to the Indian tourist authorities in 2003.

It's a popular place with Indians playing tourist in their own country, as we discovered when we sat down to feed biscuits to the squirrels. Groups of holidaying families, student lads on tour and honeymooners immediately begin circling at a distance, working up the courage to ask if they can take our photo.

Before long an expectant queue has formed, so, after posing for about twenty-five rounds of photos in manifold permutations — the economist with a group of young men, the economist holding someone's baby, the new bride and me, the both of us with Uncle Sanjay — we flee, heading for a small building in the far corner of the grounds. Inside, a charming artefact of white flight to the Antipodes hangs disregarded in a room once part of the Red Fort's seraglio (apartments reserved for the women), then a prison under British rule, now a museum. It is a notice from the *Delhi Gazette*, Wednesday 6 September 1848:

Houses to sell or let:
For sale, considerably below prime cost, owing to the Proprietor having retired to New Zealand: 3 large houses situated at Nainee Tal.

As we exit the Red Fort, the tout I said 'Sure' to earlier rushes up, like a waiter with the cheque: '*Now* you are ready to buy?' he asks. Explaining that I don't want to purchase an ankle-chain crafted in questionable silver results in a total meltdown involving loud imprecations to bystanders and vehement accusations of cheating on my part. I expect the hosts of the Indian version of 'Target' to appear any minute. Shamed, I buy two ankle chains.

'I told . . .' begins the economist. 'Don't even . . .!' I cut him off, stalking along the cracked footpath. The tiny bells around my ankles jangle shrilly.

It is 35°C at the Jama Masjid. The paving stones are on fire. Carpet-runners direct a path across the courtyard. European women are given an all-in-one tent-dress fastened with Velcro, to cover their shameful lack of apparel. The economist is handed a sarong to cover his board-shorted knees. He looks great in his. I look like a loaf of rain-soaked bread wrapped in a tea towel.

The mosque is wonderful, a space of calm and contemplation, completely divorced from all the sheepheads, flies and grubby stalls of hard-by Chawri Bazaar Road. Also commissioned by the Mughal Emperor Shah Jahan, the Jama Masjid is sublimely grand, its lofty towers and forty-foot-high minarets striped in red sandstone and marble, and yet spartan as well. A place of community, 25,000 people can pray here at one time. The Muslim families sitting in the shade of the pavilions' porticos smile at the silly tourists; mad dogs all of us, out in the noonday sun.

Leaving the Jama Masjid, in a moment of starved foolishness, I order a kebab from one of the street stalls ringing the mosque's crenulated walls. Tentatively poking my tongue out, some ancient, primeval human wisdom tells me not to eat it. I give the kebab to a beggar crouched on his haunches with his back against the stonework. He looks thoroughly insulted. I hope he lives.

Turning to gaze a farewell, I see the fine white spires of the mosque rising out of the muck, utterly disinterested in the surrounding dirt and commerce — like angels standing on the rooftop of a brothel.

Raj Ghat (King's Bank), on the banks of the Yamuna, near the busy ring road off Mahatma Gandhi Road, was the site of Gandhi's cremation on 31 January 1948. A black marble slab marks the spot. Surrounded by red earth, it is a fitting reminder of the simplicity of Gandhi's life; as is your respectful barefoot approach, across the stone footpath and spiny grass, to where an eternal flame burns.

Nearby, the Gandhi Museum (the house where Gandhi spent the last 144 days of his life) is our last stop and the highlight of the day for the economist. I'm dizzy and disoriented, close to tears. Mogul to Martyrdom in one day is pretty overwhelming — or maybe it's just heat exhaustion.

Gandhi's life of poverty and non-possession means little is left behind in the way of worldly goods with which to enrich a museum, so the National Gandhi Museum is designed to preserve his written word and disseminate his message to the curious.

'I feel and I have felt during the whole of my life that what we need, what a nation needs, but we perhaps of all nations of the world need just now, is nothing else and nothing less than character building,' wrote the Mahatma, proposing eleven vows essential for the fulfilment of his constant endeavour for universal welfare:

Truth	Swadeshi, or buying locally
Non-violence or love	made
Chastity	Fearlessness
Control of the palate	Removal of untouchability
Non-stealing	Tolerance
Non-possession or poverty	
Physical labour	

Apart from untouchability, I'd fall at every one of these hurdles. Maybe they're not so much rules as suggestions, lofty ambitions.

I think back to Rajeev's class, 'Where would the Indian economy be today if Gandhi's economic vision had been adopted?' he had asked wryly, answering, 'Ruralism.' Had it all been for nothing? 'The freedom fighters asserted that, with the British in India, the indigenous people experienced a triple loss: of wealth, wisdom and work — yet freedom comes and loss is still something the majority of Indians know all too much about.'

Today, every third Indian is poor and the central government measures poverty by calorific intake — but Gandhi *did* make a global difference, his legacy of civil disobedience flourishing anew in the ructions and recent and currently erupting rebellions across the Middle East.

Blue concrete footsteps make stepping stones to the 'site of the martyrdom of Mahatma Gandhi'. This path to where Gandhi breathed his last is a tad Disney, however even a cynic like me is brought to tears in the Hall of Martyrdom, a small room containing a few fond relics of a man whose life and death profoundly affected the world. Gandhi's blood-stained dhoti, his pocket watch and 'one of the bullets that took our Bapu from us' on that fateful day in 1948 lie swaddled in small wooden cases. When he died, people scraped up the dirt he had bled on. His last words were, 'Oh God!'

A cartoon on the wall in the Hall of Martyrdom shows Martin Luther King and Gandhi standing on a heavenly cloud. Gandhi says to King, 'The problem with assassins is that they think they've killed you'.

❖ ❖ ❖

Day three
Sound asleep in the fabulous cool of the Bombay Orient (*fut . . . fut . . . fut* complains the slowly revolving ceiling fan, in danger of overheating from constant use and with one blade bent from contact with the economist's head), we are woken at 3 a.m. by a furious banging on the door of our room. Thinking the hotel is on fire, we leap out of bed and panic blindly in the pitch black until we remember it's Ramadan. 'Not Muslim!' shouts the economist. The banger goes away. We drift back to sleep. At 4 a.m. the cannon at the Jama Masjid goes off, rousing even the deafest of worshippers to the pre-dawn meal. We leap out of bed again and stand there swaying, shaken and weird with sleeplessness.

Let's talk about drinking — or rather, not drinking. While the entire state of Goa is basically sponsored by Kingfisher beer, Delhi's Muslim quarter is as dry as a Betty Ford picnic. The evening before we had fallen off the beaten track looking for an alcoholic beverage to take the edge off our sobriety. While the sight of fly-covered sheep's heads and dirty chickens squawking their last in horribly overcrowded cages has been enough to turn us both vegetarian, a cold beer would be nice. Indulging in fantasies of mild intoxication proves dangerously distracting. We're lost.

Not nearly lost, we are *absolutely* lost, going round in confused circles, walking down identical alleys which keep ending up against a high blank wall — the red stone sides of the Jama Masjid. Were it not for the man on his way to prayers who guided us through the labyrinth of tight alleys, rubbish piles and washing lines, we'd have been long gone, trafficked to an unscrupulous flesh peddler specialising in the discombobulated.

'Shukriya,' I say, as our saviour heads off. He doesn't say anything but his eyes widen and he smiles. We're so drunk with the happiness that comes from not being kidnapped, we don't need beer anymore.

As the economist is buying deodorant inside a shop teetering on the edge of a road-works canyon in Connaught Place, I peek into the entrance way of the mosque next door. A bearded man passes and points at the bookstand outside the door, to a copy of the *Quran.* 'Good book,' he says, stepping beneath the blue and white tiled archway. Before disappearing into the puddles of shadow to join his fellows already kneeling in prayer, he turns to give me the cheekiest come-on grin ever. He is extremely tall, dark and handsome. It seems so strange: the flirting Muslim. I'm besotted. Even when the economist emerges with his smellies, I can't stop beaming. 'I know that look,' he says. 'Muriel, you're terrible.'

❁ ❁ ❁

The flame of the immortal soldier, which commemorates the 90,000 soldiers of the British Indian Army who died fighting for the Raj in the First World War, is cupped by the All India War Memorial, or India Gate. As with all these shrines to slaughtered soldiers, whether standing at arms in hazy drizzle over small towns throughout New Zealand, or looming 42 metres above a scorched Indian park thronging with ice-cream sellers and picnicking families, it is a sad place, speaking of senseless death.

Beside the India Gate, a man proffers a baby cobra in a bamboo tiffin container. The little snake hisses angrily and strikes repeatedly at the man's hand, drawing blood every time. 'It's just been milked,' says its owner. In lieu of a breeze the economist's rapidly beating heart flutters his shirt.

We walk the length of the Rajpath in the broiling heat, stopping every 20 metres to buy another iceblock, shoving the sticks into the mouths of penguin-shaped rubbish bins. Wandering up the hill to peer through the wrought-iron railings at the pink/red parliament buildings — here is the 'Indian Tiger', sleeping in the sunlight of a lazy yellow afternoon. Red, ribbed with columns and pilasters, the silent ministries lining the avenue look like they've been carved whole out of the sandstone of Uluru (Ayers Rock).

Security is being stepped up with the advent of the Commonwealth Games. There are a lot of unmanned yellow metal barricades.

The sun beats down. There isn't a soul around, apart from the guards, sheltering in their huts from the hammering heat. Their uniforms are a pageant: long white buttoned spats, waist sashes in regimental colours and rooster-comb hats. Every now and then a saloon car with tinted windows roars up the hill, rousing the sleepy sentinels to slapdash salutes, before disappearing behind the curlicues of the iron gates — the tiger's back, striped by jungle creepers.

Time pants, the heat hums. A hoopoe fluffs its crest and laughs before flip flop flying off. Nothing happens.

Amid the torpor, scandalous news breaks. The Pakistani cricket match against Australia was fixed. Suitcases bulging with money feature in damning indictment on a video, televised in continuous repeat, of a sting perpetuated by the *News of the World* (before the British tabloid's own subsequent demise, itself stung by the scorpion of public opinion). Mazhar Majeed, the Pakistani players' London-based multi-millionaire agent, is shown accepting a £150,000 bribe from an undercover reporter. In return Majeed guaranteed that bowlers Mohammad Amir and Mohammad Asif would bowl 'no-balls' at specific times during the match.

'I *told* you they were playing suspiciously crap!' shout the Aussies.

Indian television sports casters are apoplectic, incensed beyond all decorum, screaming and pounding their fists on their desks in outrage.

India only forgave Pakistan its numerous sins — weapons of mass destruction, that funny walk they do at the border guard changing ceremony — because they played halfway decent cricket. Well, now you can forget it! The Pakistani cricketers are dead men walking, militants having put a price on their heads. They had better stay in England.

BBC World News is plunged into the doldrums: 'Cricket is not a gentlemen's game anymore', tearfully intones one commentator, an old red-nosed booze hound, his wattles swaying like a sad Saint Bernard.

❀ ❀ ❀

After multiple false starts and considerable language difficulties, the economist books a driver through the concierge at the Bombay Orient. Today's meeting is in Gurgaon with the IT boys who had originally invited us out for dinner our first night in Delhi, young Indian go-getters on the up and up. Gurgaon is one of Delhi's major satellite cities and the only Indian city to have electricity connected to all its households. A wave of multinational companies followed General Electric there after they set up store in 1997, and now American Express, Ericsson, Coca-Cola, Nokia and Motorola have made Gurgaon one of India's biggest outsourcing and call-centre employers, despite the frequent power cuts, dust, dirt and a scarcity of water.

There is so much building in this 'electronic city' that, as so often also happens in Bangalore, it's hard to tell whether buildings are going up, or crumbling down. The meeting venue isn't a particularly attractive place, a charmless tower block, like one of the less alluring products of Soviet architecture. Our hosts proudly lead us up to their state of the art cubby-hole on the third floor.

Sleekly groomed boys with dreams of venture capital, they talk the usual business twaddle: unique selling points, going forward, adding value. The building is a little creaky for such lofty mythologies; seeping concrete walls, rickety banisters and particle board punched through to admit wires — it looks as if the KGB have only recently abandoned it, taking their listening devices with them.

Who cares? There is a restaurant on the ground floor and I've been promised lunch as my reward for coming along and being charming non-stop. It's all I can think about. After a week of nauseous abstinence (the food on offer at Delhi's roadside conveniences too disgusting to eat), I'm in the business of being fed.

Better than I could even imagine, lunch is a hearty bender of endlessly replaced kebabs cooked on a grill set into the table. The waiters only stop bringing them when you signal that you can't manage another bite. The meal costs more per person than we've been spending on hotel rooms and transport combined.

Faced with non-stop meat kebabs (chicken: the good kind, where you don't see the bird first, and beef from cows I haven't met), I manage to put away a staggering amount. And drink two beers. A couple of chefs come out of kitchen and hover nearby watching me eat, whispering behind their hands. The couple at the table beside us look on, fascinated. Gurgaon has never seen such champion eating. They'll talk about this for years to come, speculation rife, 'The carnivore girl — was she a tiger in disguise?'

As we leave, our hosts politely walk us out, help locate the rental car and rouse our sleeping driver. They are aghast at the state of our transportation — a clapped-out, dinged up hatchback with a rear passenger door crushed shut by what can only have been an unsurvivable accident, no wing mirrors and windows that don't wind down, and no door handles in the back. As our driver emerges groggily from the back seat, our hosts are visibly terrified. He does look like a murderer.

'Really, you can't go back to Delhi in this!' they protest, offering to call us a taxi, find another driver, take us there themselves, anything but this.

We laugh. You should have seen the Hotel Capital.

Corruption-wali Games

It seems the gods had it in for the Delhi Commonwealth Games, or the 'Corruption-wali Games' as the local kids were calling them. This is nothing to sneeze at in a country like India, where Hinduism alone has 33 million deities.

At this stage of the chaos, Delhi's top elected official, Sheila Dikshit, admitted to hoping for divine intervention. 'It's over to God now,' she said, in response to questions about the countless delays caused by the never-ending monsoon. 'If the rain does not stop, then I can only pray, and request the whole country to pray.'

With the Games coming in on a wing and a prayer, one engine on fire, Games officials seem strangely unfazed.

'We can host events at an hour's notice,' boasted organising committee chairman and comb-over king Suresh Kalmadi (who somehow still kept his job despite all the lying he had been doing), brushing aside concerns about leaking roofs and water-logging at stadium gates. Despite clear evidence deadlines will never be met, Delhi builds on. Major roads are still blocked by construction work and landscaping projects appear to have been abandoned halfway through.

High fences have been erected to hide the unsightly Delhi slums from the anticipated visitors. In the words of the *Indian Express*: 'If you don't see it, it doesn't exist.' An ostrich attitude to the shambles seems to prevail: Sabkuch ticktock hai. All is well.

New Zealand Olympic Committee chef de mission Dave Currie was in Delhi at that time, deciding whether security measures and Games' preparedness was satisfactory. His assessment included showers and toilets, a little precious surely, when 700 million Indians do not have access to a toilet. 'Let him come!' thundered a defiant Randir Singh, organising committee vice-chairman.

I can't speak for Mr Currie, but Delhi certainly made an impression on me. Not normally lost for words, I was speechless upon first seeing the bomb site that is Connaught Place. Speechlessness was followed by anger, as I assumed the tuk tuk driver had cheated us and dropped us off in the middle of nowhere. Was this rubble-strewn bog really the Delhi CBD?

'This isn't the centre of town!' I raged. 'It can't be!' It was.

'Do they *really* expect to pull this off?' I asked, shell-shocked by the scale of the destruction.

It seemed there wasn't a footpath that hadn't been dug up in the mad treasure-hunt of excavations. No electricity, no internet. Agencies had been 'over-ambitious in trying to improve infrastructure and beautify the city ahead of the Games', Ms Dikshit explained.

Deep craters filled with water punctured the roads and above the street, roofless rooms were open to the rain, blue tarpaulins flapping. Twisted skeins of shredded metal cast menacing shadows. The wreckage called to mind the aftermath of a world war, with India on the losing side. Negotiating the mire and the twisted coils of rusted wire, you imagined an Armageddon where entire buildings had been vaporised, but the truth is they were never there to begin with.

The heat squatted on our shoulders. The economist went on another popsicle bender: 15 cents each (for the ones that taste like petrol), he downed six in five minutes, the sugar high making him as giddy as a toddler.

At Delhi's monstrous Old Fort (Purana Qila), monkeys scream among the ramparts. The children of Hanuman, the monkey god, Salman Rushdie writes in *Midnight's Children* that 'these long-tailed and black-faced monkeys dedicate themselves to the dismemberment, stone by stone, of the entire fortress'. The destruction practised by Rushdie's monkeys seems an ironic premonition of the slow progress of the stadiums rising, rag-tag and brick by brick, on the other side of town.

Barefoot, hard-hatless workers (and their naked children) doze atop piles of gravel outside the Shivaji Stadium. Sleeping is probably a safety measure, as nearly one hundred construction workers have died already.

'Finished!' said the auto driver proudly as we passed.

The economist and I looked at each other open-mouthed. Was he blind? All we could see were stacks of building materials and daylight shining through a pitted concrete shell held up by bamboo scaffolding. This was 'finished' only in a deranged fantasy.

Next door to the stadium, a vast raft made of a thousand discarded plastic bottles bobs around in a lake of water. Everywhere in Delhi, there is the crunch and snap of empty plastic water bottles; burnt in piles beside the road, they exude a noxious toxic vapour twinning with the fumes of exhaust and clouds of red dust.

Shivaji Stadium, which was supposed to have been ready by 30 June, was subsequently abandoned as the practice venue for hockey, the completion date a smile and a shrug. Yet the juggernaut kept rolling, sort of. The Games' theme song, written by the Oscar-winning composer of the soundtrack to 'Slumdog Millionaire', was launched to Bollywood fanfare and more than a few raspberries (it's very 'Lion King'). Shera the Tiger merchandise was still to come, there being a hold-up with the supplier. Thousands queued for the promised tickets, only to find they weren't available. Some sort of problem with the printer. At every stage, money dribbled through the organisers' fingers like water through cupped hands.

A metro station and elevated road for transporting the athletes from the village to the stadium (the stink off the rising Yamuna River will hopefully blow away from the Games Village) was still being completed by shrivelled little women carrying concrete in baskets on their heads. Government sources continue to display mindless optimism.

Hosting the Games promised India the chance to promote the shining New India of 10 per cent annual growth and global software giants. The world would learn that the Old India of chaos, poverty and delays was no longer. This is a country which has higher rates of child malnutrition than sub-Saharan Africa, but which also puts satellites into space. Meanwhile, Kashmir burns, dengue fever rages and the Naxals (militant Indian communists) blow up trains and behead cops.

In what may become the saddest story ever told, in terms of the Games' human and financial cost (rising 1575 per cent since the original bid), Delhi was spending immense sums on sporting venues which may never be used again — even diverting funds earmarked for anti-poverty measures. Now, the city on lockdown, thousands of slum-dwellers forcibly evicted, the cow-herding teams are standing by, the rat-catchers ready; 175,000 paramilitary troops are waiting to be deployed to guard against terrorist strikes.

'The CWG is the biggest and most blatant exercise in corruption in independent India's history,' said best-selling novelist Chetan Bhagat, writing for *The Times of India*. 'But if you worry about whether the work will be finished on time, imagine the plight of Delhi's residents (the wealthier of whom are leaving in petrified droves).

'The dug-up roads will never be repaired, the potholes left as souvenirs. The Indian people will be called upon to support the Games and save India's image, but don't,' implores Bhagat. 'This is a chance to put this corrupt and insensitive government to shame' — using what Gandhi pioneered in his time; non co-operation.

'Do not watch them; do not go to the venues. You cannot become a cheerleader to an exercise in cheating.'

'Only a miracle can bring about in-time-readiness,' admitted opposition general secretary Vijay Goel. This is a country of miracles though, a place where the supernatural is a part of the everyday, where cannons are fired at night to celebrate the birthday of Ganesha, the Remover of Obstacles, God of Hopeless Causes. Perhaps India is the only country that could pull something like this off at the last minute. With untold labour resources and boundless enthusiasm, maybe it can happen. What a wonderful opportunity to say, 'We told you so'.

Hopefully, the rubbish and uprooted trees outside the Delhi stadiums will be cleared up, the terrorists stay at home and any cases of food poisoning will be no more than the travel sickness the city lends its name to. But the question was, will anybody go?

In the event, attendance was woeful, with 60 per cent of seats unsold due to a lack of actual tickets and the prohibitively high admission price of those that did manage to get printed. Organisers resorted to drafting in schoolchildren to fill the empty stands, and giving away thousands of tickets to the very people they had being trying to banish, the poor.

Death & the Maiden

Female deities are some of the most powerful in the Hindu canon, but even friends in high places can't help the girls of India. Viewed as chattels, moved from one household to another, if they manage to live through a childhood of being unwanted, adult life is no less perilous in a country where domestic violence is epidemic. Every seventy-seven minutes there is a 'dowry death' in India; every twenty-nine minutes, a rape. Wives are commonly hanged, burned, knifed, shot and poisoned.

More than 6000 brides die annually in India because their dowries are considered insufficient. Most dowry deaths occur when the young woman, unable to bear her in-laws' continuous harassment for more money, commits suicide by hanging, poisoning or self-immolation. Sometimes the wife is murdered, killed by setting her on fire; this 'bride burning' is often disguised as suicide or accident. Wife-killing is so common in India, 'murder' is the first thing people think when anyone's wife dies young.

During the Hindu marriage ceremony, bride and groom walk together around a flame. Bride-burning casts a rather ironic pall over this ancient tradition, a cloud not lifting anytime soon. A dozen Indian brides die every day in 'kitchen fires' thought to be intentional. Figures released by the Indian National Crime Records Bureau show dowry deaths have increased by 46 per cent, from 4648 in 1995 to 6787 in 2005.

In August Bangalore was rocked by the sensational murder of a twenty-nine-year-old teacher. Priyanka Gupta was found in her home, tied to a chair with her throat slit. Priyanka's husband, Sathish Kumar, told police he had been out for a jog when she was killed. Sathish said he got a call from Priyanka about two strangers claiming to be delivery men and cautioned his wife against letting them in. He told the police he found the house locked from the outside upon his return, and had to travel to his office to get duplicate keys. Doctors said Priyanka was first strangled and then tied to the chair.

Mobile tower records made a lie of Sathish's alibi. Attempting to dispatch his wife in a phoney home invasion, it turns out his parents had been pressuring him to get rid of her after three years of marriage had produced no children. Sadly for all involved, and of absolutely no consequence to his murdered wife, sperm tests later proved the couple's infertility was his fault all along.

'It is true that dowry deaths happen in India even today, but (to my mind) they are not as rampant as they used to be. Or it may be that only few get reported,' says Suparna Chatterjee, best-selling author of *The All Bengali Crime Detectives*. 'In today's society, it is very, very rare amongst educated Indian families, which is probably why this particular case [Priyanka Gupta] caught media attention. Given the diverse cultural influences, social and economic strata, religious belief systems, it would be unfair to generalise about a one-off incident such as this, and draw a blanket inference on the stature of women in India.'

The horror of dowry deaths lingered long after my return to New Zealand. As Suparna and her husband Kanchan Mukherjee (a very successful IIMB academic who struck up a friendship with the economist after attending one of his seminars) had been kind enough to invite us to dinner at their home in Bangalore and explain some of the idosyncrasies of Indian culture, I send her an email, looking for answers, or just a salve for my sickening dread.

I ask whether Indian men are afforded a superior social status (as relates to women) to that men in other countries have. What happened, I write, to the loud and flourishing Indian women's rights movement of the 1970s? Indian women are so very successful in politics, academia and publishing and yet there is this terrible disconnect, why?

'There is no clear yes or no answer,' Suparna answered. 'As I am sure you have noticed, India's belief systems stem from spirituality/religion. While in the western world, God is always depicted as a man (thus an automatic superiority is implied), in India, god is half Shiva (male) and half Shakti (female) — the yin and yang, if you will. The goddesses Durga, Lakshmi, Sarawati (responsible for valour, wealth and prosperity, knowledge and learning respectively) are worshipped with fierce devotion during the nine days/nights of Navratri by both men and women.

'Traditionally, men have been the bread-earners and women have been the care-takers of the family, with both getting equal respect (although the north-east part of India has a predominantly matriarchal society). It was only after the influence of western education and western civilisation that somehow having a career and earning money started being regarded as "superior". And thus perhaps, in the past few generations, men have assumed social superiority, although, as you say, educated women in India today have excelled in every single field. Even our president is a lady, which has not yet happened in a country as "equal" and as "progressive" as the United States.'

Indian women may be outstanding in their fields, yet indoors they are killed, poisoned, strangled with their own dupattas — strung up from kitchen fans to look like a suicide. Their husbands then remarry, sometimes doing this as many as three times without being caught. A new law has recently been passed, stating that if a wife dies in the early years of the marriage, and was poorly treated before she died, the husband and parents-in-law are automatically held responsible.

Section 304-B of the Indian Penal Code reads as follows:

'Where the death of a woman is caused by any burns or bodily injury or occurs otherwise than under normal circumstances within seven years of her marriage and it is shown that soon before her death she was subjected to cruelty or harassment by her husband or any relative of her husband for, or in connection with, any demand for dowry, such death shall be called "dowry death" and such husband or relatives shall be deemed to have caused her death.'

It sucks to be a woman in India.

'The hallmark of a healthy society is the respect it shows to women,' said Indian Supreme Court Justices Markandey Katju (now retired) and Gyan Sudha Mishra, in the aftermath of the trial of Sukhdev Singh. 'Indian society has become a sick society. This is evident from the large number of cases coming up in this court and also in almost all courts in the country in which young women are being killed by their husbands or by their in-laws by pouring kerosene on them and setting them on fire or by hanging/strangulating them.'

Appearing before the New Delhi court, Sukhdev Singh had challenged the life sentence given to him for the murder of his wife Daljit Kaur, who was 'strangulated' so badly that her neck broke. Kerosene was then poured on her body and set afire. 'Some of the convicts in bride burning cases must be hanged,' said justices Katju and Mishra. 'Too much of ahimsavadi [reliance on non-violence] is bad. Now it is time to punish these sick minds with the death penalty.'

The doctor's report in Daljit's case showed that some of the bones of her neck had been fractured and there were burns all over her body. 'These could clearly not be self-inflicted,' said the justices, unnecessarily. 'Crimes of this nature outrage the modern conscience.'

The 'modern conscience'; isn't that a nice distinction?

Train in Vain

There was a terrible train accident near Lucknow. Ten people were killed when the Gorakhdham Express collided with a stationary locomotive. 'For the time being, we have imposed some speed restrictions,' said divisional railway manager D K Singh.

I'm a bit nervous then about travelling by train to Agra. 'What could possibly go wrong?' asks the economist. 'You've got a better chance of being hit by a bus.' Actually he's right, India leads the world in road deaths of the four wheels/pedestrian variety; however I still feel a little hinky about the Indian railway system.

I pick four years at random: 1981, 1990, 1998 and 2006 (boyfriend anniversaries: handholding, car-crashing, marrying/divorcing and finally, love) and look up the accident statistics:

6 June 1981: Bihar train disaster, hundreds are killed (300–800) when a train falls into a river after the driver brakes to avoid a cow.

17 July 1981: Freight train slams into the back of a Narmada Express train in Madhya Pradesh, near Bhanwartonk Station, killing 700 people and injuring 43.

19 July 1981: In an incident blamed on sabotage, a train travelling to Ahmedabad from New Delhi derails in Gujarat, killing 30 people and injuring 70.

31 July 1981: 6 coaches of a train derail near Bahawalpur, killing 43 and injuring 50.

16 April 1990: Patna rail disaster, 70 killed as shuttle train is gutted by fire.

6 June 1990: 35 killed in a train accident at Gollaguda in Andhra Pradesh.

25 June 1990: 60 killed as a goods train rams into a passenger train at Mangra in Daltongunj in Bihar.

10 October 1990: *40 killed in a train fire near Cherlapalli in Andhra Pradesh.*

4 April 1998: *11 people killed near Fatuha station on Howrah–Delhi main line as Howrah–Danapur Express derails between Fatuha and Bankaghat stations.*

24 April 1998: *24 killed and 32 injured at Parali Vaijanath railway station in Maharashtra as 15 wagons of a goods train ram into the Manmad–Kachiguda Express.*

13 August 1998: *19 killed and 27 injured as a bus rams into the Chennai–Madurai Express train at an unmanned level-crossing on the outskirts of Karur town.*

24 September 1998: *20 people, including 14 school children, killed and 33 injured when a train engine rams into a bus at an unmanned level-crossing near Bottalaapalem village in Andhra Pradesh.*

26 November 1998: *Khanna rail disaster, over 212 people die as Jammu Tawi–Sealdah Express rams into three derailed bogies of Amritsar-bound Frontier Golden Temple Mail.*

11 July 2006: *A series of bomb attacks strikes commuter trains in Mumbai, killing at least 200.*

18 August 2006: *Two carriages catch fire on the Chennai–Hyderabad Express near Secundrabad station.*

9 November 2006: *40 die and 15 injured in a West Bengal rail accident.*

20 November 2006: *A bomb explodes on a train near Belacoba station in West Bengal, killing 7 and injuring 53.*

1 December 2006: *Bihar, a portion of the 150-year-old 'Ulta Pul' bridge, being dismantled, collapses over a passing train, killing 35 and injuring 17.*

So far this year, 264 people have died in collisions, derailments, or been blown up in Maoist attacks on passenger trains. Just saying . . .

❀ ❀ ❀

Quite possibly an Indian Railways safety initiative, the train to Agra isn't moving at all. This doesn't mean we won't be savagely rear-ended by the three o'clock from Kolkata.

The economist insisted on buying the $3 tickets, saying, 'You've had luxury, now let's see what the other is like'. I try to remember what luxury I've had.

We are the only white people. Tourists don't take this train, and with good reason.

For an hour now the train to Agra has been stalled on the tracks at Delhi station waiting for who-knows-what, and during this pause in the proceedings everybody has taken the opportunity to go to the toilet.

In cattle class, or 'rolling stock' trains, the facilities consist of what's known as a 'hopper toilet', essentially a chute in the floor bridged by metal 'pedals' on either side, ridged like spacemens' footprints. Opening onto the tracks below when the train is moving, the toilets are automatically locked when the train pulls into a station.

The minutes crawling like a legless zombie, we sit in the airless heat and steadily worsening reek of other people's waste. As the shallow stainless steel fixture at the end of the carriage simply can't take it anymore, finally overflowing, people resort to shitting on the toilet floor. A tidal bore of excrement begins to ooze out beneath the door, slowly lapping the bottoms of the furthest seats.

We are on the Poo Train. The economist is pretending not to notice.

A man is staring at me. Tall, skinny, imperious. 'White girl look at me,' he telegraphs with his eyes. This time I refuse to engage in the usual staring contest. As we pull out of the station, leave the city and rock into a countryside being covered by the falling dusk, the staring man doesn't even blink. 'White girl, I demand you look at me and acknowledge my manhood.' I won't. Even with my head down, resolutely reading my book, I can feel the laser beam of his eyes boring into my head, commanding I submit to his gaze.

Indian men have a variety of staring styles: total disbelief; mere curiosity; look at the freak; the sexual predator . . . I AM all that, Baby.

We lurch into the hot night. At some unspoken sign, all of us stand up, unhook, pull down and chain up the moveable panels of the hard vinyl carriage seats to create sleeping berths, six to a compartment. Sitting back down, looking through my eyelashes, I can see the staring man's legs shuffling impatiently in front of me. I won't raise my head.

The staring man is at long last defeated by my ignoring him; I hear him complaining as he moves off. It's a Pyrrhic victory. Looking up, I am surrounded by male passengers, lying on their bunks, all heads turned my way, eyes gleaming yellow in the dusk. My protector is swinging out the carriage door with the other boys. India, where the majority of men look at you like they want to fuck you, chop your head off and set you on fire — and not necessarily in that order.

An hour away from Agra we pull into a tiny station, brightly illuminated despite the hour, where thousands of Krishna devotees are sleeping on the platform. This is Mathura, the birthplace of Lord Krishna. His birthday is approaching. Pilgrims are pouring into this little town from all over India. If it is at all possible, the poo smell is getting worse. India is so human. Too human.

'I love having you in my life,' says the economist, sensing my unrest. I don't say anything.

The train breaks down for a while.

At three in the morning we desolately chug into Agra Cantt, reeking of shit and covered in mosquito bites. My hair is so greasy my forehead feels like it's smeared in chicken fat. Looking down at my dirty feet, I notice a peculiar patch of skin just above my ankle. I have been scratching at this red raised circle for hours, without realising what it is. I've got ringworm.

❖ ❖ ❖

Agra, on the banks of the Yamuna River, in the state of Uttar Pradesh.

Agra, where 80 per cent of the city's sewage flows directly into the Yamuna, making it India's twentieth most-polluted city.

Agra, home of the Taj Mahal, monument to eternal love.

The site, hopefully, of the economist's proposal.

'*Of course* he will propose!' reassured Mother, via email. 'It's the most romantic place in the world, how could he not?'

Failure to Launch

'It's the most beautiful thing in the country,' yelped the Australian standing beside me, 'but they'll still find some way to fuck it up.' His Kelpie-haired wife scratched at a bite on her leg, narrowed her eyes against the glare, and said nothing.

Indians pay Rs20 to get into the Taj Mahal, foreigners pay Rs970. Maybe this is what makes them act so badly. That and the prickly heat rash of unfulfilled expectations.

To be honest, I wasn't really surprised when the economist failed to propose. A monument to love and the most romantic of World Heritage sites, the Taj Mahal is a voluptuous memorial, kissed by sunrise and sunset in pink and gold. Visitors sigh upon first seeing its beauty. A pity then, that amid this perfect setting, the object of his affections wasn't looking quite so lovely.

I believe things might have been very different on the proposal front if it weren't for my suppurating mosquito bites, ringworm and worse — four inches of natural hair colour dulling my aspect. I'm too scared to find a hairdresser after the bikini wax episode (now growing out, adding to the itching) and other than a slash of lipstick to identify my sex, have gone completely feral: eyebrows, underarms and legs all as nature intended — in 3000 BC.

It's 40°C. Sitting in front of one of the wonders of the world, stomach roiling from a roadside samosa, striking a sulky Princess Diana pose, I looked like a leprous raisin.

Inspire great love I did not.

'Will you?' escaped not the economist's lips.

Bah.

It's such a shame. Beautiful and empty, like a giant marquee made of marble, the Taj Mahal so lends itself to thoughts of summer weddings.

The calligraphy on the pishtaq arches recalls the elaborate writing on wedding invitations; the intricate jali screens look just like wedding lace, and the great white domes of the Taj like cakes covered in marzipan, or the bell skirt of a bridal dress against a blue, blue sky.

I waited hours for the economist to pop the question, turning winsomely towards him every time he spoke, flashing an engagement smile as we walked in and out and around the stone cold mausoleum. I sent him telepathic messages that the time was ripe. I talked at length about the beauty of a love so abiding it withstood even death: Elizabeth Barrett Browning, Catherine Earnshaw.

Nothing.

In my defence, it's impossible for European women to look glamorous in India. Veins swollen, beetroot in the face, we lumber about palaces and ruined forts while Indian women wearing jewel-bright saris lit by a thousand tiny mirrors glide like tropical butterflies, giggling and hiding their smiles behind the corner of a crimson dupatta.

Indian women are the most exotically feminine on the planet. Tinkling ankle bracelets announce their gorgeousness. Golden nose rings, hennaed hands and feet, jasmine pinned into their hair — Indian women are even more ornate than the jasper, jade and lapis lazuli inlay of the Taj walls. They are splendid. Looking upon us sweating behemoths with compassion, their pity is no sop to our discomfort.

The effortless beauty of Indian women is pretty hard to take, giving rise to the green-eyed monster: envy, that barren emotion. Dribbling across red-stone plazas, fair skin mottled, dressed in sensible khaki (Urdu for 'dusty'), we white ladies look like Stonehenge walking. Our fingers are fat pink worms, ringless and turgid. Faces like paste. Our make-up slides off, puddling around the chin. A glowing yoke of sunburn rings our clavicles.

Even the poorest Indian women, in road crews shovelling concrete, or breaking rocks in the hot sun, look a million dollars in comparison.

I can just imagine how this must have pissed off the plain Jane Memsahibs shipped out from Old Blighty. Rescued in the nick of time from spinsterhood or a lifetime of governessing, only to blister and chaff under the sun of the Raj while the local ladies fluttered by without a care in the world. No wonder they took up drinking gin at Olympian levels.

While 'going native' would be a huge step up, the throngs of Hollys, Mollys and Kates who try to be 'ethnic' by wearing a sari make you think of oversized saveloys wrapped in five metres of limp, sweat-stained bunting. Braying into each other's faces, swigging Kingfisher beer . . . the flower of European womanhood.

Yet how the Indian men stare at us! If staring were a Commonwealth Games event, India wouldn't need stadia to scoop the medal pool.

Lockjawed from simpering, I finally fall quiet, realising a proposal isn't going to happen. Sweating with impunity, a strange feeling came over me: inside the Taj Mahal, here it was again, *Passage to India*'s ominous echo — 'Boum'.

Set in 1924 India against a backdrop of the last days of the British Raj and the Indian Independence movement, Dr Aziz, the hapless central character of E M Forster's classic novel, invites two white ladies on an expedition to the Marabar Caves (not an actual place, instead a fictional hat-tip to the Barabar Caves) to hear their famous echo. After numerous difficulties the trip is eventually achieved, involving a train, an elephant and dozens of porters, all at great expense to Aziz, and in defiance of his friends, who have warned him against it.

One of the ladies, Mrs Moore, is overcome with claustrophobia, the press of people nearly smothering her. Worse, the caves' echo, 'Boum', makes the same sound no matter what noise one makes.

The echo disconcerts the other guest, plain and uptight Adela Quested, so much that she temporary becomes unhinged. India has stripped her of her mantle of psychological innocence. Innocence is an impossibility in India, says Forster — no country more batters you with the unfairness of the lottery of birth and man's callous indifference to poverty.

Running shrieking from both the cave and the echo, Adela accuses Aziz of molesting her, fuelling the colonial conviction that Indians constantly lust after the flesh of white women. There is a trial and Aziz is acquitted when Adela confesses her mistake. Mrs Moore ships back to England and dies on the voyage. The rioting students take up her name and turn it into a song of freedom, heralding Independence.

Here at the Taj Mahal, the echo is caused by the voices of the people moving through the tomb. The echo, the terrible echo of India. My feelings of TMI, the press of unwashed bodies, the noise, the commotion, all echoes of one message: this is not your place. No wonder Adela went a bit mental.

She ended up a spinster, you know.

❖ ❖ ❖

The Taj is under threat from acid rain, as there is an oil refinery on the banks of the Yamuna River belching out poisonous fumes. The surrounding area has recently been declared a no-pollution zone. Stable door, closed. Horse, bolted.

Built by Mughal emperor Shah Jahan in 1653, grief-stricken at the death of his third and favourite wife Mumtaz Mahal (who died giving birth to her fourteenth child), the Taj Mahal's construction was a bit like that of a Commonwealth Games' venue. Discrepancies in completion dates arose due to differing opinions on the meaning of the word 'completion'. Estimates of the cost varied wildly, but back then, you could have someone beheaded. With this incentive no doubt in mind, a labour force of 20,000 completed it in twelve years. The Shah's other wives were left to quietly organise construction of their own smaller mausoleums nearby. Nobody ever goes there.

Myths abound about the ethereal Taj Mahal; most enduring is the legend of the black Mahal. There never was a mirror Taj Mahal built of black marble on the opposite bank but for some reason people persist in believing this. However, the scurrilous myth that Lord Bentinck (governor general of India from 1833–1835, charged with turning around the loss-making Honourable East India Company and famous for his ruthless financial efficiency and total disregard for Indian culture) planned to demolish the Taj Mahal and auction off the marble possibly arose because he had actually been doing this at other monuments.

In an example of how much sharper than a serpent's tooth is an ungrateful child, the Shah Jahan was usurped and imprisoned in Agra Fort (Qila i Akbari, not to be confused with Delhi's Red Fort, Lal Qila) by his own son. Qila i Akbari has strong, high walls surrounded by a twelve-foot moat. The hewn stones are, according to the *Book of Akbar*, chronicling the reign of the third Mughal emperor, 'polished like the world-revealing mirror, and as ruddy as the cheek of fortune. So joined together, the end of a hair could not find a place between them.' Ramparts possessing a battlemented parapet, merlons shaped like sloping oblongs to foil arrow-fire, Agra Fort is designed to be impregnable.

Thus confined and with no hope of escape, Shah Jahan's view from his prison window was and is dominated by the Taj Mahal crowning the banks of the Yamuna River. Every morning and every evening for the rest of his life, the Shah gazed out at the splendour of his cenotaph. The dying sun glinted off the crescent-topped finial. He had plenty of time to think about the wisdom of his choices, day in and day out, the Taj Mahal shimmering in the heat haze like a hallucination of matrimony.

Staring at the cold marble and remembering her warm embrace, I expect he kicked himself for not demonstrating his great affection for Mumtaz while she was still alive. He probably thought what a shame it was that he hadn't made a public declaration of his love, got down on his knees before her. Even if on that day she was a little puffy, a tad red in the face and squitty from a roadside samosa. Regrets, he had a few.

❖ ❖ ❖

I have finally reached World Heritage Site overload. It's not the Taj but the decrepit shanties of the surrounding town and the avaricious locals. It's like that awful Tarantino movie starring Salma Hayek, 'From Dust till Dawn', where the desert truck stop is a vampire haunt. At the end of the movie, as the camera pans up and above for a bird's-eye view, we see hundreds, maybe thousands, of semi-trailers dumped in a canyon behind the bar. Somewhere in Agra, there is a cellar filled with backpacks and Birkenstocks.

Amid the half-finished construction, the paucity of technology — no internet, no ATMs — Agra grasps onto tourists with all the desperation of remoras fastening to sharks. Tuk tuk drivers, touts and toddlers harass you ravenously the minute you step foot outside your hotel, clinging to your legs, beseeching.

Bargaining and haggling, holding out dead camera batteries vacuum-packed for resale, the locals eye you with a covetous longing. How they would like to sink their teeth into your creamy skin, suck out the marrow of your wealthy Western life, devour you whole. Get in, get out. See the Taj, pop the question and leave on the afternoon train. By night these hills will be swarming with Orcs.

The economist hasn't noticed my extreme pique at his lack of bended knee. Last night we even stayed in the honeymoon suite of a local hotel — no proposal, but His and Her towels. He is either the cruellest man on the planet, or the thickest. Perhaps a 'marriage proposal' is a mythical creature: a Cockatrice, a Shellycoat. People believe in them, but nobody ever sees one.

The next morning: 'I'm thinking today we might go a little downmarket,' announced the economist.

I thought of the Poo Train and shivered with revulsion.

The Eliminated Multitude

Even the piss of a son brings money; let the daughter go to hell.
  Bengal proverb
A daughter is a source of misery while a son is the saviour of the
  family. Aitareya Brahmana
Having a daughter is like watering a flower in a neighbour's garden.
  Tamil saying

Those busloads of eager, unmarried young Indian men spilling out
onto the Goan sands to play soccer and take sneaky snaps of the female
tourists pose an obvious question, 'Where are all the girls?'

In a normal population, the number of females equals or surpasses
the number of males. In New Zealand there is such a man-drought
that women, often better educated than their male counterparts,
are being forced to marry down. The opposite is the case in India,
due to centuries of murdering girl babies and more recently, thirty
years of concentrated female foeticide. Nobel Laureate Professor
Amartya Kumar Sen, in his article 'More than 100 Million Women are
Missing', posited that during the last century at least that number have
gone missing in South Asia due to 'discrimination leading to death'
experienced by them from womb to tomb in their life cycles.

Female infanticide (dudhapiti, from doodh piti, drowning a new-
born girl in a pot of milk) has long been common practice in India.
Traditionally, female babies were killed by putting opium on the
mother's nipple and feeding the baby, by suffocating her in a rug, by
placing the afterbirth over her face or simply ill-treating daughters. The
scope of the problem first became clear in 1871, the year of the country's

inaugural census, when it was noted that there was an abnormal sex ratio of 940 women to 1000 men, prompting the British to pass the Infanticide Act. However, it's almost impossible to police neo-natal murder in a country where most children are born in the home. Nowadays, the gross misuse of technological advancements, such as amniocentesis and ultrasound, have seen this ancient bias go in-utero.

Back in Bangalore, sitting in on another lecture: 'After generations of systematic female infanticide there is a scarcity of woman in India,' Rajeev informs his predominantly male class, 'especially in rural areas. Women in these parts of India are an important part of funeral rites and dowry is an economic necessity, not to mention the birth of sons, so essentially women are responsible for birth and death — the two most important aspects of life.' One girl child dies every day in India. By murdering these daughters in the womb or shortly after birth, those prejudiced against girl children have painted the country into a tricky corner.

New research published in the *Lancet*, led by Professor Prabhat Jha, Centre for Global Health Research, University of Toronto, shows that in Indian families in which the first child has been a girl, more and more parents are aborting their second child if prenatal testing shows it to be a girl, so they can ensure at least one child in their family will be a boy. This is not just a rural phenomenon. These declines in girl-to-boy ratios are larger in better educated and in richer households than in illiterate and poorer households, and the geography of incidents implies that most people in India live in states where selective abortion of girls is common.

Affluent south Delhi, known for its flashy markets and lavish consumer goods has only 762 girls for every 1000 boys, meaning about one in every four girls is aborted. Most offenders are members of India's growing middle class, who have the means to find out the sex of their baby and abort if they choose. Professor Jha and his colleagues from India estimate that selective abortions of girls numbered between 4 and 12 million over the decades from 1980 to 2010. Despite the Indian government implementing the Prenatal Diagnostic Techniques Act in 1996 to prevent the misuse of technologies for the purpose of prenatal sex determination, the authors conclude: 'The selective abortion of female foetuses, usually a first born girl, has increased in India over the past few decades, and has contributed to a widening imbalance in the child sex ratio.'

Rajeev points out that there are some fascinating paradoxes when India's situation is compared to that of the West. 'In the West, women have long campaigned, in the face of religious condemnation and social scorn, for freedom of choice over abortions — while girl children in India are cavalierly aborted every hour of the day.'

'In the USA, abortion is demanded by the "Right to Choose" section of society, who emphasise a woman's right to choose whether to have a child or not. In India abortion is legal, but is often used to abort female foetuses, possibly with the consent of the potential mother and her female relatives.'

Historically, India faced a massive population problem. One factor was son preference. Families would keep having children until they had a son. In 1974, Delhi's prestigious All India Institute of Medical Sciences came out with a study which said sex-determination tests were a boon for Indian women. No longer would they need to produce endless children to have the right number of sons, and it encouraged a policy of determination and elimination of female foetuses as an effective tool of population control.

By the late 1980s every newspaper in Delhi was advertising ultrasound sex determination. While these tests were very expensive in other countries, in India they could be done for between Rs70 and Rs500 (US$6–$40). Today there are 40,000 registered ultrasound clinics in India and many more trading in secret. According to *The Washington Times*, there are about 6.7 million abortions in India annually.

The much-vaunted sex-determination policy of the 1970s is now totally out of control, with female foetuses being aborted at alarming rates. This year, UNICEF reported that 43 million of the estimated 100 million women worldwide who would have been born if not for extraneous circumstances, including gender-specific abortion, would have been Indian.

While sex determination of foetuses has been illegal in India since 1996, it is very hard to police and there have been few convictions. The process is very discreet, with the doctor usually beginning by referring to the baby by gender, or suggesting parents buy clothes of a certain colour.

Prime Minister Manmohan Singh described female foeticide and infanticide as a 'national shame' and called for a crusade to save girl babies. Answering this call, some states are trying to come up with policies that change the economics of having girl children. Karnataka's Bhagyalakshmi scheme creates a bank account for every girl baby where the government deposits money . . . 'encashable at eighteen or slightly earlier for education purposes'.

In 1992, the leaders of Tamil Nadu (a state in the southernmost part of the Indian Peninsula, bordered to the north by Karnataka) started the Cradle Baby scheme, Palna, where parents who didn't want to keep their girl babies could leave them in cradles kept at government reception centres. As of 1 June 1 2007, the government had received 2589 children, most after the year 2000. This year, the Cradle Baby initiative is being launched countrywide.

Tamil Nadu also currently holds out a tempting carrot to couples with one or two daughters and no sons: if one parent undergoes sterilization, the government will give the family US$160 in aid per child. The money will be paid in instalments as each girl goes through school. She will also get a small gold ring, and on her twentieth birthday, a lump sum of $650 to serve as her dowry or defray the expenses of higher education. Four thousand families enrolled in the first year.

Overall, Indian state governments are trying to promote equality through increasing education opportunities, delaying the age of marriage and helping women to become economically independent. Changes in societal attitudes are hoped for as a result of the policy of reserving 50 per cent of all seats in local government bodies for women, thus ensuring men get used to having women in leadership positions. But as T V Sekher and Neelambar Hatti point out in their article 'Disappearing Daughters and Intensification of Gender Bias', published in the Indian Sociological Society's *Sociological Bulletin*, January 2010, better opportunities for women's education, increased labour force participation and greater exposure to urban life do not necessarily guarantee equal status for daughters.

Where families cannot afford ultrasound, girl children, once born, are strangled, smothered or neglected unto death. A study of Tamil Nadu by the Community Service Guild of Madras found female infanticide rampant in that state among Hindu families. Of the 1250 families covered by the study, 740 had only one daughter and 249 admitted that they had done away with an unwanted girl child.

In an article for the journal *Canadian Woman Studies* titled 'The Girl Child in India: Does She Have Any Rights?', Malavika Karlekar discovered deficits in nutrition and health-care overwhelmingly targeted female children. She found boys ate better, were better clothed and first in line for medical care. Karlekar's research indicated a definite bias in feeding boys more and richer food such as milk, milk products and eggs. 'In Rajasthan and Uttar Pradesh,' says Karlekar, 'it is usual for girls and women to eat less than men and boys and to have their meal after the men and boys have finished eating. More is spent on clothing for boys than for girls, which also affects morbidity.'

Apathetic neglect is a contributor to lower numbers of girl children, with widespread evidence of lower levels of nutrition and under-immunisation of girls from one to fifty-nine months. Karlekar found a higher death rate among girls in this age group, especially from 'miscellaneous' causes. 'Don't know' was usually given as cause of death.

Indian society is patrilineal (property passes from father to son) and patriarchal. The phenomenon of female infanticide is arguably the most brutal and destructive manifestation of this patriarchal society, the most extreme form of violence against women. Indian sons earn/inherit the money, continue the family name and provide security in one's dotage. In Hindu custom, boys perform the funeral rites — a father cannot attain moksha (redemption) unless he has a son to light his funeral pyre. Sons add to family wealth while daughters drain it. Sons defend or exercise a family's power, while daughters have to be defended and protected.

Recent changes in work, education, marriage age and marriage costs, while liberating women to join the workforce, also seem to add up to disaffection for daughters to a greater extent than before. These days families must invest more in a daughter's education and, now that she may have a job outside the home, simultaneously worry more about the loss of her labour should she marry.

A girl is considered to be a 'double loss' (paraya dhan — another's wealth) as she not only leaves her family when she gets married, but she is the source of marriage expenses, including dowry (despite the payment of a dowry having been prohibited under the 1961 Dowry Prohibition Act). The combination of dowry and wedding expenses can add up to more than a million rupees. The average Indian civil servant earns about Rs100,000 a year.

Any wonder doctors aggressively marketing amniocentesis advertise, 'Invest Rs500 now, save Rs50,000 later'.

In a 2004 article called, 'No Girls Please, We're Indian', India's national newspaper, *The Hindu*, recognised the country's sharp decline in girls as a national emergency. The author, Kalpana Sharma, called sex-selective abortion, infanticide and the neglect/discrimination of India's girl children '. . . an epidemic that will have far-reaching social consequences'.

Probably the most poignant social consequence of killing girl children in a country that loves weddings as much as India does is a scarcity of brides. In the old days, viewing his bride for the first time, the well-brought up groom would exclaim that he had seen a face as beautiful as the moon's. In a future bereft of women, many Indian men will never see the face of the moon. With several northern states now experiencing a serious shortage of brides, approximately 20 per cent of all Indian men will remain unmarried.

Demand always leading to the creation of a market, there are already reports of brides being 'imported' from poorer eastern states and bride-buying. In Madya Pradesh, Rajasthan and Punjab, the sex ratio is extremely adverse for women. There, a wife is shared by a group of brothers or sometimes even by cousins. In Haryana, men can buy a woman for as low as Rs3000, not minding mixing caste and region as long as the bride is from the same religion.

The Rod community in Haryana barters girls — give a girl in marriage and the family gives one back, over time this process of bartering, called 'Roda' has transformed into an inter-community black market trafficking of young girls. The bride drought has also seen a rise in the forced remarriage of widows — specifically younger sons forced to marry their sister-in-laws upon the death of an elder sibling.

For better or worse, richer or poorer, some of the usual social, cultural and economic norms in Indian society's choice of mates may, of necessity, be swayed. Even the unthinkable — inter-caste marriage — might soon become a must.

Ironically, the scarcity of females hasn't increased their value, made them a precious commodity or seen a decrease in violence to women.

'Massive resources are being invested in Operation Tiger [a World Wildlife Fund conservation programme],' said Dr Vibhuti Patel, speaking at the UN Convention to Review the Status of Women.

'When shall we start Operation Girl Child?'

Rajasthan Ramble

'I really *have* changed,' said the economist, on the luxury air-conditioned bus to Jaipur. 'There is absolutely no question where I would have slept last night (outdoors under a newspaper) — that is, before I met you, my Princess.'

The economist is in the midst of a metamorphosis all right, but I fear it may be merely bacterial. Strange gurgles have started sounding from his nethers, and he's off beer.

Jaipur, the Pink City, is the capital of Rajasthan, most famous for 'the width and regularity of its streets'. When the Prince of Wales visited Jaipur in 1853, the whole city was painted pink to welcome him. Some of this pink still remains, or they bought quite a lot of that paint.

The Hawa Mahal flutters its eyelashes above Jaipur's main street. A pink five-storey sandstone structure honeycombed with tiny windows, it was built in 1799 by Maharaja Sawaj Pratap Singh for the ladies of the royal household so they could peek through small panes of coloured glass at the goings-on down in the street, allowing them to nosey-parker while still preserving their modesty. After hours of bitching about whose son was going to be the next maharaja, I can imagine it would be a welcome diversion — climbing five floors of cramped stairs to watch a world tinted green: 'Look, I can see a camel!'

Jaipur's Hotel Kailash is as narrow as it is old, a creaking Escher staircase with rooms attached, squeezed between a bead shop and tea-towel emporium in the Old City. The desk clerk is so obviously a crook, he would fit in easily amongst the villains of London's East End. His sparse and greasy comb-over a flag of treachery. His string vest is viscously dirty.

The economist can hardly fit his shoulders around the stair bend and like a giant, cake-eating Alice, squeezes his way through the door and into our stuffy room. We're still doing it cheap (about NZ$30 a night) and nasty.

No time for wallowing in squalor, we're off exploring. In the space of an eight-hour walk around Jaipur, we say 'No' hundreds of times. 'No. No, thanks. No. Not for me, thanks. No.' The repetition drives you crazy.

Toothless spruiking hags, wide boys and oily peddlers scurry up, all with something to sell. 'Hello, my friend! Come and see my shop,' they coax, their faces fixed in an obsequious rictus. Who would have thought such an innocuous phrase could become first tiring, then threatening? We make our way through the crowd, who chant a canticle of commerce like a broken record. 'Come and buy, come and byeeee . . .'

It's like being Rosemary in 'Rosemary's Baby', encircled by gibbering Devil's minions.

After the first five hours the rot really began to set in. Saying 'No' makes you frown, saying it too much gives you a furrowed scowl. Brittle with courtesy, by mid-afternoon we were snapping it out, hunched curmudgeons, resorting to shouting 'No!'

'Fuck off,' muttered the economist (for him, the height of rudeness) at a small dirty boy proffering a dog-bitten neon frisbee.

We started to cower at each 'Hello'. The mercantile orphans, the snapping gums of stinky septuagenarians — the endless, rapacious retailing. Exhausted by our own negativity, we crawled along trying to make it back to our hotel, utterly defeated, just shaking our heads at the beads, dolls, bangles and trinkets. No, we didn't want a hat shaped like an elephant. No, we don't need a shiny box. 'No. No. Noooo . . .' The shopkeepers bar our escape, pen us in. We cringe at the unimaginable horror of yet another 'Hello my friend . . .'

'Chop me up and steal my wallet,' I think, just make it stop.

We are so fatigued and fucked-off by the time we get back to the Hotel Kailash's gaunt accommodations that, despite being half-starved, we hide in our room, refusing to go out.

Well, that's not entirely true. Driven to it by my rumbling stomach, I eventually venture out onto the street and find a couple of men standing around a pot perched on top of a gas cylinder, selling some kind of potato thing. Tasting one, I immediately spit it out into my hand. It tastes like a phlegm-clot fried in rancid human fat. The vendors look sympathetic. They wouldn't eat them either.

And then I get lost. I'm literally five steps away from the hotel entrance but I simply cannot see it. Blinded by tears of hunger and sorry for myself, I wander back and forth, up and down the same street five or six times looking for the hotel's tiny door. It's like snow blindness, and I stagger back and forth, a weeping yeti, dazed and vertiginous. The stallholders fall silent; I'm obviously a woman on the edge.

A gap suddenly opens up in my eclipsed vision, and through the murk I pick out the Hotel Kailash's door, right where it was all along. I make it back to our room, collapse in hungry tears, yell at the economist and fall asleep. The economist's gastrointestinal tract plays Dixie all night long. On the upside, Jaipur is much cleaner than Delhi.

The next day, the economist buys me an exquisite carnelian bracelet saying, 'Would you like that? Let me get it for you, Sweetie,' and I'm reminded that while you can't always get what you want, if you cry sometimes, you just might find you get what you need. The precious gemstone carnelian (a red-orange, sort of a cross between amber and ruby) was used extensively in the delicate lapidary inlay decorating the walls of the Taj, so now I have my own little bit of the Mahal.

Jewellery makes even the most difficult women happy, so I'm over the moon and temporarily distracted from the whole not-getting-married thing, additionally cheered by the thought that I must be getting thinner after all this walking around and no dinner. I'm bound to fit back into my smallest jeans when I get home, for at least a month. Although, if this is a weight-loss regime, it's not one you could easily market to Hollywood wives. Covered in mosquito bites, the red blotchy residue of receding ringworm, I have crotch rot and sunburn. I smell like King Kong's gonads.

However I haven't cut myself; I don't have dysentery, dengue fever or malaria, so it's all good.

The street noise last night outside the Hotel Kailash was incredible. It hadn't occurred to me that there was a reason the front rooms were so much cheaper. The economist though is no stranger to the hidden hazards of low tariffs, and for this reason he had remembered to bring the Blu-Tack, using it to stop our ears against the siren-song of cab horns and revving scooters. I slept as if underwater, the plug in my ears translating the crashing and shrieking to the gentle shooshing lull of ocean waves. Awoke to blaring, my gob of Blu-Tack having fallen out and stuck in my hair.

If I wasn't already alerted to the possibility that the economist might be delirious by his feverishly spending money on carnelian bracelets, he is also weak and shivery. It's obvious he's sickening. The daily watery gripe we have both been experiencing has become tidal on his part. We might need to stop somewhere quiet so he can recuperate.

❊ ❊ ❊

Ajmer, surrounded by the Aravalli Mountains, is 'an oasis wrapped in green'. With a temperature of 40°C, shivering like Lawrence Oates, the economist definitely needs to be wrapped in something.

We take a ride in a grubby plastic pedal boat in the shape of a swan and make a circle of rubbish-filled, man-made Lake Anasagar. The locals don't seem to notice/mind/think it wise to clean up the pontoons of plastic waste spreading in a mat from the dock, like a net of scum.

Our hysterical laughter at the idea that this stinking vat of sewage is a holiday resort attracts the attention of another pedal boat, filled with young men on vacation. They pedal frantically to get closer, pointing and staring at my breasts.

I don't care anymore.

Teeth chattering, the economist pedals around in circles, trailing his hand in the water like a consumptive hero. I help him out of the boat as he giggles at things only he can see and half-carry him to a rest stop beneath the marble baradari looking out over the lake.

Lake Anasagar is surrounded by fifty-two bathing ghats, segregated and used every day. Pilgrims bath in the sacred waters, and locals have a scrub-up at dusk. In a marvellous contortion of modesty, the ladies manage to wash their entire bodies under a sari without revealing anything but their lower backs.

Ajmer's Soniji Ki Nasiyan (Jain red temple) was built in 1865 and is filled with a colossal golden diorama depicting the Jain concept of the ancient world. The opaque glass windows defy photography of the main chamber containing the Swarna Nagari (City of Gold), a room brimful of gold-plated wooden sculptures representing Jain heaven. I love the Jain concept of 'harm nothing' — Jains only eat an apple if it has fallen from the tree of its own volition, as picking it might hurt the fruit.

The man selling silk prints outside the temple proudly says, 'I am Jain'.

'Tarzan, pleased to meet you,' replies the economist, as we leave.

I can tell he's been saving it up.

The economist is very sick. He is experiencing first-hand the Jain concept of arekantred, or the many-sidedness of reality. I find a chemist and buy him some Imodium. He takes it, lies down on our hotel bed, and passes in and out of consciousness for the next twelve hours. Strange farty noises are the only proof he isn't dead.

❊ ❊ ❊

The wistful Colonel James Tod, in his 1829 *Annals & Antiquities of Rajasthan*, called Udaipur 'India's most romantic city'. Udaipur's central Lake Pichola is framed by the ancient Aravalli Mountains, the old city dominated by the cupola-crown of the City Palace. Out on the lake, fairy-tale islands are topped with a confection of palaces, gleaming like icing by day and lit at night by multitudes of twinkling lights. After the hatchet-faced carnies of Jaipur and Ajmer's Lake Scummy, Udaipur feels like heaven.

The economist is now extremely sick. He started to get really sick on the bus coming here, sweating in cold rivulets, stomach churning, oesophagus lurching. We thought it couldn't possibly be a very long journey, after all it's only 200 kilometres from Jaipur to Udaipur. Instead it took eight hours, the bus stopping at every village water pump and peanut stand along the way, the poor economist clenching against every bump in the road. His pitiful groans caused the other passengers to keep a wary eye on the emergency exit, fearing an explosion.

'Breathe, just breathe,' I coached, rubbing his back like a midwife who knows the hospital is too far.

After eight hours of painful contractions, we are enormously relieved to be here. The economist is the most relieved, comforted by the knowledge that he didn't embarrass himself on the bus. Staggering from the bathroom to the bed with his pants around his ankles, he passes out. Looking at his waxen face, I am surprised to find myself dying for a beer.

I'm pretty sure Udaipur is a quiet, relatively clean, lakeside paradise. Right now though, demoralised by our Rajasthan rambles, I'd probably weep with relief over a bucket of water and a cold flannel.

Lake Pichola is only a little polluted, covered by a skim of oil so thin as to be negligible, the obligatory floating plastic bottles bobbing politely out of sight in the culvert by the bridge. Plastic bags have been banned here for several years now, so things are markedly improved on the visible garbage front. The cool air off the lake soothes the prickles of heat rash on my arms. My ringworm has responded to antifungal treatment. Things are looking up.

The economist leans over the balcony and moans his appreciation of the vista before lying down again. He may be some time.

The Hotel Lake Ghat Palace is utterly beautiful. The rooms are painted teal and white, with crazed blue glass globes cradled in antique metal filigree hanging from the ceiling, blue and white ceramic tiles on the floors. A chaise longue is parked against the wide bifold windows overlooking the lake.

Refugees from India, fatigued and shell-shocked by running the gamut through Rajasthan, from our hotel room window we can see the palace on Jag Niwas Island, built in 1754. On neighbouring Jag Mandir Island, the equally OTT palace twinning its towers to the sky, was built by Maharaja Karan Singh in 1620. Lake Palace and Monsoon Palace were used in the 1983 James Bond movie 'Octopussy' (the Bond attitude to women persists in Udaipur), earning Udaipur the sobriquet 'the Venice of the East'.

A great deal of Udaipur's fabled romance can be found in the vibrant colours worn by the inhabitants. Scarlet, yellow and saffron saris. Beads of glass glitter on traditional Rajasthani skirts and dupattas. On the men, turbans whose colour may signify caste, religion or occasion. Brahmins wear pink, Dalits brown and nomads black. White, grey, black or blue turbans are worn by Hindus to signify sadness. Shades of blue-green and white are believed mournful colours and typically worn by widows. Married Hindu women are marked as out of bounds with bichiyas (toe-rings), and chudas (bracelets) galore . . . and a stripe of vermilion down their hair parting.

The Hotel Lake Ghat Palace has an extensive room service menu and cold Kingfisher Blue in the big bottles. This discovery forms the routine of the next three days. First, I wander around the town, sightseeing and shopping for papier-mâché and pashminas, while the economist lies upstairs contemplating his mortality. The shopkeepers coo at me as I swing by, humming a happy tune, clutching the day's purchases.

'*How* much?!' The economist weakly complains, as I show him my booty. He's far too sick to stop me punching the plastic.

'One hundred rupees? But that's nearly three dollars. Surely you could have got it for a dollar?' He's not strong enough for a decent rant.

'You must have spent fifteen dollars today, including souvenirs,' he admonishes, his head lolling back on the pillow.

After my daily shopping expeditions, I have a shower and recline, reading a book before changing for dinner. Walking upstairs, I order a cold Kingfisher and sit at my favourite table on the balcony of the rooftop restaurant. The breeze kisses my neck and I look out over the inky velvet of the lake — pricked with the reflection of a thousand lights.

Every day a member of the hotel staff asks, 'Mr, he is sick?' making whooshing gestures with a hand held against their stomachs. 'Still sick,' I confirm, nodding and making a corresponding raspberry, indicating violent diarrhoea. We all smile sympathetically.

What a blessing to stop the relentless Quest to See the Real India, and just be. This is the life: lounging by the French windows of our resplendent room, reading Nancy Mitford's *Love in a Cold Climate* and Ian Rankin's Rebus series, bought at exorbitant rates from the second-hand bookstore downstairs.

I wonder what Rebus would make of Udaipur.

'Seems like a nice place from where I'm lying,' croaks the economist.

Playing nurse to his feeble doctor means I can rest and recoup, after a journey best described as 'India done the hard way'. While it has been great to peek behind the tourist façade and share the footpaths, trains and smog-clogged roads with the teeming millions, the chances of catching typhoid, malaria or dengue fever are that much higher, making it a bit of a false economy. Although, in hindsight, I wouldn't have done it any other way — especially if it meant somehow not appreciating Udaipur as much as I did. I loved it there.

Too cheap to pay for malaria medication before we left New Zealand, I'm beginning to wonder if this is what the economist has. Headache, nausea, fever — vomiting and flu-like symptoms, isn't that malaria? Then again, the vomiting is mostly rectal. The economist won't let me call for a doctor. I go to the chemist instead and buy hundreds of little pills designed to ameliorate fever, pain and excessive pooing. I give him eight times the recommended dose, in the hopes he might get better quicker.

Briefly turning to my own needs — you can't take care of others if you aren't looking after yourself — I try to find something on the room service menu that doesn't taste like Chicken Tikka Masala, and eat my dinner alone upstairs again (the economist can't abide the smell of food, retching at my omelette, which is a bit off-putting).

At the temple across the lake, a cultural display involving lively drumming begins every night at 5.30. I have a wonderful view from my private rooftop grandstand. Black-faced langur monkeys, their babies tiny jockeys on their backs, clamber over the balcony to see what I'm doing and whether I'll give them a piece of naan. Their curious fingers feel like small, warm leather gloves. It's sublime, even if my boyfriend *is* dying downstairs.

He rallies enough to see one corner of Udaipur, the City Palace. The maharanis used to stage elephant fights here: hopping the beasts up with hashish before the battle and building a knee-high (to an elephant) wall for the jumbos to break down before they could get to each other, using their sharpened and gilded tusks to gore the loser. Now politically incorrect, the last pachyderm punch-up was in 1995.

The Rajput Kings (formerly the Mewar) were independent, staunch bastards who fought off the Mughals and refused to marry into families who had wed Mughal princesses. They didn't want to dilute/pollute their stock. Concerned with improving the lot of their people, the Mewar organised massive, highly sophisticated hydro-engineering of the area's several lakes during the 1500s. In the portrait gallery of the City Palace, the great Mewar warrior king, Maharana Pratrap, cradles the head of his favourite horse as it lies dying of injuries sustained in battle. The noble steed's pained, martyred face looks a bit like the economist's.

On the way back to the hotel, as a final fling, I pop into my favourite emporium ('Lisa!' exclaims the shopkeeper with an ecstatic smile) and buy a silk scarf.

'Stop. Spending. Money,' gasps the economist, sagging against the doorjamb. He possesses some mad fantasy that we will return to our apartment at IIMB via a forty-hour train ride. While he has a shower, I slide his credit card out from under his sweat-soaked pillow and book a flight from nearby Ahmedabad back to Bangalore.

As we climb into our airport taxi the next morning ('Are you *sure* we should be doing this?' asks the rickety economist), the retailers of Udaipur tearfully line the streets and wave hankies, as the best thing to happen to them all year departs.

The Bowels! The Bowels!

Except for in my neighbourhood, where feral cats and hoarded washing machines are the only garden ornaments, there are many places in the South Island of New Zealand where people own neat, well-kept houses, drive to work each morning on comparatively deserted roads, buy a new car every five years and honestly believe they lead 'normal' lives. I daydream about this normality the way guests at Guantanamo do about jumpsuits that aren't orange.

Right now, or if not right now then tomorrow, standing behind the deli counter at a certain supermarket in Dunedin (on the days he is not at university studying Information Science), occasionally singing 'Bohemian Rhapsody', is a young man called James Brown.

He is not the Godfather of Soul. While he cannot manage the falsetto of 'Beelzebub has a devil put aside for me,' he does have impeccable hygiene standards. My daughter Sophia, whose boyfriend this clean James is, works in the delicatessen of a rival supermarket, when she is not at her beauty therapy course. Their hairstyles are strangely similar. Hair-netted and begloved, these deli twins would never dream of touching your Parma ham with their hands.

Indian food workers are not so conscientious. I haven't seen a single hairnet. As for gloves, you only have to look around to realise thin latex shields aren't exactly popular here.

I will admit it right now, I was cocky. Warned, I paid no attention. 'Cast-iron stomach,' I boasted. Rambling Rajasthan, I ate my way around the state, putting anything and everything into my mouth, playing Russian roulette with my gastrointestinal tract. Emboldened by my example, the economist did the same. Quite possibly this explains why we both now have amoebic dysentery. The economist is so sick, he has entirely gone off beer.

I had thought making it back to Bangalore would be enough to cure him, but he remains unwell, a pale dribble of a man, and now I have gone out in sympathy. It's almost as if my body was just holding out for an apartment with two bathrooms before surrendering its dignity.

We have spent pretty much the whole of this month prone on the floor of our apartment, rising only to do the needful. The bathroom is thick with the odour of spastic colons.

I have decided not to dwell on this painful period too much in my recollections. 'And then I went to the toilet. Again' is pretty boring.

On the upside, being presently unable to travel further than four steps from plumbed porcelain means there's plenty of time for contemplating the differences between New Zealand and India. I still love India, but at the moment it is a bit of a Bad Romance.

Beggars: Walking down George Street of a workday afternoon, someone might apologetically shake a bucket, collecting for Daffodil Day. However, it is highly unlikely that, waiting at the lights on an eight lane thoroughfare, you will be accosted by a woman with only one hand who will thump you with a stump, ask for money, and then look disappointed by the amount you give her. As you drive away, she will spit on the ground and call you a stingy bitch in Hindi.

Littering: Apart from those people who eat Hot 'n' Spicy parked up at the beach and toss the empty red boxes down the sandhills, most of us don't throw our rubbish just anywhere. Should I ever litter, I have no doubt that my old religious studies teacher, Sister Mary Rose, will materialise in front of a stand of pohuehue and yell 'Scott! Pick up that wrapper!' Catholic guilt hasn't made it to India. Discarded plastic water bottles and potato-chip packets choke every waterway in India. Glaciers are covered in rubbish. Nobody seems to care.

Perving: In New Zealand, women over a certain age often complain that they are invisible. Well, not in India! Sure, having men constantly gawping, tripping over while staring, and pleasuring themselves against your leg sounds great. But really, it's like being the Elephant Man.

Quiet: There is never a moment in India when someone isn't tooting their horn, firing a cannon, shouting or screaming. I often lie awake on the more clamorous nights fantasising about New Zealand's vast, empty tracts of noiselessness. Winton . . .

Marriage: In New Zealand, you can marry pretty much anyone (good luck getting a proposal though) and relatives will not chase you down and hack you limb from limb in the name of caste purity.

Corruption: David Garrett? Oh, please. While New Zealand regularly tops Forbes' list of the world's least corrupt countries, Indian members of parliament kidnap and rape, loot and abscond. Indian police stomp people to death. Cover-ups and shonky deals rule. Backstabbing is an integral part of the Indian culture, only with real backs and real knives. Not xenophobia though. Screaming at servants, bullying students, cruelly teasing the dark-skinned; Indians hate each other much more than they hate foreigners.

As well as sick, I am homesick. I miss familiarity. Let it breed contempt, just as long as I can smell that expensive hair product my daughter uses, hear my mum whistling as she sweeps and watch my stepfather fix yet another thing at our house that has broken.

Under the mosquito net I dream of Lake Aviemore, picture slipping into that cold, clear water. It's strange, the things you pine for: verdant bowers of yellow gorse, fluoridated tap water, *Pinus radiata*. In the land of Gobi Manchurian, I crave my almost-mother-in-law's home-made vegetable soup. I even miss the guileless way she exclaims 'You're eating well!' when I put on weight. What is it with people from Gore? Anyway, I digress.

People come to India with a specific goal in mind: outsourcing deals, seeing the 'real' India, finding themselves, whatever. And they will always achieve these ambitions. In India, everyone (apart from the poor) can have what they want. But in India, as in no other place on earth, life and death are so close you also get what Paul Theroux calls the 'Indian Surprise', which can be different for everyone: amoebic dysentery, spiritual enlightenment, a sadness that clings like a fever . . .

Having lost 13 kilograms, the economist's Indian Surprise is rediscovering his ribs. A born entrepreneur, he can see a business opportunity in this new-found skinniness.

Inspired by both the full catastrophe of his long-ago first marriage and now, amoebic dysentery — fancying himself a weight-loss guru — the economist has an idea for a slimming programme involving dysentery and unhappiness.

'I'd almost guarantee my work,' he boasts. And he knows what he's talking about; his former lovers have all been very thin. Misery will do that to a woman.

My ex-boyfriends always leave Lisa Land a lot heavier due to stress eating. If this professor lark falls through, laughing boy plans to open a chain of clinics specialising in cruelty and parasitical regimes: tapeworms, intestinal amoebiasis, protozoan infections . . . all the while showering abuse on clients who have paid dearly for the privilege.

'It's genius,' he says, 'I'll franchise it.'

My Indian Surprise is realising how much I love Dunedin. And let's not forget I couldn't wait to leave. Packed a month beforehand, I declared the city 'boring and provincial'. Now, I long for Dunedin's 'ramshackle, struggling-to-function charm', as *Otago Daily Times* blogger Anna Chinn puts it: the dilapidated buildings leaning over Princes Street, the baroque beauty of the Wolf Harris fountain, pubs and art galleries, windy beaches, steeples against the sky, freezing mornings presaging blue-sky days, cold and salty, wool-clad and awkward, bogans and Presbyterians.

They say the grass is always greener. But then, it's the grass I miss.

The Queen's Hinglish

This week I'm reading *The Death of Mr Love* by Indra Sinha. God bless Blossoms Bookstore in Bangalore's Church Street — three floors of new and second-hand, able to satisfy even this most ravenous of bookworms. Like *White Mischief*, Sinha's book is based on a real murder which electrified Bombay society in 1959. Navy Commander Kawas Nanavati, after killing his English wife Sylvia's lover, Prem Ahuja, found public opinion solidly behind him. The jury acquitted Nanavati on the grounds that Ahuja had it coming, the outraged judge refused to accept the verdict. Nanavati was eventually pardoned by the state governor and sensibly left the country a short time afterwards.

Anything but a linear narrative (who am I to talk about sensible, sequential stories?), nevertheless *The Death of Mr Love* provides a wealth of detail about Indian life.

Sinha notes that 'babu speak', a phrase the English used to denigrate the way Indians speak English, is actually perfectly preserved eighteenth century English, as spoken by Lord Nelson and battalions of bored subalterns like Winston Churchill, playing polo at the Bangalore club and running up whiskys on tick, or the overheard 'fark, fark, fark' droning above the *donk* of bugs and clink of glasses on hill-station evenings.

This unchanging language architecture has preserved such gorgeous antique-speak as 'Kindly do the needful, and oblige', still written today at the close of formal business letters and essentially meaning 'Please take care of this matter'.

One of my particular favourites 'doolally', meaning crazy, was Raj military slang for a town near Mumbai called Deolali, where there was a sanatorium for Brits gone bonkers.

Are these corseted words and stiff-upper-lip idioms a lovely linguistic echo of a more polite and formal age? Not as far as Sinha is concerned. He maintains that the culture this language preserves, in reality, never existed: 'The dashing colonels and majors of myth were as extinct as the brontosaur — [by the time of the Raj] the British in India inhabited a world of their own dreaming.'

Whether a language homesick for dreaming spires, or a figment of nostalgic imagination, 'Hinglish' — what is today a mix of Hindi and antique English — has in all probability been around since the first trader stepped off a British East India company ship in the 1600s.

Hinglish has undergone a remarkable cultural makeover of late — going from deprecated to acceptable to almost patriotic over the course of the last decade, becoming the lingua franca of India's young urban middle class. A charming hotchpotch of phrases and English-sounding words which only have meanings in Hindi, such as 'badmash' (naughty) and 'glassy' (in a need of a drink), Hinglish is now the hippest slang on the country's streets and campuses.

'While once considered the resort of the uneducated or the expatriated (the so-called 'ABCDs' or American-Born Confused Desi), Hinglish is now the fastest-growing language in the country. So much so, in fact, that multinational corporations have increasingly in this century chosen to use Hinglish in their ads. A McDonald's campaign in 2004 had as its slogan "What your bahana is?" (What's your excuse?). In Bombay, men who have a bald spot fringed by hair are known as stadiums, while in Bangalore nepotism or favouritism benefiting one's (male) child is known as son stroke.' (From the fifth book in lexicographer Susie Dent's 'language report' series, *The Language Report: English on the Move, 2000–2007*, Oxford University Press.)

Sometimes the base of Hinglish phrasing is definitely English: 'Careful yaar, woh dangerous hai!'; sometimes English with just a sprinkling of Hindi. Film director Mahesh Bhatt catered to the Hinglish audience (and caused sniggers amongst filthy-minded foreigners) when he called his latest movie 'Murder, Gangster, Jism, Crook' (jism means body in Hindi).

This collusion of languages generates flavoursome phraseology.

Below some exquisite turns I've eavesdropped on the streets, read in the papers, or read subtitled in Bollywood movies:

Time-pass (doing something trivial)
Himalayan blunder (a *very* big mistake)
Prepone (move forward, of a meeting)
Jungli (uncouth)
Jocundity (humour)
Cent per cent (completely)
Gone for a six (ruined)
Kitty party (a regular gathering of women, usually over a meal)
She is innocently divorced (not the party at fault)
Stepney (spare, can apply to either a tyre or mistress)
Would-be (fiancé/e)
I'll give you such a tight slap your ancestors will feel it!
You must be tired, isn't it?
Don't try to butter me!
I took them off because I was getting shoe-bite.
Why are you acting so pricey?

Hinglish is evocative, archaic. Colonial leftovers blended with Hindi, Urdu and the odd cricketing term mashed and morphed into a whole new language, one that's poised to take over the world. In conjunction with the increasing 'chutnefying' of English and the growing influence of the Indian culture globally, what with so many Indians working in information technology, in time Hinglish may quite simply *be* English.

Anglo-Indians have already brought Hinglish home to the place from whence the Empire's much-lauded phraseology sprang — England, where it is, in turn, colonising the utterings of urban Asians. It is so popular, even white boys try to speak it, as witnessed by the irrepressible contagion of the superbly meaningless 'innit?'

'This will be an increasing trend,' says Jeremy Butterfield, editor-in-chief of the Collins dictionaries, in an article called 'Kiss my Chuddies!'(undies) which appeared in *The Observer*. 'If new words are used enough, they end up in the dictionary, and once they are there they become English words, too. With our increasingly multi-cultural society, in fifty years English will have adopted a mass of words from all the different cultures living on this island.'

Those who complain about the loss of the purity of the language are simply misguided. 'English is a mongrel language, and always has been,' says Butterfield.

Many Asian words have already been naturalised into English. Bungalow, bangles, cheetahs, ganja, shampoo, toddy and thugs have all been shipped over from the subcontinent. And every time Jamie Oliver kisses his fingers and cries 'pukka!' he is speaking Hindi.

In 2006 acclaimed author Gurcharan Das predicted that by 2012 the largest number of English-speaking people in the world will be in India. 'The British defined English at the end of the nineteenth century, the Americans at the end of the twentieth century,' explains Das. 'At the end of the twenty-first century it will be Hinglish that will define the language for the world.'

Hooray for a richer vocabulary, innit?

One for You, a Billion for Me

There is a distinct lack of voting in the Indian democracy. One, it's hellishly difficult — voters must first have an identity card (only 300 million issued so far) and then circumnavigate the slippery coils of the electoral roll, computerised in only a few states. And two, most people don't really believe their votes will make a blind bit of difference in political waters so murky and shark-infested.

'Karnataka's biggest industry was kidnapping until several of the kidnappers got into politics,' says Rajeev. He's not joking.

Corruption is a way of life in India. Government officials steal state property, doctors sell fake medicines, defence stores are sold on the black market. Indian Army generals gift their mother-in-laws apartment blocks in swanky Delhi neighbourhoods. Yet even in this mucky milieu, Karnataka is hands-down the most corrupt state in India, managing to out-filth them all.

In Karnataka, the rot starts and finishes at the top. The car bombings and knife attacks carried out by the local dacoits (bandits) are a Sunday drive with Aunty Mildred compared to the murderous goings-on of Karnataka's ministers.

The economist and I are invited to the IIMB auditorium to watch a screening of 'Blood and Iron', a documentary produced and directed by renowned journalist, activist and film maker Paranjoy Guha Thakurta about the 'convergence of crime, business and politics in southern India'. Paranjoy has been working for years to expose the heartless dealings of the villains of the piece: the Gali Reddy brothers. Two of the Reddy brothers are ministers (Tourism and Revenue respectively) and the family is the moneybags of India's biggest political party, the

Bharatiya Janata Party or BJP, the Hindu Nationalist Party.

Everyone who voted for them got Rs500 and a sari.

The three Gali Reddy brothers came from a humble background (their father was a police constable in Bellary) and become fabulously rich by the filthiest of means. Pig iron magnate G Janardhan Reddy's mining crews have been accused of trespassing over the state boundary between Karnataka and Andhra Pradesh in their greed for iron ore, which is then illegally exported out from under the feet of the Indian government (30 million tons in seven years) — mostly to China, where the ongoing demand for steel (soaring in the lead-up to the 2008 Beijing Olympics) continues to make these activities worth it.

For years the Reddy brothers have seemed invincible, their influence not diminishing, despite reports prepared by the Indian Bureau of Mines describing blatant violations of the laws of the land, destruction of the livelihoods of local people, degradation of the environment and rapacious depletion of mineral reserves.

The Bellary region, where one fifth of India's iron ore is extracted, is the biggest and dirtiest example of Karnataka's unchecked pillaging, with miners, government officials and ministers all colluding to defraud the government of mining revenues, while decimating the locals' land.

In the first decade of the new millennium, extraction of iron ore in Bellary became even more lucrative than mining for gold and diamonds. The people who live there never saw a cent.

Poor Bellary has the misfortune of being rich in metallic minerals including iron ore, manganese ore, red oxide, gold, copper and lead, and non-metallic minerals such as andalusite, asbestos, corundum, clay, dolomite, limestone, quartz, soap stone, granite and red ochre. The iron ore found in Bellary is of superior quality, one of the finest in the world, known as 64Fe. This 'red gold' has created a class of Indian oligarchs; extracting huge profits from their brazen endeavours, riding helicopters, driving luxury cars and laundering money through international tax havens. Bellary's inhabitants live in abject poverty, forced to eke out a living grubbing for the specks or 'fines' of ore the miners have missed while thick clouds of poisonous dust swirl over a once fertile landscape.

Drilling and invasive mining for any and every speck of mineral and non-mineral wealth has ruined the health and livelihoods of the local agricultural peoples, who have no option but to stay, as their villages are turned into red dust deserts, the very air they breathe a carcinogenic death-cloud of iron ore. The sloth bear has disappeared from Bellary, medicinal plants do not grow there anymore, and the red earth surrounding the mining area is denuded of greenery, bereft of farming activity. Even the rain system has altered.

While the Reddys stand out for their shamelessness, criminalisation festers in Indian politics across the board. In July 2008, *The Washington Post* reported that nearly a fourth of the 540 Indian members of parliament faced criminal charges, including human trafficking, immigration rackets, embezzlement, rape, even murder.

Politicos with convictions for rape and murder never serve any time; most never get charged in the first place. Our friend and host Rajeev (himself a political aspirant with integrity, so probably destined for failure) explains that it costs so much to stand for government, only criminals can afford to. Plus, it's a given that you must accept bribes to get anywhere in Indian politics. Ergo, it's impossible to be an honest politician. Chalta hai.

Chalta hai (just the way it goes) is an attitude of acceptance and apathy prevalent across India: crime, corruption, social issues and inconveniences; the chalta hai mentality means most people think the status quo can't change, so why fight it? This omnipresent, lackadaisical manner is often cited as the reason why Indians happily accept mediocrity in almost every aspect of life.

India's rampant corruption extends to the everyday. It's widely accepted in Bangalore that the bribe/fine for any minor traffic violation (speeding, drink-driving, knocking over a fruit stall) is Rs500. No ticket is issued, the money is just handed over to the police officer who pulled you over and you're on your way. Everybody keeps a cache of bribe money in the centre console dish where we would normally keep the parking meter change.

If you think about it, this is a pretty good deal. All-day parking is really expensive and Rs500 is only NZ$18, a mere trifle. Or three Boston

Buns. The daily application of little bribes would certainly make *my* life easier. I once hit one of those parking meter wardens, knocking him right off his little scooter. Looking in my rear-view mirror I could see him getting up off the road, mouthing something. A month later I read in the court news that he had been sentenced to undertake a course in anger management. Don't imagine I don't feel just sick about it.

And then there are the conscience-less gazzillionaires of India's ruling families . . . without naming names, let's just say that India beats the world for black money, with ill-gotten gains totalling almost US$1456 billion squirreled away in Swiss banks. According to data provided by the Swiss Banking Association Report (2006), India has more black money than the rest of the world combined; in fact Indian-owned Swiss bank account assets back then were worth thirteen times the country's national debt.

Hard upon the heels of the sickening waste of money that is the Commonwealth Games, an even bigger corruption calumny has just been exposed. One that makes the US$13.38 billion spent on the Games look like a sound investment.

The '2G scandal' revolves around the head of India's Telecommunications and IT ministry who pocketed millions in bribes and issued 2G licences at throwaway prices to private Telecom players back in 2008, when India launched 122 new licences onto the world's fastest-growing mobile phone market. As a result of this grafting, India may have lost up to NZ$60 billion, a quarter of New Zealand's GDP, in revenue. This in a country where 80 per cent of the population earns less than $2 a day and every second child is malnourished.

Telecom ministers pillage like pirates, trillions are stashed away in foreign havens by greedy Indian politicos slicing the fat off the nation's rump. It's disgusting, cannibalistic, and hopefully not the status quo for very much longer. Anna Hazare's India Against Corruption movement is picking up speed and winning global support. Indians from all walks of life are sick of the profits from India's booming economy washing into the swimming pools of the few.

'It seems as if the only honest people in India are the poor, who want to get rid of their poverty by education and migration, whereas the corrupt rich are getting richer through scams and crime. India is a wealthy country filled with poor people,' said the organisers of Dandi March II, India's 'second freedom movement', a worldwide march against corruption held this year, modelled on Gandhi's Salt March.

Petitioning to what seem to be resolutely deaf ears, at least the anti-corruption campaigners haven't lost their sense of humour. Putting their money where the greediest mouths are, 5th Pillar, Corruption Killer (An Eruption Against Corruption — www.5thpillar.org) led by anti-graft activist Anna Hazare — who dresses, talks and fasts like his hero Mahatma Gandhi — have created a zero rupee note, designed to be given to officials who request a bribe.

❊ ❊ ❊

Once back home in New Zealand, I received an email from Paranjoy Guha Thakurta, announcing the arrest of illegal mining king Janardhan Reddy, now former Minister for Tourism, Youth Affairs and Infrastructure Development. Also clapped in irons was Janardhan's brother-in-law B V Sreenivas Reddy, managing director of Obulapuran Mining Company (OMC), and his brothers and associates.

The arrest came not a day too soon, but almost twenty-one months after the Central Bureau of Investigation (CBI) first lodged a report against OMC, in itself testiment to the political clout of the Reddy brothers in the states of Karnataka and Andhra Pradesh.

Janardhan Reddy, who continues to protest his innocence, had ample opportunity to remove evidence, cover his tracks and wipe clean any fingerprints. Which is why it's rather surprising that the CBI still managed to seize more than 30 kilograms of gold and over Rs1.5 crore (US$275,000) in cash from his office.

'The only explanation,' says Paranjoy, 'is that the greed of this former minister and his family knew no bounds.'

Hiding Out in the Real India

The son had come to see his parents off. Sitting next to them on the train, his cell phone chirruped importantly. He was new India. They were old. The father was skinny in that painful way only elderly Indian men can be. Shank, sinew and spindly arms. Teak-faced, white-haired, dressed in a crisp white shirt and dhoti.

Unable to help himself, the father leaned over and cupped his son's chin in a weathered hand. His look was one of tender pride. The train began to pull out and the young man got off. The father rushed to the carriage window for one last glimpse. The old couple slept all the way to Hampi.

❖ ❖ ❖

A month since our return from Rajasthan, we'd been hiding out, afraid of the communal violence predicted in the wake of the Ayodhya verdict (damages awarded after the destruction of the Babiri Masjid, and a decision on just who the land belongs to — a court case that has been pending for half a century), due to come out on 23 September 2010. According to the press, riots between Muslim and Hindu were all but certain, not to mention that age-old Indian crowd violence standby: hacking to pieces and burning. The country had been holding its breath. Army and air force had been deployed. Entreaties to keep the peace were being constantly broadcast, 'India First', the slogan; religion second, the implication.

A fleshy, long-haired poet repeated calming verse on the television news. Sales of alcohol and petrol were banned, as was text messaging in bulk. Notorious 'rowdies' had already been locked up as a preventative measure. Last time this issue had flared up (1992), over 2000 people were killed and more than a few lifelong enemies murdered, as people took advantage of the chaos.

The economist had retreated to experiencing the world via Wikipedia. 'Did you know dragonfly larvae can suddenly and rapidly propel themselves by expelling water through their rectums?' he asked. To insulate my own fears, I'd turned to Evelyn Waugh's *Decline and Fall*, and was deeply immersed in the annual dinner of Oxford's Bollinger Club, where, from all over Europe, old members had rallied for the occasion: 'Epileptic royalty from their villas of exile, uncouth peers from crumbling country seats, smooth young men of uncertain tastes from embassies and legations, illiterate lairds from wet granite hovels in the highlands.'

The sun was low; soon the verdict would come out. Meanwhile, the squirrels peeped and the crows went *wak-waa*. Outside the door, India glimmered and seethed. I was on lockdown. Paws buttered. 'You're NOT going out today,' said the economist sternly. 'No mall, no grapes, no nothing. Am I making myself understood?' His eyebrows beetled, his nostrils might even have flared. I love it when he gets all Heathcliff.

No argument from me. Bannerghatta Road is one of the most divided areas of Bangalore. Muslim on one side, Hindu on the other. There was no way I wanted to be chopped into pieces small enough to mail.

Drink o'clock, the economist made me a vodka and cranberry. 'I didn't ask for lemonade,' I complained peevishly. 'Everyone thinks you're so *nice*,' he said, blowing his nose with every accent of emotion. His super-silliness masked the malodorous dead elephant in the room: fear of India. The news came on, the Ayodhya verdict had been delayed until 30 September (sixty years after it first went to court, the three-judge bench would eventually find Hindus and Muslims were joint title holders). There would be no riots, no bloodshed. Bit of an anti-climax, really.

❖ ❖ ❖

It was time to leave the house. Go where that great epic poem the *Ramayana* (an Indian *Iliad*), claims it all began. Hampi: the site of the wondrous medieval city of Vijayangara, the City of Victory.

Hampi: forlorn ruins surrounded by piles of precariously perched giant boulders (volcanic activity and erosion at its best), miles of palm groves, banana plantations and paddy fields. A World Heritage site, relaxed and laidback. In the *Ramayana*, Hampi is called Kishkinda, the realm of the monkey gods. Monkeys saunter, clamber, swing off every building, shoplift from the fruit stalls and generally run amok.

In 1336, the Telugu prince Harihara Raya chose Hampi as the site of his new capital, Vijayanagar. By the sixteenth century Hampi/ Vijayanagar was a thriving cosmopolis, exporting goods as far as Venice and boasting luxurious palaces, imposing temples, bustling bazaars and ostentatious festivals. Held up as the epitome of power and might, this hubris would eventually be its downfall when a confederacy of huffy Deccan sultanates laid siege to it in 1565. Robbed and pillaged, the city was razed to the ground and left desolate. Its temples and pavilions standing forgotten, the world moved on.

Across the Tungabhadra River (which happened to be in full monsoon flood at the time — mean and quick and dirty) is Anegundi, an ancient fortified village which predates Hampi. Sounds cool, but we're never going to get there, the river is too dangerous. The only one going in the water was the temple elephant, and even she was sticking to the shallows.

Bounded by the natural defences of the torrential Tungabhadra on one side and impassable ranges crowned by monumental boulders on the other, and originally enclosed by additional fortifications and massive gates, Hampi is named after a torrid love affair between the river goddess Pampa and the god Shiva. Despite this romantic hedonism, Hampi is a straight-edge town; 'No Drugs!' shout placards tied to every lamp-post. No chemist, no doctor and no beer either. No matter, the economist is still off it following the amoebic ravages he suffered in Rajasthan. My body has resisted any and all dysenteric slimming. Typical.

We toil past the monolithic Nandi statue and up, up, hundreds and thousands of steps. Around the goats and over the hills, we climb and climb, scaling the large, round, flat-topped boulders and looking down into the valley below. Slippery, and with a sheer drop to the valley floor 400 metres below, it's like clambering up the sides of an enormous balloon. I had no idea I was so afraid of heights.

The mute remains of Vijayangara's grand temples and royal enclosures are glorious. Ornate and exuberant, although not overly florid, made as they are of hard granite. They are a rare example of what every traveller craves: the feeling that they are the first to discover them. The economist, as happy as any boy who once built a private museum in his cellar, leaps from boulder to boulder, enjoying a delusional voyage of self-discovery. It is the Indiana Jones effect: rounding a corner and finding a tomb, a monument, and thinking to himself, 'I am the first person to have ever seen this'. Hampi does indeed have that feel: a lost civilisation rich with the possibility of finding treasure, in the form of a deserted temple.

Or the fire-blackened bones of a goddess. The practice of sati was once common in Hampi, though voluntary and mostly among the upper classes. A woman choosing to enter the fire after the natural or heroic death of her husband was raised to the status of demi-goddess, proclaimed by the sculpture of a sun and crescent moon inscribed on the satikal (sati-stone). These cult stones sometimes record the efforts made by the widow's family and friends to dissuade her from this extreme step, only to be rebuffed. Traditionally the sati donated her land, cattle and jewellery to a temple before jumping into the pyre.

Should the economist snuff it, I certainly won't be making the ultimate sacrifice, something of which he is well aware. He has taken measures to ensure my loyalty after his death. 'Mr Puck gets everything,' he threatens. 'If anything happens to that cat, you'll not see a cent.'

Outside the Virupaksha temple, a snake-charmer playing a pungi, a wind instrument with two reeds, encourages three cobras to dance by whacking them on the head with a stick. At intervals the largest repeatedly tries to escape. I don't blame him — life in a too-small wicker basket and constant aggravation. Cobras are deaf, so 'charming' is a cruel pretence. Inside, the temple elephant Lakshmi receives offerings of bananas and coconuts with the girlishness of a born coquette.

At twenty-one, she is very pretty, little (for an elephant) and black.

Regal and gentle, her trunk is a strange mix of soft and bristly. Snuffing up rupee notes, and giving them to her trainer, she lays her trunk on your head for a 'blessing'. An ugly chain around her ankle spoils her pedicure, appearing to cut her foot off below and above, making me think of an umbrella stand I once saw in a Dunedin stately home. Snatching the keeper's lathi, she scratches her tummy, dancing from foot to foot. Lakshmi's eyes are brown pools. I want to give her everything. 'You are beautiful,' I say. She knows. Yes, she is a chained elephant, but this is a pretty good life.

Like India, Lakshmi is proud, gentle, imperious, frighteningly large and unpredictable. Bathed, painted, pampered, gorging herself on gifts of fruit, Lakshmi bats her lashes at the tourists' cooing. She belts an urchin with the lathi, showing her displeasure at his repeated attempts to steal her limelight with his capering.

The temple grounds are home to several breeds of monkey. Twitty Hanuman langurs sit primly beside Sita's shrine, politely eating pieces of mango. They raise a preposterous eyebrow: 'Another? Don't mind if I do. Terribly kind of you, old bean.'

Common Rhesus swagger maladjustedly about the courtyard, like Travis Bickle from *Taxi Driver*, 'You talkin' to me?' Staunch little macho-man pickpockets, they're only interested in your bananas if they can steal them.

Thanks to the economist's discovery of a Wikipedia function allowing the creation of a booklet of factoids, I share the benefit of an extensive library of printed background notes, double-sided. The economist has been reading up on the *Ramayana* and much more. 'Any questions, don't hesitate to ask,' he says.

The Hazara-Rama temple abutting a corner of the King's palace enclosure is a small but highly ornate temple dedicated to Vishnu in the form of Rama. The shrine is a veritable picture gallery, its walls and pillars commemorating the legends of the *Ramayana* in stone.

Translating to *Rama's Journey* the 24,000 verses in seven books and 500 cantos of the *Ramayana* tell the story of Rama's defeat of the demon king of (Sri) Lanka, Ravana, with the help of his best mate, Hanuman the monkey god. The story presents several Indian character ideals: the ideal servant, the ideal brother, wife and king, and explores the concept of dharma, your role/fate/place in the world.

Rama (the incarnation of the Hindu god Shiva) has to fight Ravana to get back his wife Sita, who has been kidnapped by the many-armed, many-headed monster and imprisoned for years on the island of Lanka.

Rama (like Odysseus and Heracles) is actually a bit of a misogynist bastard — accusing his poor hostage wife of willingly having sex with the demon who kidnapped her. She ends up ostracised and sent into exile with her sons but, far more charitable than he deserves, forgives him in the end.

The Vijayangara Empire exported cotton, spices, jewels, ivory, amber and perfumes to China, Venice, Burma, Persia and Palestine. It was finally conquered, plundered and destroyed by the Sultanates of Bijapur, Ahmednagar and Golkonda (ferocious, bogan warriors on horseback) in 1565. The ruins stood untouched for centuries.

The Hampi children smile shyly, just children, not Artful Dodgers. Far away from the liars and touts of Delhi, the rheumy-eyed hobgoblins of Jaipur, is India — the way it has been forever: Hindu and Muslim living side by side; history and religion warming the stones, like heat from a fading sun. The smell of clove cigarettes, nights coloured orange by kerosene lanterns, cows stopping to lick the soles of your propped-up feet. An elephant stepping daintily down to the bathing ghat to get a good old scrub. Finally, I found it. My India.

This is the India I was looking for, lost under the noise, the rubble, and the constant 'Give us all your money'.

Walking to the Mango Tree restaurant (another one), thunder booms and lightning flashes on the swollen Tungabhadra River. They say travel broadens the mind. The teacher in the economist believes that, if you're lucky, you can broaden someone else's mind.

'The *really* interesting thing about the Egyptian Mau [a cat] is that its presence in Israel could help prove the Exodus,' said the economist, over dinner.

The monsoon crashed and shivered over the flooded river. Water lapped the steps of the restaurant and swallowed the trees at the shoreline. Lassi, Southern Thali, Aloo Gobi and Chapathi. No alcohol, no meat. 'This vegetable curry is actually very good,' I thought. 'But it would be better with an ice-cold beer.' Although I've never felt healthier — five hours of walking every day, fresh air, sunshine. Chocolate-coloured children lining up to shake hands, 'Hello, hello, hello!!'

I am really enjoying myself.

'You might as well,' says the economist, 'it's all the same price.'

The last day of our week in Hampi, and the sunset flambéed the red-stone boulders, palm trees and banana plantations. We climbed the hill to look out over the ruins of that once-great imperial city and say goodbye. Having walked for hours, biked up hills and climbed mountains in my jandals, I was stinky, exhausted and utterly, blissfully, happy.

As we passed, the snake-charmer was noticeably absent from his spot outside the temple. Savagely bitten and unable to seek medical treatment, hopefully. The economist cast about for a Honky in need of comprehensive explanations, distributing his Wiki-notes like sermons to the bewildered.

A motley group of humans watched the pinking sky while on another rise, a troop of monkeys did the same.

'Did you know,' began the economist, 'that in the fifteenth century Vijayangara was the second-largest city in the world?'

A feeling rose in my chest. A fluttering, a rushing, a bumping. My heart smiled.

It was love.

❀ ❀ ❀

It is probably symptomatic of a much larger problem, however, that I have begun to strike small children. While we were in Hampi, an eight-year-old boy attempted to hitch a lift on the rear rack of my rental bike as I was cycling along a tranquil, palm-lined road.

On my way to attaining a higher level of consciousness, only to be suddenly and violently yanked backwards, incensed, I lashed out behind me with a closed fist, a right-hook, a real haymaker. He saw it coming and leapt out of the way. Little brat probably gets clobbered all the time.

'Nice work, punching a toddler,' said the economist. I hadn't realised he was watching.

I'm afraid this kind of thing has been happening rather too much lately. After our life-and-India affirming visit to Hampi, walking out of the IIMB compound to buy tomatoes, cucumbers and grapes at the neighbourhood market, an adolescent boy with arms like pipe cleaners shot at me with a spit-ball pipe. I gave chase clumsily through stalls, awnings and piles of coconuts, arms outstretched like Frankenstein's monster — but he was just too fast for me.

His friend, waiting in ambush on the other side of the market, ducked down behind the potatoes and put pipe to mouth, intending to get off a head shot. He was stopped in his snotty little tracks by the fruit and vegetable ladies, who yelled something along the lines of 'Leave that grumpy white woman alone, she buys all the grapes'.

Face red, frown lines damn-near unbotoxable, I stomped back to our apartment. There is something going on with this irrational rage. I don't normally have an overwhelming urge to beat children.

On the bus yesterday, catapulted by a pothole, a woman lurched into me and knocked my shopping to the floor. Snapping, 'Stupid bitch!' I elbowed my way to the exit, not a very nice person. Today a tuk tuk driver harassing me for business at the intersection of Brigade and Mahatma Gandhi roads stood open-mouthed when I told him on no uncertain terms to 'Fuck Off'.

Watching myself from above but unable to intervene, I could hear a horrible voice, unpleasantly nasal. It was mine. As I trampled everything in my path, the tuk tuk driver looked close to tears.

My mother would be horrified. 'Lisa, you're still working,' she used to admonish when, as marketing manager of Dunedin's Fortune Theatre, I hankered after quite a few drinks on opening night to erase the taste of ham. A professional public face being all-important, if she could see me now — swinging at minors and swearing on public transport, she would have me sectioned.

'Be the change you want to see in others,' said Gandhi. It's his birthday today. There's no way Gandhi would approve of my child-beating ways.

Let the Games Begin

Things were going fine until the rains came. About twelve months behind schedule, but fine. In September pictures of venues no more than rubble-strewn puddles started appearing in the media, malaria hysteria mounted and everything got carried away in a torrent of corruption. Since then, the countdown to the 2010 Commonwealth Games in Delhi, opening on 3 October, has floundered in a mire of sleaze.

As late as August, while the whole organisation lurched from shambles to shameful, and stories of nepotism, bribery and special favours followed one after the other, New Zealand Athletes' Federation boss Rob Nichol was stating — 'hand on heart' — that he could not say whether we would send a team. Safety fears for supporters, too, grew amid the chaos.

'My family were going, but I have told them to stay at home,' Silver Ferns captain Casey Williams revealed to the New Zealand media. 'We, as players, have protection. The public don't.'

The story was picked up in India immediately. 'Silver Fern captain tells family to skip Commonwealth Games!' shrieked the local newspapers. *The Times of India* attempted to gauge the mood of major Commonwealth nations. It's verdict? Jamaica: supportive; Malaysia: upbeat; Canada: keen; New Zealand: cold.

Meanwhile, an outbreak of dengue fever was topped by the discovery of a new strain of typhoid. The monsoons have devastated Pakistan; Naxal rebels just beheaded a cop. Williams' sentiments were echoed by fellow Kiwi netballers Joline Henry and Leana de Bruin, and they weren't alone. Australian long-jump champion Fabrice Lapierre seriously considered joining stars Usain Bolt and Jessica Ennis in pulling out.

Those infamous treadmills looked like standing empty — a symbol in India of everything rotten about the Games and an example of the sense-defying contracts that have been awarded, treadmills for athletes to exercise on were hired for forty-five days at $33,000 each, when it would have cost $9000 less to have bought them outright.

On the streets of Delhi, people joked that the Commonwealth Games' organising committee was planning to give out medals to spectators simply for attending. In a country where bureaucracy is a slow-turning elephant and sports federations are personal fiefdoms, the gargantuan size of the Games scandal eventually forced Prime Minister Manmohan Singh to end his maun vrat (vow of silence) and step in. Heads will roll — but after the closing ceremony.

Steeped in bureaucracy, the organisers have also suffered from a chronic outbreak of acronyms: 'An OCCWG officer brought questions about the security of the CWG to the CAT, despite the government giving an NOC. Now the CVC, the PMO and the CAG have stepped in, sensing things are spiralling out of control.'

There is history to consider. Hosting the 1982 Asian Games in Delhi was a proud moment for India, a nation seeing itself on screen for the first time. Now, with the whole world watching, the 2010 Games could either win global recognition of how far the country has come in sixty-three years of independence, or a gold medal for corruption.

And what glorious skulduggery it is. Company directors have listed bogus addresses in Karalla village, an unauthorised settlement of overflowing drains and temporary roads where, as *The Times of India* put it, 'unwashed children and flies abound'.

One such company, Jubilee Sports Technology, was registered in September 2006, and until March 2007 did absolutely no business at all, before suddenly pocketing a series of lucrative contracts at exorbitant rates to supply turf to Games' venues. Baying like bloodhounds, the Indian press followed the money trail to London, Sydney and Switzerland, hoping to catch Shera, the Games' tiger, by his tail.

Before they make up their minds about coming, everyone wants to know, what's India really like? Well, I'll tell you. The smells of India: marigolds, sandalwood incense, excrement and coriander. The largest obstacle: cows. Ambling across four lanes of traffic, they know they're holy. Monkeys will steal your biscuits. Walking down a wretched street, you'll stumble upon a temple to a 4000-year-old religion, with colourful gods and goddesses frolicking on the bas relief. The people are gracious and nosey. Like a Bollywood heroine, India is beautiful, mysterious and capricious. Ancient and modern, in cities and villages.

Here, visiting Kiwis can experience wealth for perhaps the only time in their lives. People will call you Sir and Madam. Food, clothing, shoes — everything is cheap, especially unskilled labour. And life.

Oblivious to the fuss, the Games' venues continue to be laboriously erected by frail men in dhotis and wizened little women in saris — faces harrowed like a tilled field — carrying panniers of red dirt on their heads. Labour laws have been flouted and workers have died, but at least the daily six-to-ten-hour power cuts don't affect construction done by hand. Maybe the non-building is a kind of passive resistance?

As a plus, there aren't any beggars left in Delhi. Delhi's massive 'clean-up' means visitors will miss out on seeing children lovingly disfigured by their parents to ensure a lifetime of earnings as a beggar. Slum evictions, 'no-beggar zones' and the widespread arrest of the homeless mean tourists won't be hassled for spare change by those missing limbs, eyes or pants.

Despite the corruption, delays and shoddy work, most Indians remain optimistic. 'We are hopeful,' says our dear friend Professor Rajeev Gowda, 'that the Games will be a success. Not to mention a way to promote sports that are not cricket.' Like netball.

So, has all the media fuss just been unnecessary drama? 'Everything in India is done at the last minute,' a Delhi rickshaw wallah told me, smiling to reveal teeth stained by paan.

'I'm not worried,' said Australian Commonwealth Games Association CEO Perry Crosswhite. 'The athletes' facilities are the best I've seen. Plenty of other Games have been in the same state by this time.' The Australian delegation (the largest ever) has no security concerns, according to Perry. She'll be right, mate.

Thousands of volunteers turned up last week to receive their red and white Commonwealth Games uniform kits; consisting of two polo shirts, trackies, shoes, socks, a cap, a sipper bottle and waist pouch. Most (volunteers and outfits) never to be seen again.

The lead-up to the Delhi Games has been like production week in a theatre. The sets aren't finished and the box-office phone is silent. At the dress rehearsal, the actors flub their lines. It appears the stage manager has spent the entire props budget on an armoire which will look very handsome in his living room. But come opening night, as the audience rustles its last and the curtain begins to rise, the cast can put all that behind them. After all, the show must go on.

❖ ❖ ❖

A postcard home right now would say, 'Wish I Wasn't Here'. Thanks for nothing, Paul 'Bhopal' Henry. And while I'm at it, Michael Laws, what is your problem? Also leaking lethal gases: Mike Hooper, CEO of the Commonwealth Games Federation. This toxic trio of New Zealanders are enough to make you dread that ubiquitous Indian question, 'And your good country?'

It's no fun being a New Zealander in India at the moment. Paul Henry has an attack of verbal diarrhoea on TVNZ's 'Breakfast' and by tiffin time in Bangalore, Kiwis are about as welcome as a beef patty at a Hindu barbecue.

Worse, there have been numerous stories in the media here about Indian-bashing in Australia, so we automatically get lumped in with our less-couth neighbours. Right now, the Pacific Rim has all the charm of a ring around the toilet.

And when Indians get upset, they get really upset — effigy-burning, rioting-in-the-streets upset. Striking drivers soak themselves in petrol and demoted cabinet ministers threaten suicide.

Annoying India is a bad idea, especially when you're trying to negotiate a free-trade agreement with them. As Paul Theroux writes in *The Elephanta Suite*, 'India is not a country but a creature, a big horrific creature sometimes angry and loud, sometimes passive and stinking, always hostile'. Who wants to make 1.2 billion people mad? Doubly aggravating then, that before the Paul Henry hoopla could die down,

Michael Laws decides to be the naughtiest kid in Year Eight and call Governor General Anand Satyanand a 'fat Indian'.

'Just who is Michael Laws?!' shouted an incensed Indian newsreader, going on to explain that Laws was (ahem) 'a respected former New Zealand politician, mayor and columnist.'

For the record, Sheila Dikshit's name is pronounced exactly the way it is spelt. But it was Henry's asking if the next governor general would 'look like a real New Zealander', while our prime minister tittered nervously, that really did it.

Incidentally, what is it with governors general? When Theroux wrote in the *Happy Isles of Oceania* that Dame Cath Tizard was bossy, shallow, unimaginative and a piggy eater to boot, New Zealanders went ballistic. Theroux also said that New Zealanders were 'the hardest people to compliment' and that Dunedin is cold and frugal. Some things are incontrovertible.

New India has risen from direst poverty, morphing an antiquated language of 'miscreants' and 'jocundity,' and combining it with call-centre American English ('sure thing') to become an outsourcing giant speaking the language of tomorrow. However, Old India still hovers like a starved spectre and not surprisingly the phenomenally wealthy emerging Indian middle class has a bit of a chip on its shoulder about it. Though judging by the crassness of Henry's and Laws' sneering mockeries, New Zealanders have chips on *both* shoulders.

Despite the brouhaha, everyday Indians remain dignified in their politeness towards we Antipodean scum. Walking into a sari shop, the proprietor enquired the eternal, 'Which country, Madam?'

'New Zealand,' I admitted.

'Oh dear, Madam,' he replied.

Noam Chomsky said: 'If freedom of speech doesn't apply to those we despise, then the term has no meaning.' Lovely sentiment Chommers, but it doesn't quite cut the mustard over here. Henry and Laws are as bad for New Zealanders living in India as it is for Americans in Afghanistan when some redneck Bible-thumper starts burning Korans.

I'm considering dusting off my French: 'Ou est le Taj Mahal?' Either that, or New Zealand public figures could just stop embarrassing me.

rac·ism: n. 1. The belief that race accounts for differences in human character or ability and that a particular race is superior to others. 2. Discrimination or prejudice based on race.

Racism, according to the economist, is ascribing the aggregate tendencies of the group to individuals. For instance, in New Zealand more Maori are in prison for violent crime than white people, ergo, all Maori men are violent. Racism is a bit stupid, in other words.

'Racism!' has oft been organisers' cry in the run-up to the Commonwealth Games. South African swimmer Roland Shoeman accusing the crowd of 'acting like monkeys', Paul Henry's demented giggling over Sheila Dikshit's name, Melbourne Indian-bashing, racist emails circulated by the New South Wales police — all these and more hot news stories are in the Indian media at the moment.

'Is the whole world prejudiced against Indians?' is the question most often asked.

When Mike Hooper said that the Delhi population 'was to blame for delays in athletes getting to venues', Sheila Dikshit was outraged. Just wait a minute though, 17 million people use Delhi's under-developed transport system — it might not be entirely unfair to say some of them got in the way.

According to Ms Dikshit, it was 'racist' of Mr Hooper to say the Commonwealth Games organisation was hampered by bad management. But it *was* bad, even criminal, management.

The massive population of Delhi *are* to blame for traffic delays, how could they not be? The management of the Games *was* ludicrously bad. Sheila Dikshit's name is ridiculous (to an English speaker) — I admit to laughing the first time I heard it. All this righteous anger, yelling and pounding of desks by countless television discussion panels only makes Indians appear childishly defensive, monumentally over-reactionary.

Yes, it's very embarrassing. Yes, the whole world is watching, but the complex India has about perceived slights and slurs seems to act as an impetus to unnecessary defensive manoeuvres that do more to emphasis, rather than diminish, differences.

If India doesn't want to be seen as a poverty-stricken backwater, then a sidestep into blaming the world's perceptions — leading Indian sports official Lalit Bhanot defending the country's preparations in the Games village (dirty and uninhabitable) with statements like, 'Foreigners have different standards of cleanliness' — 'Huh?' said most Indians — are a nonsense, deliberately avoiding the real problems: too many people and massive corruption.

Am I racist? With my bouts of TMI caused by space-invasion and the wearying weight of staring, I worry I might be prejudiced (of course I could never be as big a bigot as Paul Henry has made himself appear).

I'd defend to the death Paul Henry's right to be an idiot, but from here it seems there is a dull boorishness creeping about parts of the New Zealand mainstream media. An icky meanness, a small-minded attitude of mockery and sneering, infecting the country like a virus. Where does it come from? And more importantly, have I got it?

It's only when you are abroad, looking down from atop the mesa of someone else's mountain, that you can actually see your own country, every fault line and foible, as if from space. This is normally the cause of much misty-eyed patriotism. Right now though, thanks to Henry and Laws, I feel nothing but shame.

It's cringe-worthy to have these cheerful morons speaking for a nation of decent people, and unsurprisingly Indians are judging us by the motley of our media fools.

At the end of *A Passage to India*, as the tragedy of partition looms, the novel poses the question: can the English (and by extension, their colonial cousins, white New Zealanders) and the Indians ever be friends?

In answer, Aziz explains to Fielding that even the earth and sky seem to say, 'Not yet'.

Perhaps, eighty-nine years later, it is still too soon.

Cobra in the Garden

Nature is rising up against us. We have disturbed a massive cobra, at least six feet long and as thick as a man's arm, in the garden. Alerted by the vibration of our footsteps, it reared up, within striking distance of the both of us. I leapt to the other side of the path. The economist, as curious as a simpleton, followed as it sinuously muscled the garden aside.

This cobra was nothing like the pipsqueak kept in the tiffin box under Delhi's India Gate, or the juveniles wriggling to escape captivity outside Hampi's Virupaksha temple. This was a free-born monster, dappled with diagonals — its hood open, swaying above the foliage. Absolutely the most beautiful and frightening thing I have ever seen.

Adrenalin is amazing stuff. In the space of a second, I found myself ten feet away without even realising I had moved while the economist jogged after the cobra, captivated by the spectacles on the back of its hood.

It's obvious which sex is more evolved.

The frustrating thing is that, like prophetic Cassandra of Greek mythology, nobody will believe us. 'We saw a massive cobra in the garden!' we tell everyone, from the manager of the campus canteen, to the guards and the professors. 'Oh, no,' they say, shaking their heads, 'not anymore.' The cobras are gone, they repeat, the city has grown up and scared them out into the country. 'But we saw it!' we insist. The tourists who cried 'snake'.

❖ ❖ ❖

At the moment the economist and I can't see each other properly either. It's become so bad, I've even stopped talking (to him). You know I'm in a bad mood when I stop talking. For three days now, I've uttered nothing more than grunts.

We don't often fight. After the pre-nup stand-over of '05 and the great retaining wall fight of 2008, there has hardly been a cross word between us. Until three days ago, that is.

Like anyone with a short attention span, I'm almost over the economist's comments about how difficult it seems for me to make any money writing. My writing career about as beneficial as a pet disease. There was even the implication, spoken in that jocular tone at which he so excels, that I had two months to finish my book and make it big, after which I would have to find a job. I called him 'cheap'. He commenced a scathing diatribe on the subject of the cost/benefit ratio of having a waged partner.

In retaliation for this cruel sensibleness, I stopped talking to him. Sulking, it's called.

Quite frankly, lack of money is a lifestyle choice with my people: our family motto is *Prodigo is Totus*, loosely translated as Spend it All. However, a vow of poverty doesn't preclude expensive tastes. As the economist made his derisive, anti-literary pronouncements, I was eating Lindt chocolates — he finished off the stale bread, rather than waste it.

I silently offered one of my caramels.

'Oh no, too good for the likes of *me*,' he said. 'I'm too *cheap*.'

Time passed.

The economist fetched up a pneumatic sigh. After a long while he finally said, 'I'd just like to ask you what we're going to live on when we're old'.

'Obviously I'll be a famous novelist by then,' I thought, but didn't say. It's this pedagogy that I can't stand. The economist is always explaining things to me. He once tried to explain 'living within your means'.

Travelling together is the greatest test of any relationship. Landing in a strange country, bombarded by yucky smells and cows; I defy the happiest of couples to survive intact.

Plus, at the moment there's no food, which makes me extremely grumpy. On the IIMB doctor's orders, we are on a strict, amoebic-dysentery-curing diet consisting of green coconut water, plain rice and yogurt. Marooned with only ourselves for company and nothing good to eat, I sometimes feel like the naughty wife in Maugham's *The Painted Veil*. A cholera epidemic would be a relief. How did the memsahibs of the Raj cope? Triple gins at the club, I suppose.

Close confinement in challenging conditions is often a recipe for the flowering of deep love — but just throw a little gastrointestinal backlash in there and see what happens. Nothing says 'I love you' quite like amoebic dysentery.

We don't often fight (with him so sick it would have been like picking on a kid in a wheelchair) but we *do* negotiate carefully, gradually demonstrating greater and greater courtesy ... 'After you,' 'No, you' ... as we get more and more annoyed — sort of the middle-class equivalent of a *Once Were Warriors* punch in the face. Instead of passive aggressive, the economist is polite aggressive — the angrier he is, the more polite he becomes. Lately we have become so excessively considerate, we're almost mailing thank-you notes.

But let's face it, quarrels between boon companions are nothing new. Captain Oates was so sick of Scott's mithering on about Amundsen that he stomped out onto the ice, declaring huffily, 'I may be some time'. Tenzing thought Hillary had tall-man syndrome. Dr Livingston was just trying to get some personal space.

The trick is not to exacerbate an already fraught situation. Celebrate difference. Allow for foibles. Recognise an alternative. Try strolling instead of running (the economist always makes me run for things and he has much longer legs. It's unnecessarily stressful. I defy anyone to show me something so urgent you have to run for it). Embrace shopping as a lifestyle choice. It turns out shopping is a great cure for homesickness.

The economist hates shopping. He thinks shopping is a private matter, something one wouldn't want to be seen doing, like buying German porn. This is a man who, despite his place of work being called the 'commerce' building, requires water-boarding and electrodes on his man-jellies before indulging in any kind of conspicuous consumption. While spending money is not quite anathema, the purchase of non-sale items still makes the economist as angry as that time my GBF (Gay Best Friend) called him an accountant by mistake.

RIGHT: Soft-drink seller, Delhi.

BELOW: Teased by its handler into displaying its hood, a baby cobra is justifiably annoyed at the economist's attentions, Delhi.

BELOW, RIGHT: The quiet and often overlooked resting place of Isa Khan, ruler of medieval Bengal, is hidden within the elaborate Persian gardens surrounding Humayun's Tomb, Delhi.

LEFT: Dowry Death poster illustrating the new penalty of seven years in prison for her husband or in-laws, should a bride die in suspicious circumstances within the first seven years of marriage.

BELOW: A couple share the Shah Jahan's final view of the Taj Mahal from Agra Fort.

LEFT: Graveyard in Jaipur.

BELOW: Hawa Mahal or Palace of the Winds, Jaipur. The honeycomb lattice of 953 small windows allowed royal ladies to watch everyday life in the street below while observing strict purdah.

The Scottish historian Thomas Carlyle called economics the 'dismal science' and this shopping allergy is probably why. The embarrassment the economist feels trying on jeans and shirts in the company of other people is acute. Avoiding all eye contact, mortification colours his face. If he has to actually speak to someone, he'll leave the premises. It's probably a disorder.

Why do men hate shopping so? You may as well hate breathing as far as I'm concerned. I'll admit, shopping expeditions in Bangalore are fraught with danger. On average three pedestrians a week are struck by traffic, ground under the KSTC buses. Vast piles of rubbish obscure people's vision. Cows cause swerving. Marooned on an intersection, little Indian grannies see my fear and, holding my pink hand in their turmeric-stained one, stop the traffic with the other and help me cross the road.

Finally arriving in a store, breathless, heart pounding, one must first negotiate the twin obstacles of 'Where from madam?' (I've started saying 'A-ha!' to avoid any Paul Henry/Michael Laws-related embarrassment; people assume it's a town in Sweden), and over-enthusiastic service.

Making a brushing-off gesture similar to that used to discourage a pesky sparrow from hopping about your café table in search of sugar, ford the ranks of obsequious assistants and head for the object of your desire. Before trying it on, check for peepers above the cubicles and cameras in the changing rooms. Now begins the fun part. Haggling.

Initially, I was exceedingly bad at haggling. For me, shopping consisted of skidding to a halt outside a boutique, rushing inside, professing admiration to the surly shop girl for the item that had caught my eye and then paying whatever she asked. Not in India. If you gave the proprietor of an Indian store exactly what they asked for, they would assume you were a congenital idiot.

Indians are naturally confrontational. For the shop-keeping class, non-cooperation never ended. My patience worn as thin as my marital hopes, I'm feeling more than a little truculent myself.

In India, there is the dance of purchase to be danced. Refusing to execute the steps is very poor form. The first step is asking 'how much?'

This figure takes into consideration the quality of your shoes, hair colour, posture and whether you speak convent English. State that you are prepared to pay half that sum.

The shopkeeper will then perform an arabesque of amazement involving piteous hand gestures, soulful eyes and complaints about being unable to feed his children.

Twirling, you have now reached the point where you are so far in you cannot get out. The shopping equivalent of 'I do'. Leave and weeping minions will cling to your ankles and get dragged along in your wake, a bit like Torvill and Dean doing a bolero in the red dirt.

In the ensuing pause, give the shopkeeper a look of absolute disdain, hands on hips. Say nothing. A duel of passions, this is the final tango to the cash register. Face as red as the tikka on his forehead, he will name a sum Rs100 higher than your offer. Realising that this still makes the total price less than NZ$10, try to keep a leer of avaricious delight from your face. Grudgingly agree to buy. Bowing to reveal the comb-marks of his parting, the seller capitulates, but only because you are: so nice/ the first customer of the day/Swedish.

Smiles all round. Depart exhausted and wondering what it *really* cost.

'Been shopping,' I deign to tell the economist (forgetting we are on no-speaks), holding up my purchases with pride.

'Really?' he answers, looking up from his laptop. 'Why?'

❈ ❈ ❈

One evening, as we watch the news, still not talking to each other, a swarm of Kali bugs invades the living room. Hundreds all at once, soft fat moth bodies flying in the open window, bashing against our mouths and eyes, caroming off the walls and getting stuck in our hair, writhing about on the floor. They taste like dust.

Kali bugs hatch out of the ground, fly about and die all in one day after the monsoon rains, in their last paroxysms shedding their transparent wings, leaving their ribbed bug-bodies squirming along the ground. Their death throes sound like a thousand wet paper fans beating against the tiles. The fallen writhe about and get squished beneath our bare feet. It is terrifying and revolting.

Running around batting the air, screaming, we finally realise they are just attracted to the light. At the flip of a switch, every Kali bug in the room immediately drops to the floor, where they die slowly, shuddering. The lizard hiding in a crack in the kitchen wall breaks from cover and scutters around, gobbling them up, masticating their foul little bodies with relish.

Traumatised, we shiver and scratch at ourselves, finding the grotesque, wingless grubs for hours afterwards, blindly squirming along the floor tiles, wedged in books, drowned in half-empty glasses. Now I know how the Egyptians must have felt about locusts. Plagued with uncertainty.

Completely Bonkers

In the end I seriously considered going home without the economist. There was a time when I loved him so it made me want to shed my skin. I used to dream of being inside him, being him. I thought that was what love meant, disintegrating into each other, until we were one person. Now I want to kill him.

I contemplate my former self with a wry fury. That I used to marvel that someone so ordinary could attract a man so handsome. How gormless. In the early years of our relationship I thought only of him, saw the world through his eyes, echoed his words. The arrogant, wealthy economist was my Mr Rochester, complete with something nasty lurking in his attic.

I've been reading too much, crossing the line between words on the page and words meant to be spoken. Expecting a great literary romance, and finding instead the ghastly grubs of a loveless monsoon, I choose no words at all.

Estranged, permanently strange, yet living in the same apartment, I think about the nature of entwining oneself completely with another person, and its inherent dangers. All-encompassing love is like a snake eating its own tail. It's an important lesson for me to learn that we are separate people. I can't reach into every part of him, to that place where he sometimes disappears, and just so, I need to have something for myself. Clarity comes at a high price.

Ever since that fateful morning when the economist suggested I couldn't survive without his money, a simmering, slow boil of resentment has welled up between us, a curdled casserole of hurt feelings and things-not-said. Never mind the fact that it is true: I'd starve to death without his patronage. The truth has nothing to do with this.

The economist hates it when I don't speak to him, retreating in turn, so now I feel his heavy lack. Even when present, he is simply not there. All our tentative conversations are so loaded, they collapse into silence, like a verbal house of cards. It is the hyper-sensitive behaviour of the neurotic. But I cannot help it. India has undone me and in the undoing ripped something open, spilling out a toxic landfill of little hatreds, dead rats of hurt, snippets of slurs written on scraps and crumpled in pockets. These fish-bone skeletons, these brown-petalled blooms are now unearthed and stinking to high heaven.

I lie awake through the long watches of the night, upstairs to his downstairs. He refuses to come to bed. Silent crying puffs up my face until my eyes are slits surrounded by a bog of swollen skin. Soggy, useless thoughts plod through my mind like a fat hamster on a wheel. If I *do* fly home, I'll need to find somewhere else to live, so that I'm not there when he returns. I'll have to kick the house-sitter out.

Trying to figure out the logistics of how I will cope (finding a flat, moving all my furniture, rehanging the paintings, paying for everything), I have loony thoughts — does the couch in the living room count as mine because I picked it out? Long, unspoken conversations spool through my head. Promising rants dwindle into non-sequiturs. I'm unravelling.

I can't come up with a solution that doesn't have the economist in there somewhere. Even my plans of singledom involve him standing on the periphery with a bunch of flowers and a poem that rhymes. I know I would be lost without him. But I am lost *with* him, too.

During the day I chat, chat, chat, filling the silence that might otherwise be used for conversations too painful to be endured. There is a sick desperation in my laugh. I do not meet the economist's eyes. My garrulous gabbing wears the guise of warmth and closeness, when the truth is frosty enough to make air visible. Anger sharpens my vowels.

The economist is clearly dementing, going round and round the same arguments like a ferret in a bucket, 'What you said . . . it's very hurtful . . .' Beset by insomnia, he shuffles the apartment in the wee smalls, spending all his time sneaking articles about Multi Criteria Decision

Making onto Wikipedia, even though he's banned. I have a theory that his madness is caused by extreme thinness, the after-effect of amoebic dysentery. Everyone knows that skinny women are completely unable to think rationally, due to a lack of brain fat. The same anorexic psychosis is obviously affecting the economist.

This doesn't mean his wallowing in self-pity is any less annoying. The economist's first marriage proved he could take a punch — I'm sorely tempted to smack him out of it. But I fear I'm not the sanest myself. More like an extinct volcano rising up in the middle of a placid country town, a hillside formerly covered in cool green grass and fluffy white sheep, suddenly dangerously warm and giving off vapours.

India is smothering me. I'm squashed by the constant noise, the corruption, the callous indifference to poverty, the endless need for interaction. I feel obliged to warble 'Good morning! Good morning!' to the gardeners, the guards, the street sweepers, greeting everyone with a big fake Hollywood smile. Just so nobody can think I am a rich white snob or a bad person. Nightly the economist and I lie rigid under the sheets, unspeaking (and *certainly* not touching), beneath the mosquito net's hole-punched netting. And it's become a lot colder. The floor's marble tiles sear our feet in the mornings.

The mongoose in the garden turned out to be a bandicoot. A bandicoot is a type of rat. An exotic rat, but a rat nevertheless. When I see him trundling past, out for his evening constitutional, I don't feel charmed anymore, just nauseous. The bandicoot and his thick black tail seem a damning indictment of all things Indian — nothing's ever what it seems; it's usually worse.

❁ ❁ ❁

Thanks to an ugly first marriage involving tantrums and husband-bashing, the economist can't abide a screaming woman. 'Fuck no,' he says, flinching, when reminded.

All too aware of this aversion, I've hardly ever shouted at him, not wanting to be considered a shrew.

Well, the quiet years are officially over. It happened like this:

We were walking to the Reliance Mart, the traffic grinding its gears and gunning its engines, when, without warning, I simply explode. I scream my head off, wave my arms about. Spit comes out of my mouth. I have found my voice and my voice is LOUD. I squall, cry and holler things I never dreamt I would. Condemnations. Accusations. Points of Order. A small crowd gathers at the dusty wayside of Bannerghatta Road.

The economist is shocked, and relieved.

'Why didn't you just say so?' he asks, when I'm done.

Immediately I feel much better.

'My father grew up eating horse,' said the economist, apropos of nothing, as we walked home, his arm slung around my shoulder.

'Because there wasn't any meat?' I queried, with a sniff, sensitive to post-war hunger. Red dirt striped the tracks of my tears.

'No, there was plenty, he just liked it.'

I laughed like a drain, reminded of why I love the economist — and that I should have done those pelvic floor exercises the maternity ward nurses told me to.

❖ ❖ ❖

In an effort to assimilate, I've begun speaking Hindi, never mind the fact that I know how awful it is to murder someone else's language. Bravely trotting out the few words I've picked up, paratha, doodh (milk), earns the gleeful ribbing of the boys at the shop. Now, every time I pass they grin ecstatically, roll their eyes and yell, 'Dooodh!' whispering to each other behind cupped hands the Hindi equivalent of 'You don't need binoculars to see those'.

'Where you from?' asks the shopkeeper, every single day, when he's finished laughing.

'New Zealand,' I say, 'we're quite good at cricket. Do you have cricket in India?' The boys in the shop break-up and fall about. I'm pretty sure they haven't a clue what I'm saying. I'm just hilarious as a concept.

❖ ❖ ❖

The house-sitter emails. She feels trapped and isolated. The neighbours make her nervous; the man living in the house in front is a pervert. She just can't take it anymore. What is it about people who go in for house-sitting? Our last house-sitter left everything sticky, and pulled all the hooks out of the back of the bedroom door. Maybe she was just a heavy secretor with an overweight coat, yet I wonder.

While I worry about our little house being left unguarded in a neighbourhood filled with the light-fingered and chemically addled, I'm not as depressed as the current house-sitter sounds, despite living in southern India: the 'suicide capital of the world'.

It was pretty weird to discover, in *The Bangalore Times*, that homosexuality has only been legal in this country since last year. 'Companies are going to great efforts to sell products to gays,' asserted the article, 'but are they welcome here?'

There is an anti-prejudice campaign afoot; television ads feature immaculately coiffed boys hugging. Unsurprisingly, in this ferocious sell-or-be-sold economy, even though it would be suicide for Friends of Dorothy to be flagrant about it (ironic to the extreme in a country where the straight men hold hands on the street), corporations are chasing the pink dollar with everything they've got.

Market segmentation notwithstanding, suicides amongst gay Indian men are massive in number every year, but then so are the number of suicides full-stop. Death by suicide in India is booming, nominally at 10.5 per 100,000 (the actual rate is thought to be at least five times higher, as data from police records is not considered accurate due to religious taboos associated with post-mortems and suicide being a crime) with larger numbers of women than men killing themselves, reversing the worldwide trend (in Western countries, men are three times more likely to commit suicide than women).

Housewives and the self-employed made up 62 per cent of all Indian suicides in 2006. The Indian 'suicide gradient' rises to the south. Kerala, the country's first fully literate state, has the highest number of suicides. On average thirty-two people kill themselves there every day.

Southern India may be the country's information technology hub; however the region also has the sad distinction of the world's largest number of suicides by young people. The highest rate of suicide in the world is reported here, amongst young women.

In a research letter published in *The Lancet*, paediatrician Dr Anuradha Bose from the Christian Medical College, Vellore, found that females in the fifteen to nineteen age group around Vellore in Tamil Nadu killed themselves at a rate of 148 per 100,000, compared to 2.1 in the same age group in the United Kingdom.

Bose posits that poor countries that are developing rapidly have higher rates of suicide. She suggests there are stress factors that affect Indian women in particular, such as issues of matrimony and dowry. One common suicide method is unique to Indian women, that of self-immolation. Sacrificing oneself on a fire was the third most frequent method of suicide recorded in the study and carried out almost exclusively by girls, followed in popularity by hanging and ingesting pesticide.

Another big user of pesticides (to kill themselves) are farmers. In 2006, 1044 farmers killed themselves by consuming pesticides, which ironically hadn't worked on their cotton — the subsequent crop failure and resulting huge debt burden driving them to suicide in the first place, because they couldn't repay government agencies, who are also the pesticide suppliers.

Suicide prevention organisation Maithri Kochi estimates there are 100,000 suicides every year in India. But it's actually more like 126,000. Why is the rate so high? Or is it simply a question of scale — 10.5 per 100,000 of 1.2 billion people is a lot of deaths.

'Aren't we supposed to be spiritual people, content with our lot, with strong religious beliefs and a fantastic attitude to life?' asks freelancer journalist and blogger Nita J Kulkarni. Looking for reasons for the growing Indian suicide rate, Kulkarni blames globalisation, industrialisation and affluence.

'Indian society is becoming more individualistic,' she says. 'At one time, one brother supported another, or a father supported a lazy son. Today depending financially on someone else is something to be ashamed of. And the typical Indian family — often acting as a buffer in times of stress — is breaking up. Getting into IIM, scraping up a loan, desperately trying to win a job in a multinational — people stake everything they have.' If they don't succeed, it's not just failure, it's a disaster.

Indian suicide numbers seem epidemic because the Indian media have no scruples about reporting, in lurid detail, the manner in which people take their own lives. Reporting on suicide is banned in the New Zealand media for fear of copycats, yet this patently does no good whatsoever as, amongst young men at least, our numbers are much higher.

Academic pressures and unfulfilled romantic ideals, a voracious appetite for high-end consumer goods spurred on by moneylenders, a wide gap between aspirations and capabilities, mental illness and the disintegration of the traditional social support mechanism of the wider family . . . it's a desolate litany, and one which rings familiar. Perhaps my calm in the face of a house-sitter mutiny has to do with hailing from the suicide capital of the South Pacific?

According to a Ministry of Social Development report, last year New Zealand had the second-highest male youth (fifteen to twenty-four years) suicide death rate in the world, and the second-highest for female youths. Each year in total about 540 people, 50 per cent more than the road toll, take their own lives. In contrast to India's 10.5, in 2010 the suicide rate amongst New Zealanders aged fifteen to twenty-four was 15.3 per 100,000, although young New Zealand men prefer firearms and vehicle exhaust gas as their method of self-annihilation.

The suicide helplines in Bangalore are open from 9 a.m. to 6.30 p.m. After hours, there's an answering machine. Perhaps you'd be kind enough to tell them where to find the body.

In India, you can be charged with inciting or driving someone to suicide, as happened recently to a secondary school teacher who taunted a pupil about his bad grades in front of the rest of the class. The student went home and jumped off the roof of his apartment. The teacher was detained and charged with inciting suicide. If found guilty, he could face five years of 'rigorous imprisonment' and a fine of Rs5000 (about NZ$160).

A Night at the Bangalore Club

It is in the spectre of the Raj that we visit the exclusive Bangalore Club, invited to the eightieth birthday of the paterfamilias of one of the country's most influential families. The Bangalore Club is the oldest and most exclusive club in the city, founded in 1868. The waiting list for membership is a lifetime.

The economist and I squeeze our unaccustomed feet into fancy shoes, put on our gladdest rags. Here, in what was once the sole domain of the English (one particular bar is still men only: 'you may look through the window, Madam, but you cannot go in') is the old club ledger, open to a page listing 'irrecoverable debts' including Rs13 owed by Winston Churchill, eventually written off due to his 'financial penury'.

Palladian windows, yellowing volumes. The precious tea-stained ledger sits atop a pedestal, propped against the wall beneath an elderly elephant head with a shrivelled trunk. Various dead furry things pose, teeth bared, glass eyes dusty. A moth-eaten tiger splays out on the floor tiles; his bald tail is squashed flat, his toothless mouth open in feeble protest. Tattered spoils of ancient blood sport, limp trophies of long dead hunters.

Built in the colonial style (Imperial classical — think pillars and rotundas), the Bangalore Club offers a number of restaurants, bars, libraries and sports facilities all in varying degrees of exclusivity running the gamut from 'how deep is your wallet' to 'related to the prime minister'. Originally formed solely for use by British soldiers and, after Independence, Indian military officers stationed in the cantonment, today it is a club for rich Indian civilians.

Pulling up beneath the pristine white Doric columns of the

carriageway, liveried staff open the glass doors to admit us to vast chandeliered rooms lined with teak polished to toffee. Now, *here* is the flip side of colonialism. The Indian upper class are the new elite, the conquering culture. To them now belong the spoils, the swimming pools and tennis courts, the bridge clubs, the massive sense of entitlement.

Waiters pass platters of canapés. 'Would we like a tour?' asks a young man dressed head to spats in white. He holds his right hand fisted behind his back as he walks in front, a model of perfect eighteenth century butlerese. Wandering, gawking — could the economist and I be more the poor relations? We are not shunned, but in comparison to the soft-spoken, bejewelled women and their sharply dressed husbands, we are total 'oiks'. Scruffy, ill-mannered, beaded with perspiration. We smile too much.

The ballroom's parquetry bears the patina of 140 years of the tread of dancers waltzing back and forth. Fourteen feet above, gilded chandeliers tinkle with condescension. The Bangalore Club is undoubtedly haunted. Incorporeal murmurs sing up from the floor, everywhere the echoes of the Raj. The air shimmers with the guilty ghosts of sweaty subalterns, frogged and braided. Walking through a cold spot, a shiver of memory, you glimpse the phantoms of skinny punka wallahs, pulling the cords of the carpets which once hung from the ceiling. The Raj is gone but its passing has left a phosphorescence. Gone, but the servility remains.

Despite our lack of graces, mingling with the guests we are treated to the warmest welcome, the utmost civility and kindness. At no point do we feel unwanted, even though our otherness shrieks from the tips of our hair to the soles of our shiny new shoes. A third of the people in the room have been to New Zealand, the rest tell us politely that they 'dream of visiting'. I can't see the few Indians whose presence was patronised here during the years of the Raj experiencing the same magnanimity; or Indian immigrants fresh to the Land of the Long White Cloud, for that matter.

The hundreds assembled, aunties, babies, cousins, nieces, nephews, are all off-shoots of a very distinguished family tree.

'I didn't know you had royalty in the family,' the economist jokes to Rajeev, surveying the well-dressed denizens of the ballroom.

'Oh no,' says Rajeev, 'that's on Shamilla's side. Our side were busy fighting the British.'

Freedom fighters on one side of the gene pool, friends of Nehru on the other. After the appetisers, birthday boy grabs the microphone. With what can only be described as rambling gusto, Grandfather begins to tell long and winding tales of his youth: piloting a small plane across the country, lunches with prime ministers and viceroys, jolly japes involving elephants, and naughty stories about one-eyed cricketing nawabs.

In the heavy pauses between Grandfather's dawdling reminisces, New Zealand seems very far away and very young. A baby country or maybe a teenager: acting out, full of a swaggering self-importance that we will blush to remember when we grow up.

Granddad's speech goes on forever. After the first half hour, the audience — his children's children, their wives and husbands start to talk amongst themselves, make calls on their cell phones, or simply push their chairs back and go outside to the garden bar to drink and gossip. The past doesn't interest these fair-skinned, oiled and polished scions. Heir apparent to a dazzling wealth, what do they care about the old days of regents and elephant fights?

How blessed they are, to have this incredible heritage to be so bored by. Turning their backs on history, they compare sari material and check their diamond-encrusted watches, yawning. Granddad rattles on, shuttling between now and then, drifting in and out of decades, time travelling while his descendants look on. An hour and a half later, his son-in-law manages to wrest the microphone from him. Granddad's not finished by a long shot, but those years are over.

I am confronted by the hidden subtext, ancient codes, unspoken signifiers. Everything in India has a meaning: the pattern of a sari, the number and value of the bracelets on your arm, the incense burning on your altar, your name, your individual mother tongue. Everything has an additional cultural, spiritual or social significance which can either be a perceived threat (depending what caste/religion/sex the viewer belongs to) or a marker of divinity, a sign of privilege or poverty, and all these myriad indicators are never random.

This is what constitutes true culture: the strata of meaning, history and religion layered like an onion beneath even the most prosaic event, mythology and millennia trailing behind every single Indian like a broken slinky.

❊ ❊ ❊

What does New Zealand have in the way of culture? Rugby?

Don't get me wrong, I love rugby players. Well, only one actually, I've had a rucking huge crush on Anton Oliver for years (when you're with a man as stereotypically good-looking as the economist you often fantasise about a bit of rough) — what woman wouldn't enjoy being with a man whose thighs are twice the size of hers?

But it's all we seem to have. In a world of innovators and industrial revolutions New Zealanders hold fast to that ageless angelic theme: the triumph of the underdog.

'I always root the underdog,' says the economist.

'Root for.'

'That too.'

In New Zealand, rugby has ceased to be a sport, has become instead a litmus test of patriotism. We're a nation of Pavlovian dogs, dropping a haka at the first ka mate.

Intellectual strength is what New Zealand needs now, yet men who wouldn't know a vowel from a trowel are still considered our best ambassadors. We don't value academic success, literary endeavours or business acumen nearly as much as we do the moronic activity of kicking a ball. In New Zealand, you're not a real man unless you play or fanatically follow rugby.

The model Indian male works in IT and drives a Hero Honda. Indians don't play rugby. They esteem intellect and enterprise. Maybe that's why their economy is booming.

Are we Kiwis better off without the dangerous weight of meaning which exists in India? Sure, we have our superstitions: thirteenth floors, ladders, black cats, saying 'rabbits' on the first of the month — and we desperately labour our tenuous ties with the British royal family, pump our fists over the myth of clean and green. Does our shallow lack of cultural depths make us a little safer? There would never be a riot in New Zealand over a politician's chosen dialect, for instance. And let's not forget religion. Religion isn't mere lip service in India, it is a viable part of every moment of the day, shades all relationships, saturates the political.

No wonder we New Zealanders eat, drink and fornicate so much. There are no 5000-year-old temples in our country, and if there were, we wouldn't believe in the gods they housed. I'm afraid New Zealand *has* no culture; all we have is sports and booze.

From here, New Zealand seems like a very beautiful, very boring woman. Look at her all you want, but don't make the mistake of striking up a conversation.

Outsource my Heart

The economist's field of speciality is health economics, yet he never goes to the doctor. You get that a lot with economists: the sports economist who doesn't play, the Asian economic development expert who has never been to China. A lot of the life experience of economists is purely theoretical.

Bearing this in mind, I was understandably taken aback when Blondie decided to get Lasik while we're here. 'God, that's brave,' said a friend, hearing the news via Skype. It seems everyone back home automatically thinks of disease when Indian hospitals are mentioned. 'What on earth would possess you? Taking your life in your hands, disgusting conditions . . . iatrogenic infections . . . '

What is the most sensitive, delicate, hygiene-dependent surgical procedure? Why, eye surgery. And where, exactly, are you having it done? India.

India? Home to dirt, dust and prokaryote micro-organisms? That India? Are you crazy?

Well, that's where you'd be very wrong, chums. Inside the private hospitals and speciality clinics of India, nowhere could be further from dirt and disease. Private Indian health care is expert and inexpensive, and word is spreading. Medical tourism is booming in India, as thousands of uninsured Americans board planes for the subcontinent, seeking discount hip replacements and sophisticated heart surgeries with greatly reduced waiting times.

Joining the swelling ranks of medical tourists in search of high-quality health care and cut-rate surgery, the economist is gratified to discover that rather than a squalid, post-war dump, the Shekar

Nethralaya Superspeciality Eye Hospital looks like a spaceship or something out of 'Gattaca', all modern white tiles and shiny chrome. If the women weren't dressed in saris, you'd expect Lieutenant Ahuru to appear any minute with a hands-free and a clipboard.

Indian medical technologies are amongst the best that money can buy. Then again, anyone with money can buy whatever they want in India — while the poor can't even get a prescription filled.

The eye surgeon is one of the best in the world, and the most experienced, having performed this operation over 30,000 times. 'In medicine, practise makes perfect,' pontificates the economist, lying upstairs in our apartment after the op wearing a rather fetching surgical blindfold.

In his usual pedantic way, he researched the hell out of this before committing, getting an inside word from the ophthalmologist brother of an IIMB professor, even learning everything he could about the model of laser used. He admits to having had extreme pre-surgery nerves, and a prejudice against having his eyeball cut open.

'I also needed to overcome mental prejudices — the ingrained belief that an Indian hospital would be dirty and disorganised,' he says. 'However once I realised how smooth and mechanical it was, a production line, I was happy to be number thirty thousand and one. Lasik was actually a lot less traumatic than going to the dentist.

'Plus they'd given me a sedative, of course. And there were so many staff, seven nurses and one doctor to every patient.'

Fastidious about the regime of eye drops post-surgery, 'Darling, put my drops in, would you?' he says, looking every inch the hypochondriac movie star, bedside table cluttered with pills and drops. 'Was that exactly four? Are you sure? Thank you. I think I'll have a little rest now.'

Lasik eye surgery in India costs $4000 less than it does if performed privately in New Zealand. The procedure the economist has opted for, Wavefront-guided Lasik, is a new technique approved by the United States Air Force to correct pilot vision. It sounds extremely scary.

'First they slice your eye open, and then, after scanning the topography of your lens, they sculpt the surface of your eye with a laser — sort of like remodelling a city by smoothing off the hills and reclaiming the harbour. I didn't actually smell anything burning, just heard an *eeee* noise.'

Gruesomely effective, after only one day of recovery time, the economist has experienced an immediate improvement, going from pretty bad eyesight to 20:15 vision (at 20 feet he can see what someone with okay vision can see at 15 feet).

Ever the cynic, he was surprised to find out, after asking another patient, that he has been charged the same as the locals. 'We don't do that for the international students who come to Otago,' he says, 'India's going forwards, New Zealand's going backwards.' He really should get this printed on a T-shirt.

India is the New World of Health Technologies, leading innovation in medical procedures: laparoscopic knee surgery, hip resurfacing and heart-valve surgery. Leg lengthening was pioneered in Bangalore — yet an out-dated view of the country as dirty, backwards and dangerous still persists (well, in fairness, it is all these things).

It's just like all those sheep-shagging jokes about New Zealanders, when hardly anybody does it (although there was that man in Mosgiel last year who was sentenced for bothering a pony).

'What can you see that you couldn't see before?' I ask the economist.

'Everything. I can read minds.'

❖ ❖ ❖

The economist's right leg has suddenly stopped working. He woke up this morning and fell down the stairs. His father had a stroke, so at first that's what we think it is.

Half an hour after presenting at the campus GP, we walk across Bannerghatta Road (I walk, he hops) to be seen by one of India's top neurologists at Apollo Hospital.

Wheelchairs *hoosh* down the corridors of Apollo Hospital's clean expanses, machines beep expensively. This is the Indian private health system: fast and furious for the filthy rich.

Not a stroke, it's drop foot. Quite common, sometimes permanent. In the economist's case, after a massive dose of steroids he will likely get both feeling and response back in his leg. Until then, he'll drag it around like a lame spaniel.

God, but the man is falling apart! I didn't sign up for this. I wanted a salty sea god with pecs like sculpted margarine. It doesn't bode well for our old age if bits are already dropping off him, not to mention his toilet issues.

At least we are in the right place to get him fixed, quickly and cheaply. We have the technology, we can re-build him.

Sound, Fury & an Idiot's Tale

Gagan, 15, a Secondary School Leaving Certificate student, allegedly committed suicide by consuming poison when his parents did not allow him to burst crackers. The incident occurred on Saturday night in Doddaballapur police station limits. Police said the boy was brought to Baptist Hospital, but he died on Sunday morning. The Times of India

Ding dong, a neighbour comes over this morning with gifts of sweets for Diwali, creamy pistachio halva, sunny orange ladoos, and diamond-shaped tukdi. Diyas burn inside everyone's houses, small earthen lamps filled with oil or ghee and a cotton wick. Hundreds are laid out around the home's shrine, all over the floor tiles, interspersed with intricate chalk drawings in pink and orange. With the lights off, it's like a glow-worm cave made of saffron.

Indian hospitality goes far beyond just making sure guests don't drive home skittered. It is a deeply ingrained culture of politeness and warmth, where everything revolves around the happiness of the guest, to whose desires it is an honour to yield. Indian hosts bend over backwards, not eating until their guests have, watching over them fondly like indulgent parents.

Diwali/Deepavali symbolizes the victory of good over evil and brightness over darkness. For some it celebrates the return of Rama and his consort Sita, after defeating Ravana. The villain of the *Ramayana*, Ravana is the ultimate bad guy, pure evil from the top of his ten heads to the nectar of immortality stored under his navel.

The return of Rama is celebrated by 'bursting' crackers and fireworks. Falling around mid-October, the festival of Diwali explodes into seventy hours of non-stop knees-up. 'We just look for any excuse to celebrate,' says MBA student Subhojit Sarkar, explaining the Indian propensity for partying. Indian festivals often auto-extend considerably, the jubilation spilling over into the days before and after.

'Durga Purga is actually three days but we take seven, Diwali is supposed to be one day, but we take three.'

In the south, Diwali falls later in the year and often commemorates the conquering of Asura Naraka, a powerful king of Assam, who imprisoned tens of thousands. Krishna subdued Naraka and freed the prisoners, granting the king one last request before death. Naraka said he wished to enjoy the last day of his life in a grand manner — go out with a bang, in other words.

The noise begins slowly. A few pops, enough to make you jump each time, turns into a dozen booms, a hundred, then thousands, thudding, tonking, whistling overhead until by 3 a.m. the enfilade is an absolute cacophony — a Sarajevo firestorm.

The dogs of India have very coarse fur from being outside all the time (there don't seem to be any cats). Are Indian pets terrified during Diwali? The night-time dogs certainly howl between salvos, but they are probably made of sterner stuff, or it simply doesn't occur to them that there is slightly more noise than usual.

For the next three days, Bangalore is laid siege to by the Gods of Fun. Kiwis haven't experienced this sort of thing since 1978. We have mostly forgotten what this kind of amusement is actually like, as almost everything is now illegal in New Zealand. The economist nostalgically remembers the colossal glee of lighting, and then running away from, unpredictable Red Devils, fondly looking back on the charred letterboxes of the thumbless 1970s.

New Zealand's safety-plan-and-barricades culture, while successfully halving the grim annual toll of fireworks injuries, has extinguished some of the dangerous allure that small tubes of gunpowder once held. Indian fireworks are of a kind that have long been banned in our country. Terrifically explosive.

We watch the IIMB students set theirs off with a mad joy and lunatic disregard for safety.

'Bloody good thing this isn't a drinking culture,' whispers the economist. Combining this total disregard for health and safety procedures with drunkenness would be an absolute disaster.

Lighting the fuse, standing back, watching explosions in red and blue and gold, sky rockets bouncing off trees before plummeting back to earth — Diwali is all about doing. There are no safety cordons, no fire officers. Simply the sheer insanity of a billion people running amok for three days with high-powered fireworks.

'India sees the maximum number of burn accidents during Deepavali,' announces *The Times of India*'s helpful first-aid guide, before going on to advise: 'Do not apply butter or oil to any burn. Victims with burns to the following areas need emergency medical assistance (call ambulance): face, hands, feet, genitalia. Before bursting fireworks, ensure to keep a bucket full of water handy.'

Nobody is paying these warnings much heed. Diwali is a celebration of noise, freedom, and the untrammelled wonder of high explosives. 'It's so much tamer than last year,' complains one of our neighbours, shouting above the cannonade.

A particularly close whistle has us ducking. Sheepish, cheeks pink at this show of nerves, our ears rang like submarine bells. People are throwing crackers at each other, 'bursting' them frighteningly near. I wonder how many lose fingers, thumbs and eyes every year. Not to mention genitals.

I suck air, finding myself wanting to shout, 'Look out! Be careful!' Fortunately, I hold my wussy back.

Little girls in pink party dresses grab fistfuls of rockets out of a huge cardboard box. 'Not those ones,' says Daddy, exchanging the Air Bombs for sparklers. Gangs of boys light Roman Candles and Star Bursts and then run back to shelter under a tree, but there is no predicting their trajectory. Onlookers flee a sudden shower of sparks, laughing and patting down their hair and clothes. It's a community of bedlam, unlicensed self-indulgence. Unlike the English-style Guy Fawkes night, there are no bonfires. Indians save their effigy-burning for public figures of hate like Kevin Rudd, Mike Hooper and Richard Gere.

A pall of blue smoke hovers over Bannerghatta Road. Beneath the noise of a million crackers, you feel like a helpless peasant trapped within the walls of a medieval city under attack, hunkered down. A chorus of barking follows in the deafening suction of the post-bang quiet.

By morning of the third day of Diwali the rambunctious barrage is still going, albeit with longer pauses between bombardments. The whistles and sonic booms sound fewer and fewer. It's all winding down. Time to take the cotton wool out, leaving only the residual smell of sulphur to tickle one's nose.

The night-time dogs have all fallen silent.

❋ ❋ ❋

I've forgotten how to spell fabulous. Started thinking 'Girl Power' was a company of all-female electricians. I spend my time obsessively checking the mirror, not out of vanity, but to see what else has fallen off.

I've lost my mojo.

Lured here under false pretentiousness, these past five months, I've seen sunny days that I thought would never end. I've seen riots, Rhesus monkeys and rubbish. I've seen palaces, elephants, monuments to eternal love. What do I have to show for it?

Good question.

There are so many things I haven't done in India. I didn't have a facelift, cheap Botox or liposuction. I didn't go to an ashram or a yoga retreat — but then I'm not the world's most spiritual woman. Or the most flexible.

The economist has had laser surgery on his eyes, bought a tonne of new clothes and lost 13 kilograms. I haven't lost any weight at all.

In the light of his Indian experience, I'm beginning to feel that I haven't really made the most of things. Niggling at me like a wiggly tooth is the mortifying idea that, despite being in one of the most exotic countries in the world, I'm a little bored. Who was it who said, 'Only boring people get bored'? Oh, that's right, my mother.

I am having a 'near-life' experience. These are the days that should be seized. I should be out there smoking opium with the hill tribes, finding my chakras and having them opened.

The solution was simple: a tattoo. Yes, I know this sort of behaviour is similar to that of couples who, the light of their relationship going out, get a dog. In hindsight I think I was rebelling against the endless silence of that month of mutual sulking, and the aggravation of the economist's constant polite aggression, 'Are you sure you want to buy that, wear that tight a T-shirt . . . get a tattoo? Have you thought this through?'

Quite frankly, if I was the kind of person who thought things through, I wouldn't be basically innumerate, having spent the entire fifth form standing in the corridor outside the maths classroom as punishment for talking. And I could really do with understanding percentages.

Girish of the Bramha Tattoo studio on Rest House Road is an enormous shy man with a long nose. Blue/black ink blooms in tarantulas, pentagrams and pictures of Alice Cooper from his fat little tummy to the expanse of his arms and legs. He looks like a punk Ganesha. His tiny parlour is located three floors up in a cramped retail tenement filled with Muslim stores guarded by slick boys in skinny jeans and cowboy boots.

Girish only tattoos two days a week, strict 'timings' are listed on his door. Long before he is due to appear, the queue outside flows all the way down the stairs and out onto the pavement. Most are just nervous kids with friends in tow. They don't really mean to get a tattoo, merely trying on cool for size and when Girish arrives, an hour late, at one look from him they scatter. Suddenly it's just me.

Girish indicates he will oblige my desire for permanent ink with a nod. I'm getting a trio of stars, Rock Star stars. Girish avoids eye contact. He doesn't talk much, and when he does, it's such a soft mumble I can't hear what he's saying. I'm not convinced he knows what I want, but it's too late to back out now. Charged up, his needle emits a tired whine. Girish inserts a cassette and presses 'play' on an old 50-pound boom box. Hindu Death Metal drowns out my squeaks of pain.

Sadly, when I remove the bandages two days later, the reality of the tattoo doesn't live up to the expectations. Wobbly and badly-drawn in too-thick ink, it looks like something crayoned by a sugar-cranked three-year-old.

Am a terrible, impulsive, train-wreck of a person . . . and the worst tourist ever.

'You're all right luvvy,' my friend Jo posts on Facebook. 'Want me to send you some Church Road chardonnay?'

'White woman sulks in India, New Zealand consulate alerted,' jokes my friend Roy.

Facebook is my lifeline. Ten o'clock in the morning here is about two in the afternoon over there — sometimes I spend entire mornings desperately poking, friend-ing and changing my status (single/in a relationship/single), while India waits for me to come outside and play.

My friends all seem so witty, and they look nice and clean in their profile pictures.

'Post a picture of your tattoo,' they beg.

I can't face it. My leg looks horribly foreshortened. The stars around my ankle make me look cheap, like a half-price hooker from Hamilton. I hate it.

Nice to Meat You

'Who, out of the two us, is fitting into this vegetarian vibe?' asks the economist smugly over his dhal, chapathi and yogurt bath.

'It's only because you're starving and delusional,' I counter.

'And lunch is only 70 cents. It's a hell of a country.'

'I *need* meat,' I whine. 'I can't eat anymore of this cellulose pap.' After five months of vegetarianism, I'm gagging for red meat. Desperate. I don't care how it comes: steak, patty, kebab, salami, schnitzel, bratwurst — just gimme. Hot and steaming, straight off the cow.

The economist has become a born-again vegetarian, joining some of history's vegetable-loving giants: Mahatma Gandhi, Leonardo da Vinci, Albert Einstein and the Apatosaurus. This avoidance of animal protein comes complete with a new moral high-ground.

I've begun sneaking out of the house on secret meat-eating trips. When the cravings get too much, I catch a 365 to the KFC on Brigade Road, white meat the methadone to my red-meat jones. Ordering an entire bucket of chicken, I stagger upstairs and stuff myself. Nice Indian girls out on chaste dates covertly watch me through their hair, aghast. Their boyfriends are visibly impressed. Some days I go to McDonalds, lured by thoughts of Big Macs, but sadly there's no such thing in India as two all-beef patties on a sesame-seed bun.

I am a failed vegetarian. The economist could quite happily never eat meat again. Not me. Earlier this year, some of the tigers in Bannerghatta National Park got salmonella from the chicken carcasses they were fed. Even tigers can't eat cow here. I know just how they feel. Ravenous. Annoyed.

Nobody eats the cows of India. Pushing them out of the way, trying to buy a newspaper, groaning 'Mooove', you start to develop a fellow feeling. Sort of a 'don't tread on me, I won't eat you' mentality. Yet murder lurks in my heart. Waking from dreams of golden arches, I fantasise about food I wouldn't normally consume at home: mustard-smeared hotdogs, greasy burgers. I look at pictures of meat online. The word 'steakhouse' makes me salivate. I'm a red-meat carnivore, there's just no getting away from it.

Not to worry, soon I will be a wiener. That's right, 'Ich bin ein Frankfurter'. You are what you eat after all and I'm flying into sausage central, Frankfurt. After two weeks of Deutsche gluttony ('Hardly,' said the economist gloomily. 'We'll be lucky if we can afford to eat once a day.'), I'll return to India to face haughty, holy, bovine stares. Will I be racked with remorse? Well, I'm just planning to eat anonymous German cattle; they probably don't even have names. They certainly won't be blessed every morning with a swipe of sandalwood paste on their foreheads. Drinking will hopefully assuage any feelings of guilt.

Which brings me to beer. While we have been away, the economist has gone right off beer, and I have begun to love it. He prefers a nice vodka and cranberry. It's like that movie 'Freaky Friday'. We've switched bodies. He's lost 13 kilograms and developed a taste for swishy drinks; I've become a beer-swilling chauvinist with a hankering for barbecue.

Anticipating Germany, one can't help considering the economist's Aryan looks — blonde, blue-eyed, tall, stern. Now that he's had Lasik and doesn't wear glasses anymore, he's a dead ringer for the handsome, heartless German commandant of Second World War movies. Subduing the populace with his frosty stare and relieving society of the mentally incompetent by teaching them managerial economics. 'I can see right through women's clothing,' he boasts.

He *is* Aryan, Danish in fact, the Danes and the Germans being kissing cousins. It might surprise you to learn that Danes are the happiest people in the world, because their expectations are so low. Despite this, Germany managed to disappoint them from 1940 to 1945.

'Do you actually know any German?' I asked the economist.

'Raus! Schnell! Gott in Himmel! Messerschmitt! Achtung! Englisher dogs!' he shouted.

Read a lot of war comics as a boy scout, apparently.

Fortunately, I did languages at school, though all I really need to know is 'Als Hauptspeise, habe ich steak' (for the main, I'll have steak).

So here's how I imagine it: a foaming stein in one paw, a massive sausage in the other. Squiffy and replete. Frankfurt's culinary specialities are Frankfurter sausage, Frankfurter rindswurts, Frankfurter kranz and Handkäs mit Musik (not meat with music, but marinated cheese and onions). Even writing this, my mouth is watering so much, I'm dribbling. Believe me, I'm going to eat it all. Roll me home in an empty Hefeweissbier barrel.

The economist is always astounded when I behave in a less than ladylike manner (strange really, given how many times I have). Conversation might go a little like this: 'What are you doing?' he will ask, as I gorge myself. Flecks of hock decorating my cheeks. Fingers blood-pink. Hunched over my food like a cannibal eating Cook.

Gesticulating with a ragged shank, talking with my mouth full, I'll reply, 'I'm eating myself stupid'.

Why Germany? Let's face it, if you're not in New Zealand to begin with, nowhere in the world is very far away. The economist is supposed to be giving a seminar on the economics of . . . well something terribly interesting, no doubt. I'm afraid I wasn't listening — dreaming, instead, of sausage. The point is that there will be meat, and lots of it. Museums and art galleries too, but I may need to be wheeled into them.

Forget the execrable 'Eat, Pray, Love'.

The movie about my Frankfurt experience will just be called 'Eat — One Woman's Search for Nourishment'.

Toilets & Tall Pink People

If we hadn't just spent five months in India, the toilets of Frankfurt might not seem so extraordinarily clean. Nor would we be astonished that everyone was so tall and pink, or that there wasn't a single cow on the quiet roads, and nobody was 'making urines' against the buildings.

Frankfurt is the fifth largest city in Germany (and the most ruthlessly dull, according to Berliners), but compared to Bangalore it seems almost deserted. Travels with my economist have taken me from the Town of Boiled Beans to the City of the Franks (a little culinary humour there).

Located on the site of an ancient ford on the river Main, Frankfurt's first inhabitants may well have been Frankers; today it's home to Bankers. Systematically fed by autobahns and the largest airport in Europe, its skyline filled with the colossi of chrome-and-glass skyscrapers, Frankfurt is the financial capital of continental Europe.

The city has not always been so bright and shiny. Frankfurt had the bubonic plague during the Thirty Years War and the shit bombed out of it during the Second World War. In March 1944, the once famous medieval centre of town was utterly destroyed. All that remains are six reconstructed buildings located at the east side of the Römerberg, piped white and chocolate in criss-cross hatchings, stacked up like gingerbread houses above the lights of the Christmas market.

The cold crisp air, if it smelt of anything, would smell like newly minted money. A freezing wind whips down from the Urals, barrelling through the empty plazas. Standing in front of Frankfurt's Eurotower, which houses the European Central Bank, is a giant blue Euro surrounded by twelve yellow stars. It lights up at night, flashing a greedy semaphore: 'money, money, money', at the guardians of the geld, riding past, taking the tram home.

We have arrived dressed for India; in fact the economist is wearing a pair of black Bata jandals. The subway passengers stomp the snow off their boots and lean over to politely enquire if he is cold. I think his blue toes might have given it away. Outside, it's minus 2°C. In ten days' time Europe will experience the coldest winter in centuries. I think of the poor Romans, here in the first century, guarding their crumbling Empire from the Vandals and shivering in their little skirts and sandals. Now the vandals wear the jandals.

I can understand German. Well, some of it. Guten tag, tranken, wurst — the essentials. Finally, something I learnt at high school has proved useful. Maybe I shouldn't have said all those mean things about algebra.

My scrapings of the vernacular help us negotiate the U Bahn and S Bahn. Frankfurt has an excellent transport infrastructure, ordered, timely; the subway carriages are warm and clean. The streets of Frankfurt are driven by Mercedes, BMWs and Audis, all travelling at a courteous distance. Everyone in Frankfurt looks familiar. I keep doing double-takes, convinced I've seen a friend, a neighbour.

Frankfurters are very friendly, albeit at a polite remove of about two feet. Many bowl up to the economist though, and start jabbering away, ask him for directions, assuming he is a local. Not me. Obviously my people were some kind of freckled troll race.

German men are *gorgeous* . . . Blonde, square-jawed, they all look like they would be very good on horseback. Hale, square-headed, Jilly-Cooper equestrian heros who have for some reason left their whip and jodhpurs at home today. Polite, chivalrous door-openers, they maintain a discreet arm's length which I find myself wanting to invade. Germany is historically called 'Das Land der Dichter und Denker' (the land of poets and thinkers), but should be called the Land of Hotties.

We were invited to Johann Wolfgang Goethe University, the oldest and best-known in Frankfurt, where the economist was expected to dazzle the prestigious business school's MBA programme with his academic and entrepreneurial prowess. As long as his drop foot doesn't trip him up.

As we tour the architecturally pristine, frigidly cold concrete-and-glass campus with our host Guido (so gorgeous it's almost boring) I point to a large bronze bust of Goethe and exclaim, 'Hey look, Beethoven!' thus proclaiming myself too stupid to live.

I met Guido nine years ago, when he came to stay in Maitland Street not long after the economist left his wife and met me three days later.

'You've changed!' he exclaimed, when, instead of a tall thin blonde, a short curvy redhead opened the door.

'That was the wife, I'm the girlfriend,' I explained.

'Ja! Very good,' he replied, entirely unfazed.

Tall and fussily dressed, Guido is an intense German economist with a maniacal laugh. His personality comes in surges. As we walk into his office at the Goethe Institute, he has just finished giving a radio interview explaining the Nobel Prize to the nation. As soon as he can find his tux, he needs to pack it; he is off to Stockholm for the ceremony next month.

Guido's beautiful and clever wife Mieke is blonde, as are their two perfect children. Northern European hair inclined to throw in the towel early, Guido's pale tresses are beating a ragged retreat. He owns lots of thick woollen jerseys, the kind you'd find worn beside the fireplace in a mountain chalet. Outside the blonde wood and white leather luxury of Guido and Mieke's immaculate town house, a huge orange tom sits on a snow bank swishing his tail in annoyance. He'll be sitting there for a while. Guido hates cats.

In honour of our arrival, Guido cooks dinner. Guido is a gourmet cook. Dinner is steak, mashed potato with horseradish and duck breast. Foie gras from Toulouse. Strong blue cheese, herring and beetroot. Rich, dark German bread, olive oil from a Montpellier socialist co-op. All washed down with a full-bodied red. Overcome with gratitude and gluttony, I start to cry and have to be put to bed.

The next day, the economist finds himself no less moved by the charms of Frankfurt. Waking to a foot of snow outside the windows, eating a breakfast of ham and beetroot herring on brown bread, we pad about Guido's house in jeans and T-shirts while the central heating sings of supremacy. Borrowing jackets, scarves, gloves and shoes, bundled we troll the local supermarket where, upon discovering that hefeweizen, Schwartz and dunkle beers cost a mere NZ$1.25 for a half-litre bottle, he wells up, cradling his clinking shopping bag like a baby. Meat and beer. How well you know us, Frankfurt.

A day ticket, or Tageskarte, costs €8. Getting it out of the machine requires faith and a stubborn ruthlessness. Or you could just ask someone to help you. From the Römer we cross the Eiserner Steg, an iron bridge over the Main, the pewter sky presaging snow. The Main flows slow and gun-metal gray. Cathedrals spike the lowering clouds.

East of the main railway station is the red light district, the hangout of pimps, junkies and drug dealers who huddle against the cold. The whores wear long black puffy jackets over their work clothes. In the flashes, as they light their cigarettes, they look like ski-bunny strippers.

Under the mordant shadow of Saint Katherine's church, braced against the biting wind, we warm up by drinking Glühwein (hot, spicy red wine) from a caravan set up near the entrance to the Zeil, the main shopping street. After three Glühweins I become a bit silly. It would make sense to fortify my stomach. I trot off in search of bratwurst.

'Haven't you had enough meat?' asks the economist, mildly revolted.

We head up Gruneburgweg to The Best Worsht in Town for a sausage sandwich full of habanero peppers. Chilli-fuelled tears roll down my face. I couldn't be happier.

'I love it here,' I tell him. 'I don't ever want to go back to India.'

Past Paulskirche to duck inside Saint Bartholomew's Cathedral, a chilly Gothic hump dating from the fourteenth and fifteenth centuries, built on the foundations of an earlier Merovingian church. From 1356, the kings of the Holy Roman Empire were elected here.

Frankfurt's old opera house, Alte Oper, was heavily damaged in the war, and nicknamed 'Germany's most beautiful ruin'. Former Frankfurt Lord Mayor Rudi Arndt called for blowing it up in the 1960s, earning himself the nickname 'dynamite Rudi'. It was finally reconstructed, and reopened in 1981. The walls of Alte Oper are nougaty. The window sills are iced white in thick dribbles. Everything in Frankfurt makes me think of food.

Hauptwache is the central point of Frankfurt and its most famous

ABOVE: Udaipur, like heaven but with shopping.

RIGHT: Part of the ruined Veerabhadra Temple, Matanga Hill, Hampi.

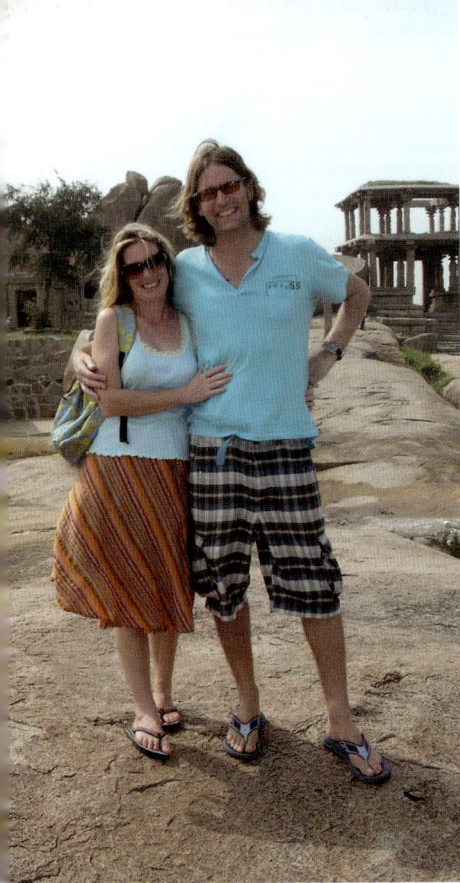

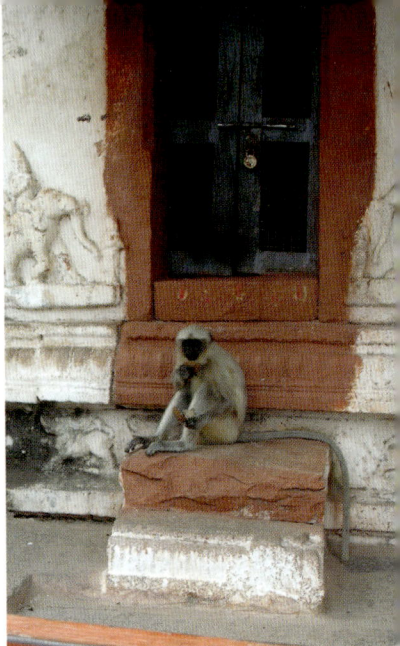

ABOVE: Langur monkey, Virupaksha
Temple complex, Hampi.

LEFT: Happiness is a week in Hampi.

BELOW: Far away from the hustle and
bustle of modern India, ancient Hampi
temples perch on a steep-sloping
volcanic moonscape.

ABOVE: Lakshmi baths in the monsoon-swollen Tungabhadra, taking care to stick to the shallows.

LEFT: Royal library, Hampi.

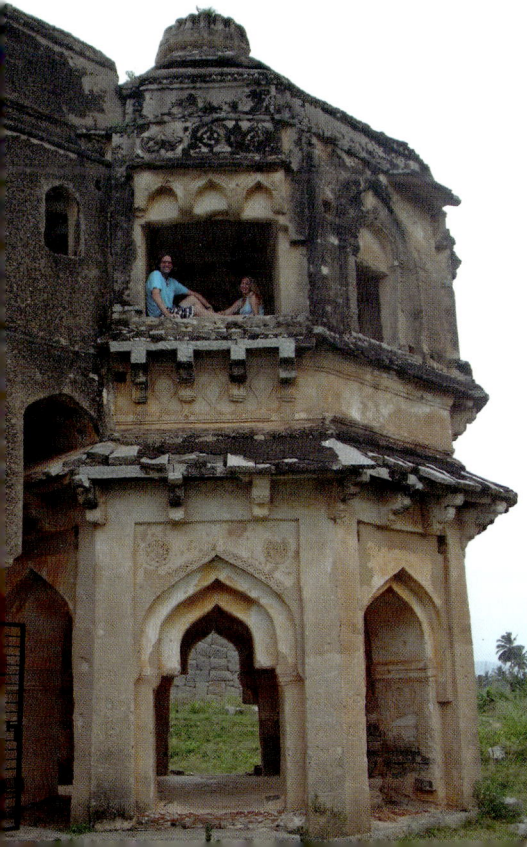

ABOVE: Opportunist monkeys, Bannerghatta Zoo, Bangalore.

RIGHT: The failed vegetarian rejoices after back-to-back bratwurst at the Christmas market, Römerberg, Frankfurt.

BELOW: Shy boys pose outside the Government Museum, Bangalore.

plaza, boasting a baroque stone building of the same name, once home to the city's militia, now a fabulous café. Their Apfelstrudel is delicious.

Almost all of Frankfurt's museums can be found conveniently spaced out along Museumsufer or Museum Embankment, on the south side of the river. Fences topped with verdigris fleur-de-lis. The bracing walk along the tree-lined esplanade is great if you're feeling a little bilious.

The Städel, or Städelsches Kunstinstitul und Städtische Galerie, is home to seven centuries of European painting. Founded in 1815 by the Frankfurt banker and merchant Johann Friedrich Städel, by the start of the twentieth century the gallery was among the most prominent German collections of classic art. In 1937, seventy-seven paintings and 700 prints were confiscated by the National Socialists who declared them 'degenerate art'. In 1939, the collection was moved out of Frankfurt to protect it from damage in the Second World War. Good thing too, as the gallery was substantially munted in air raids, but was rebuilt by 1966, following a design by the Frankfurt architect Johannes Krahn. An expansion building for the display of twentieth-century work and special exhibitions was erected in 1990 and it is here we enter, as the Städel proper is undergoing massive renovations.

The current exhibition is called The History of the World in Art. The walls are cluttered with masterpieces warring for attention. Hieronymus Bosch's tortured souls, pitch-forked and bare, Rembrandt's potato-featured peasants, Vermeer's domestic scenes, Degas' sad little ballerinas, and a leering goat with enormous balls made by Picasso. And a woodcut by Hans Baldung Grien.

I've always been fascinated by the work of Hans Baldung Grien, known by the German word for green, grun, because he liked to dress head to foot in that colour. 'Grien' comes from grienhals, meaning witch. Grien lived in Strasbourg, in the mid-1500s a claustrophobic, narrow-minded city. While the rest of Europe was getting ready to be enlightened, Strasbourg's citizens lingered in darkness. Rumours circulated of fearsome hairy men who came down from the mountains to eat children. The end was constantly nigh.

Thanks to the twin barriers of the Voges and the Black Forest, Strasbourg was stifling in the summer, a breeding ground for every plague that hankered to hitch-hike a mucus membrane.

Hot and bothered, the population of Strasbourg were easily sparked to violence. In one such explosion of viciousness, hundreds of Jews were burnt to death in the square and the rest expelled from the city.

❁ ❁ ❁

After the death of his mentor, Dürer (upon which he was sent a lock of the Master's hair), Grien became the Holy Roman Empire's pre-eminent woodblock artist, most famous for perfecting the technique of using multiple woodcuts to produce graduations of colour.

After getting into a bit of trouble over his 'provocative' chiaroscuro, Adam and Eve (Adam lasciviously tweaks Eve's nipple while a snake with a rather doggish face looks on), Grien turned his considerable genius to witchcraft and its rites — commercial talents at a time when war, the Black Death and a raging epidemic of syphilis bedevilled the city. All these calamities had to be someone's fault.

Grien's fecund witches were the printing-press equivalent of Playmate of the Month. He became successful enough to employ his own Formschneider to trace his designs onto blocks of beechwood prior to cutting, leaving him to apply his monogram, a green HGB, to the final product.

Holding onto a fear of homeopathic women far longer than the rest of Europe, Strasbourgians were still burning witches almost into the seventeenth century, but the masterpiece I have just blundered upon hails from 1523.

Walking into the Städel's gallery and suddenly coming face to face with Grien's 'Zwei Hexen' or 'Two Witches' — disturbed in the act of sorcery, the younger kneels on a rather one-dimensional goat while her friend holds aloft a jar containing the Devil — I am filled with the humbling realisation of my own fleeting, speck-like place in history.

For an art-loving girl who attended a Catholic school where life drawing was banned as too degenerate, the Städel is mind-blowing. Time to replenish the psyche. I have to say (not that I would talk with my mouth full) that Christmas is better in the snow. Glühwein, meat, tinsel, candles. Snow-covered pines decorated with angels and twinkly lights, carousel ponies bobbing with muffled-up children. The medieval churches surrounding the Frankfurt Christmas market are dark and plaguish. The dead of December must have always been the blackest, cruellest time of the year, shivering by your fireside, scraping at a frozen turnip, and freezing at the sound of a goblin-scratch on the windowpanes.

The demons of dark night and bitter cold are kept out by the ring of cheer made by stalls selling candles, bratwurst and kartoffeln (potatoes with apple sauce). Smiling red-cheeked people, golden lights. Thinking of our Pacific Christmas: holly and a hot meal on a barbecue day, I realise it springs from homesickness and a sweet nostalgia.

It hasn't escaped me that everyone in Frankfurt is my kind of handsome: blue-eyed, tall and blonde. Well of course they are. All the brown-eyed, short, dark people were murdered by the Nazis. Here in Frankfurt at least, Hitler got exactly what he wanted.

Visiting the Judisches Museum in the former Rothschild Palais on Untermainkai, I am bemused to see that after an extensive exploration of the history of the medieval Jewish population of Frankfurt complete with parchment illustrations of various pogroms, the museum's narrative goes straight from the Third Reich's removal of Jewish property rights to the settlement of Palestine.

If you didn't know any better, you'd think the Nazis were a kind of jackbooted Inland Revenue, nothing more than unpleasant pecuniary forces. No death camps for this museum. No photographs of skeletons stacked up like kindling. No piles of shoes. It's all so sanitised. Todeslager streng verboten. Too messy.

Whenever modern Germans are talking about the Holocaust (of course we mentioned the war) they say, of crimes against humanity, that 'the Nazis' did it — those other Germans. One can hardly blame them for attempting to cleave themselves from mass-murdering grandparents, from an inheritance of evil.

❖ ❖ ❖

Zooming along the autobahn in Guido's black BMW, a monster of excess and indulgence, capable of reaching speeds over 223 miles per hour. There is no speed limit on the autobahn. Guido's laugh is that of a crazy person.

We have been invited to a wine tasting at Gutsausschank Hamm, followed by a customary festive meal of goose, red cabbage and traditional Frankish knödel (enormous dumplings served with red-wine gravy). Wine tasting in the Rhine Valley, the terroir of Charlemagne . . . the things I have to put up with.

Underground in an ancient stone cellar, braziers warming our hands, rows of barrels recede forever from the light of our candelabra. The arched ceiling is covered with a black, wine-fume-eating fungus. Outside, a white Spanish galgo called Paschimo, all splayed legs and long nose, frolics about the white courtyard like a dog who has just stepped out of Brueghel's 'Hunters in the Snow'.

A small castle rises into the dark on the hillside above us — Dracula's holiday house. From here the turrets look like gnomes' hats. Down here in the valley, snug from the snowstorm behind the thick stone walls of Gutsausschank Hamm, the guests sit at a long wooden table, drinking the best Riesling in Germany. Outside it's minus 8°C. Inside, the bliss that is European central heating. Swirling the golden wine, sniffing peach and earth, smoky sunshine: spätlese, blanc de noir, spätburgunder.

After dinner a twenty-year-old brandy is served. Drink and warmth, combined with memories of India, coloured by candlelight and the telling as a succession of awfulness, cause me to become quite emotional. I have evidently died in my sleep and this is heaven. Up at the castle, a half bottle of 1700s Riesling remains. Once a year, the cellar master is allowed to taste some. 'There is nothing bad under the sun if you pay respect to it,' pronounced a fellow guest. We had learnt much about wine, and said so to the vintner. 'It's all lessons in living,' replied Carl Heinz Hamm, exuding bonhomie and the wisdom of ages.

And then something even more wonderful happens. The gratification of gastronomy cracks the cheap candy coating of the economist, a man whose eyes once rolled back in his head when I brought a $23 bottle of wine to dinner, in the days when we were courting. The benefits of indulging in the best were suddenly made apparent to him. He and Paschimo basked in the candlelight, their coats glossy with good food and fine living.

'I can see there will be some changes when we get home,' he says, resigned. I smiled expensively.

But before turning our heads for home, it's back to India.

'It's going to be difficult to convince her to go back,' I overhear the economist muttering to Guido.

Damn skippy it will. Good wine, hot men and a sausage on every corner; I could stay here forever.

Leaving Frankfurt, the economist scattered auf wiedersehens like confetti. I had to be dragged to the plane, mouth open in mute protest, like a crash-test dummy in a Trabant.

Not that I'd feel any impact — I've put on 5 kilograms in nine days.

❧ ❧ ❧

Déjà vu, all over again. The ice bath of our Frankfurt trip has rinsed the scales from my eyes and everything Indian is charming once more. The vivid colours, the smiles of commuters on the jam-packed roads, the curious stares. Wedding season; the wedding palaces on Bannerghatta Road sparkle with a million lights. We eat paratha for breakfast, Gobi Manchurian for lunch. Free cable TV. Fuchsia saris. Cows in the middle of the road.

After five years of design and development, India is set to launch a cheap tablet computer retailing at NZ$60 (at that time, the cheapest Apple iPad cost NZ$799), aimed at bridging the country's digital divide and bringing modern technology to the rural disenfranchised. The computer, called Aakash or 'sky' in Hindi, is the latest in a series of world's cheapest innovations coming out of India, including the Rs100,000 (NZ$2660) compact Nano car and NZ$2610 open heart surgery.

What a country.

News is breaking of a tragedy in a New Zealand coal mine. One of *The Times of India*'s most popular columnists, Swaminathans Anklesaria Aiyar, was in New Zealand himself last week, checking in for a flight, when the whole airport stopped to observe two minutes' silence in remembrance of twenty-nine coal miners who had just lost their lives in a mine explosion. In an article titled 'Learn from Kiwis How and Why to Grieve', Aiyar said he could not help thinking that this public display of sorrow and shared pain would be impossible in India.

Even the first-class passengers looked sad, Aiyar marvelled, as all New Zealanders, rich and poor, grieved together for the lost men. The tragedy dominated the New Zealand media, and we followed the sad saga religiously online.

The death of twenty-nine coal miners wouldn't rate more than a paragraph in the Indian media, if it even made mention. A thousand workers die every year in Indian mines, and nobody gives it a second thought. As Aiyar bluntly points out, 'these (people) are seen as a lesser breed, whose deaths are unfortunate but not catastrophic'.

India remains a heartless country, seldom held to account. Deaths caused by negligence are too often shrugged off as chalta hai (just the way it goes). Nobody demands that heads roll in the myriad government organisations where criminal negligence is a way of life.

Miners dying in mines, or pedestrians killed while crossing railway tracks — these are most often from the poorer classes and Indians are so used to treating them like dirt that they do not mourn their passing. 'Socialism is enshrined in the Constitution of India,' writes Aiyar. 'By contrast, New Zealand is among the most free-market economies in the world. Yet the mining tragedy showed that the rich and poor in that country constitute a true brotherhood.

'In those two minutes when New Zealand mourned the dead miners, I tried to grieve for the millions in India who die unnoticed and unknown; for those kept illiterate and sick, for villagers robbed daily of their entitlements by an army of corrupt officials and politicians. But for all my trying, I could not match the shared pain I saw on the faces of the mourning New Zealanders all around me.'

I want to go home.

Home for Christmas

I'm back from India and loving New Zealand. Even if New Zealand doesn't seem to be here right now. Where is everybody?

'Anything to declare?' asked the twelve-year-old customs officer at immigration control.

'New Zealand is the best country in the world,' I said. His accent was adorable, all mangled vowels and soaring sentence structure. I wanted to pinch his cheeks, muss his hair, and give him a sweetie. To my left, the multitudes with foreign passports shuffled in their pen. They would be hours yet. We few incoming Kiwis fair zipped through, striking up conversations our natural shyness would normally prevent. Nice was the common denominator.

Stamping my passport, 'Welcome home, Miss Scott,' the customs officer said, with a benign look that implied he had seen many a tearful returnee. He smiled, I smiled. I might have cried were I not so dehydrated.

There may be lots of sheep in New Zealand, but there aren't many people in Dunedin. Vast savannahs are yours for the taking. Wide plains of Leave Me Alone. Bliss. The true privileges of the rich Westerner aren't material, real luxury is being able to ignore the herd, be aloof from the crowd. Space of one's own is a precious commodity.

Strolling down Saint Clair beach, knee-high waves fling themselves at my feet. Biking along clean and lonely Princes Street to buy venison at the Farmers' Market, there is only peace and quiet, a contemplative lull. No traffic, no beggars, no uppity cows. Spacious serenity. It's a pathetic fallacy, isn't it, the tendency to credit nature with human emotions? Still, never has a summer been so balmy.

My daily 'gross' quotient drops hourly. The psychological blinkers I had adopted to avoid seeing the truly awful are no longer necessary. Even this season's camel-toe inducing short shorts fail to make me wince. I've been exposed to worse sights.

Dunedinites smell terrific. Most have all their limbs. Nobody is pooing on the intersections.

I'm not screwing up my face, I'm squinting. My olfactory functions are recovering from near-constant urine assault but my eyes hurt. The New Zealand sunlight is blinding and there's so much skin on display. Did Kiwis always have so many tattoos? This morning, buying essentials at Pak'nSave, everyone looked like they'd just got out of prison.

Shorts and teeny tops seem to be summer's must-have. Compared to the repression of Indian dress, it's almost pornographic. Put it away, I thought fleetingly, embarrassed, mortified, like a teenager realising his parents have had sex, at least once.

I need to loosen up, relax. India has somehow made me prudish and uptight. A zealous Free Churcher, all rigid and frowny.

It won't be long though before I'm shocked back to normality. At every turn there's a flash of pink neck, mottled purple calves. Remember I haven't seen as much as a knee for six months. In the bakery enormous boobs heave into view, struggling against the confinement of over-wrought tank tops, dangling above the crumpets. The women of the South Island are a real mix: netball tall, pugilistically short, WWF Smackdown wide. Faces cured to handbag by too much sun. Spunks and scrubbers. Real beauties and hard-faced bleachers sporting a smeared blue rose over one breast.

Beside the condiments, dark canyons of cleavage beckon. Dimpled thighs support sturdy buttocks, like the stone buttresses of an old bridge. Freckled shoulders gleam with self-tanner. Muffins and beer guts pout. Let it all hang out. It's flesh fest and it's fabulous. Such confidence, such aplomb, so devil-may-care. The women of India would die for that kind of freedom, and do.

Clutching half a dozen beef and garlic sausages, I couldn't stop smiling. 'Hello, hello,' I beam at strangers. Everyone speaks Kwinglish (Kiwi English) and I want to talk to them.

People think I am insane.

Tacking this way and that like a sailboat with a drunken captain, I carom about the supermarket. Cuddling bacon, grinning with impunity. Aïoli, prawns, chicken pieces on a plastic tray. Food shopping in the total absence of the heavy smells of blood, death and decay (so off-putting when contemplating things you later plan to eat). Not here. Here, in the hospital neon of the supermarket aisles, sanitary items promise consumption without consequences.

It's almost Christmas. I am notorious for my antipathy towards the season to be merry. Christmas, in my opinion, is the time when members of extended families are reminded why they do not meet during the year. Whether it's the thought of Uncle Geoff, the practical joker/alcoholic/groper, or Aunty Mary, not actually related to anyone and possessing all the charm of a cigarette butt in your chardonnay, I usually fester through the festivities.

In fact, in my haste for the awfulness to be over, last year I bundled the tree, wrapping paper and decorations into rubbish bags and surreptitiously heaved the lot out to the curb while the Irish mafia enjoyed their post-prandial liqueurs. Not this year. This year, after India-Germany-New Zealand third world, first world, third world shock-treatments, I'm more than ready to be convivial. 'Ho Ho Ho,' I say, and while you're at it, 'Deck the Halls'. I catch myself smiling at the checkout chick's earrings, a lurid sparkle-fest featuring Rudolph and his flashing nose. Call it seasonal schizophrenia.

I think New Zealanders are wonderful. Decent, if indecently dressed. Sweet, generous, well-meaning. Glorious, half-wrapped packages of niceness. They seem so open, I'm nattering away to people I don't even know. What with the economist's Lasik-enhanced perving and my loony grin, we must look like an Antipodean Fred and Rosemary West.

But we mean you no harm. We're just so happy to be back. Oh, how I love you, Dunedin. I want to hug you. Come here, you gorgeous thing.

After all the corruption and apathy, the grinding poverty and suffocating press of India's millions, a nation where more than 1000 miners die every year and nobody cares, here I am back in God's Own. A country whose entire population stood in silence and shared pain to mourn the death of twenty-nine men. A little corner of the world where, for the most part, people are still good.

Yes, Virginia, there is a Santa Claus.

❧ ❧ ❧

Upon my return from India, I'll admit I breathed a none too quiet sigh of relief — recalling the parting remark of Edward Longshanks (Edward I, Hammer of the Scots), crossing over the border from Scotland in 1296, 'It does a man good to be shot of a turd'.

The economist is surprised to learn that I hadn't enjoying vast parts of our Indian experience. 'Pee in a bucket, throw in some coriander and, Boom! You're there,' I described it to friends. Listening to me exaggerate, he says, 'I had no idea it was India that was making you so unpleasant. You should have said something.'

'What was your favourite thing about India?' I ask him.

'The cheapness.'

'There must be more to it than that,' I protest.

'What's better than cheapness?' he counters. 'No, really, I know it's a terrible cliché, but I loved the colours. And the fact that it works, *everything* works, the traffic, capitalism, the activity. I loved that. Cows, dogs, people selling stuff, buying stuff, going to work . . . a rich ecosystem where everyone is doing something, from the rat in the rubbish right up to the head of the temple. But what's all this talk about marriage? I never said anything about proposing.'

I don't want to talk about it.

The economist rather simplistically suggests that I should be happy to be in the country I love, with the man I love. He would like me to remain a trophy girlfriend — versus atrophy girlfriend, which is what he thinks will happen if we ever get married.

'Darling,' he wheedles. 'If I were going to propose to anyone, it would be you. And anyway, I know what you're like — the minute you get what you want, you won't want it anymore.'

'So not true,' I pouted, knowing perfectly well it was.

Reader, I *will* marry him.

India is an appalling country in many ways; certainly a horrible place for women, with terrible poverty on an unimaginable scale. All you can do is make yourself see everything and not shudder and not look away.

India is also a great country, a country of phenomenal growth, entrepreneurial acumen, and more returning millionaires ploughing their skills and funds back into helping solve the problems of their own country than any other. Indians are wonderfully philanthropic.

And callously indifferent.

A cauldron of contradictions, my memories of India consist of moments of awfulness and wonder, hard up against each other. Squalor and beauty in the turn of a head. A pile of rubbish, the flash of a crimson sari. I was not merely saddened and horrified but *disgusted* by the density and suffering of human life in India — but it is this very intensity of emotion which awakens you to the possibilities of your own life.

A voracious bookworm, my experience of India was one as much literary as literal: leaving New Zealand with the ridiculous intention of finding 'a passage to India', I discovered instead a 'white tiger'. And an antidote to consumer angst. Before I went to India, I dithered about the colour of our new bench top, craved the latest Carlson and agonised over the right wine to go with dinner. Now these concerns are but vapours. How pathetic, how petty the daily cares of the New Zealand middle classes seem, so meaningless, so utterly irrelevant, when compared to a country where 80 per cent of the population live on NZ$1.66 a day.

Our contemporaneous experiences (mine and the economist's) seem to have come down to seeing things versus the decision not to see. The economist being in the camp of those who, through sheer embarrassment at their own riches, never look too long at the destitute, my stricken gaze caused near-constant tears and a crushing, paralysing horror. That which is seen cannot be easily unseen.

'I just muddled through,' said the economist. 'I simply saw bargains everywhere. I even lost my fear of money, temporarily. I didn't notice any of what you're talking about.'

Methinks he protesteth too much. Ever since we got back, the economist has been spending money like the terminally ill, demonstrating such a rash of can't-take-it-with-you that his sister thinks he has affluenza. But then nothing makes you realise life is for living like staring into the eyes of a dying beggar on a Delhi sidewalk.

It's not surprising that our experiences of India were so different: the economist spent months either on the toilet or unconscious, and, when he was alert enough to appreciate his surroundings, was constantly amazed at the cheapness of lunch — while I was inconsolable at the cheapness of life. No wonder I went a bit bonkers; as Nietzsche said, stare too long into the abyss, the abyss stares back at you.

People always use that old chestnut 'life-changing' when speaking of travel to India. Well, sometimes clichés exist because they are true. The very best thing about life-changing experiences though, is that you never come back the same as you left. So I went to India and I fell in love with New Zealand. Sure, I found myself, but not the way you would think.

I found myself in the minutiae. Clear water, clean air, smog-less sunlight on my skin. The freedom to wear shorts without causing offense. The freedom to go out for a drink with my girlfriends on a Friday night and get loud and stupid. The freedom to go to the beach and flop down on the sand without a busload of unmarried men forming a circle.

It's the little things.

❀ ❀ ❀

Epilogue: Regrets, I've had a few . . .

Doctor Safari is wearing a thick Perspex face-shield, the kind that protects you from splashes of arterial blood. She hands me a pair of black-out goggles and a black rubber stress ball to squeeze. I've got my comfy pants on.

The clinic's operating room is all white: the walls are white, the ceiling is white and the operating table is white, except for a square of blue surgical gauze at the foot. White paper crackles beneath my bottom when I fidget.

'Ready?' asks the doctor. The mask lends her question a Darth Vaderish menace.

'Sure. Go for it.' I can hear the terror wobbling my voice.

The laser's intense pulsed light is so bright I can see a corona of white around the edge of my goggles. The pain is searing, excruciating. I hiss and slither away from it.

Doctor Safari stops what she's doing and holds the barrel of the laser up, away from my ankle. Her pose is eerily reminiscent of the tattoo artist Girish, poised above that same spot with his electric needle, only two months ago. A Zen contemplation, speaking of permanence.

'Would you like me to stop?' she asks, with an unspoken, 'You enormous baby.'

'Not at all,' I say, with the faux bravery of the born yellow, returning my foot to the blue square. 'Just taking a breather.'

The agony resumes. It's true: it really is much more painful than having a baby. Doctor Safari traces over the blurry outline of stupidity's souvenir. Intense Pulsed Laser doesn't actually remove a tattoo, but reactivates it, breaks it down, so that the ink is reabsorbed by the body. The tattoo is still there, forever under the surface, even if you can't see it.

'You are a moron,' says the laser's burr, 'moorrrrron.'

I'll need ten to fifteen more sessions before I stop seeing stars. Ten to fifteen more sessions before this is but a memory — fading the way a black eye fades, purple then green then yellow — to be replaced by rose-tinted travel stories and misty-eyed nostalgia for that great subcontinent.

It's already started. These last few days, I've felt the beginnings of a prickle, an itch to return to the bedlam. To re-experience that saturated stare, the totality, the reality.

India, it's under my skin.

Bibliography

I found EM Forster's *A Passage to India* (Edward Arnold, London, 1924) invaluable for its depiction of Mrs Moore's spiritual muddle and evocation of the despair and 'otherness' felt by Europeans when confronted with the enormity of India.

The Jungle Book, by Rudyard Kipling (MacMillan Publishers, London, 1894) provided a lovely romp through the India of fables, the long-gone India of the British Raj, a place where anthropomorphic morality speaks of colonial dreaming.

Aravind Adiga's Man Booker-winning debut, *The White Tiger* (Harper Collins, India, 2008), tells a tale of contrasts: the wealth and opportunity to be found in the city spaces against the crushing poverty suffered by India's working class. The central character Balram's increasing worldliness leads him to commit a murder for which he is not punished but rewarded. Adiga paints New India as a place to lose your soul.

Reading *Midnight's Children* by Salman Rushdie (Jonathan Cape, London, 1981) gave me an irreplaceable insight into Indian mythology and the Indian psyche. This tale of children switched at birth, played out against the backdrop of Partition, and written in an exuberant, pun-and-wordplay, 'Babu' English medley is as dizzyingly complex as the country itself.

My favourite book about India is Paul Theroux's *The Elephanta Suite* (Houghton Mifflin Harcourt, Boston, 2007). These three novellas brilliantly capture the inherent racism of Western visitors and their horror, hatred and fear of the many-armed monster that is India.

In *Q & A* (Black Swan, London, 2006), diplomat-turned-author Vikas Swarup creates an India of limitless potential, an India where a chai wallah can become a gameshow millionaire. A fantastical denial of the inevitability of caste, this novel also represents the hopes and dreams of the working class of New India, a place where a Dalit can be become a billionaire.

5 Point Someone — What not to do at IIT! by Chetan Baghat (Rupa & Co., Chennai, 2004) is the highest-selling English novel published in India (despite being criticised for its over-the-top-ness: 'Bollywood on paper!'), and said by fans to perfectly capture the burden of expectations placed on many Indian students, the terrible stress and associated disillusion.

The Indians, Portrait of a People by Sudhir Kakar and Katharina Kakar (Penguin Books, New Delhi, 2009) is a compelling work examining the common character of the Indian people, and a window on the Hindu world view. Cultural commentator Sudhir Kakar and anthropologist Katharina Kakar investigate what makes an Indian recognisably so to the rest of the world, and, more importantly, to his or her fellow Indians.

Additional reading

The Complete Sherlock Holmes, Sir Arthur Conan Doyle, Doubleday & Company, 1927

The Death of Mr Love, Indra Sinha, Scriber (Simon & Schuster), New York, 2002

The Discovery of India, Jawaharlal Nehru, Oxford University Press, Oxford, 1946

The Girl Child, P R Lakshman, Emerald Publishing, Chennai, 2006

The Language Report: English on the Move, 2000–2007, Susie Dent, Oxford University Press, Oxford, 2007

Articles & essays

'1990s, Chronology of Major Indian Train Accidents', *The Times of India*

'2010 The Social Report, Suicide, Current Level and Trends', New Zealand Ministry of Social Development, http://socialreport.msd.govt.nz/health/suicide.html

'A Wide Angle of the World, the Growing Suicide Rate in India — the Reasons', 14 May, 2007, Nita Jatar Kulkarni: nitawriter.wordpress.com

'Black, White and Shades of Brown', by the Man from Matunga, published in *Sulekha Select*, Smart Information Worldwide, Chennai, 2001

'Britain, the Commonwealth and the End of Empire', Dr John Darwin, BBC History, www.bbc.co.uk

'Disappearing Daughters and Intensification of Gender Bias: Evidence from Two Village Studies in South India', T V Sekher and Neelambar Hatti, *Sociological Bulletin 59*(1), January–April, 2010, pp 111–133, Indian Sociological Society

'India: the Missing Girls', Frontline/World, Rough Cut, www.pbs.org/frontlineworld

'India's Unwanted Girls', Geeta Pandey, Delhi, BBC News South Asia, 23 May, 2011

'Indian Society Has Become Sick', 28 October, 2010, *The Times of India*

'Kiss My Chuddies! (Welcome to the Queen's Hinglish)', Anushka Asthana, *The Observer*, 25 April, 2004

'Learn from Kiwis How and Why to Grieve', Swaminathans Anklesaria Aiyar, 5 December, 2010, *The Times of India*

Major Railway Accidents in India, 2000–09, Ajai Banerji, self-published paperback, first edition 25 July, 2011

'More Than 100 Million Women Are Missing', Amartya Kumar Sen, *New York Review of Books*, Vol. 37, No. 20, 20 December, 1990

'Please Don't Cheer the 2010 Loot-fest', Chetan Baghat, *The Times of India*, 29 August, 2010

Rajeev Gowda, 2010 lecture slides: 'The Missing Girl Child'

'Retrieve Honour from Some Dishonourable Men', Monobina Gupta, *Sunday Times of India*, 4 July, 2010

'Sex Selection & Pre Birth Elimination of Girl Child', Dr Vibhuti Patel, presented at the UN Convention to Review Status of Women, UN Headquarters, New York, 28 February–1 March, 2005

'Study Reveals High Suicide Rate among Young People in India': www.scienceblog.com/community/older/2004

'The Eliminated Multitude: Female Foeticide in India', Piyali Sarkar, *Centre for Social Research* newsletter, Vol. 34, No. 2, May–August, 2006

'The Girl Child in India: Does She Have Any Rights?', Malavika Karlekar, *Canadian Woman Studies/les cahiers de la femme*, Vol. 15, No. 2–3, March 1995, Inanna Publications & Education Inc.

Any mistakes are Wikipedia's.